DISTRIBUTION, DEVELOPMENT AND PRICES CRITICAL PERSPECTIVES

DISTRIBUTION, DEVELOPMENT AND PRICES CRITICAL PERSPECTIVES

Editors
Theodore Mariolis
Lefteris Tsoulfidis

SERIALS PUBLICATIONS
NEW DELHI (INDIA)

First Published - 2006

ISBN: 81-8387-044-9

Published by
SERIALS PUBLICATIONS
4830/24, Prahlad Street, Ansari Road
Darya Ganj, New Delhi-110002 (India)
Phone : 23245225
Fax : 91-11-23272135
E-mail: serials@satyam.net.in

CONTENTS

PREFACE

This Book of the *Distribution, Development and Prices Critical Perspectives* consists of thirteen papers which deal with four central and, at the same time, controversial topics of economic theory and policy analysis: (i) Theory of value; (ii) Capital accumulation, profitability and economic cycles; (iii) Effective demand and interaction between the 'real' and the 'financial' sides of the economy; and (iv) Economic development and the related policies.

The first two papers deal with the relations between labour values, prices of production and market prices. More specifically, Dave Zachariach, by using input-output data from a number of OECD countries investigates the empirical strength of the labour theory of value. His findings show that both the labour values and production prices are particularly close to market prices as this can be judged by a number of statistical measures of deviation. Furthermore, the paper subjects to empirical testing the hypothesis for the profit rate equalization across industries which is not found to be consistent with the data, a result which essentially makes labor values more relevant predictors to actual prices than prices of production. Theodore Mariolis presents and critically evaluates the so-called 'New Approach or Interpretation' to the 'problem of transforming values into prices' and argues that the 'New Approach' goes just half a way towards the full logically consistent interpretation, according to which values of commodities are their actual prices.

The next four papers focus on the process of capital accumulation. Allin Cottrell and Paul Cockshott discuss the original formulation of the theory of the falling rate of profit by Marx and the criticisms regarding its micro-foundations. They suggest an alternative macroeconomic interpretation in which the falling rate of profit is governed by demographic factors, and in this context they examine the social implications of a declining rate of profit. Dong-Min Rieu deals with the implications of the 'Okishio Theorem' and he argues that Okishio's analysis of the relation between technical change and the profit rate is logically consistent and, at the same time, constitutes a viable research program. Stavros Mavroudeas and Alexis Ioannides provide a critical presentation of the interwar discussion about the schemes of reproduction and they show mathematically that Grossmann's idea to extent the number of periods of Bauer's schemes of reproduction lead indeed to economic crisis. Aris Papageorgiou and Lefteris Tsoulfidis present and critically evaluate Kontradiev's theory of long cycles in connection with Marx's theory of the long run tendency of the rate of profit to fall. They argue that Marx's theory of the falling rate of profit is in fact associated with long cyclical rhythms of capital accumulation.

The question of effective demand becomes the focus of the next four papers, all of which emphasize the importance of the financial side of the economy.

Eladio Febrero offers an interpretation of what Keynes called a monetary economy of production, taking elements from the 'Theory of the Monetary Circuit' and from the Sraffian Theory of Production. It is argued that this approach provides a fruitful starting point for improving our understanding of the functioning of the real economy. Eckhard Hein deals with the Kaleckian models of distribution and growth according to which the equilibrium rate of capacity utilisation may persistently diverge from its 'normal rate' without endogenous adjustments. He further constructs a growth model, which accounts for the major features of a credit economy, and shows that (i) the 'normal rate' of capacity utilization is endogenous to distribution and monetary policy in the long-run; and (ii) major Kaleckian results, in particular the paradox of costs, can be retained. Oscar De-Juan considers, on Classical and post-Keynesian grounds, that, in a world of 'credit money', the interest rate is a (re)distributive variable with a monetary character, but does not accomplish the requirements of 'natural' variables. In particular, there is no a unique relationship between the rates of interest, profit, growth and inflation and, consequently, the ability of monetary authorities to influence the market interest rate is enhanced. George Argitis develops a post-Keynesian framework, which is based on Minsky's financial theory of investment that highlights the distributional and demand effects of debt and of interest payments on capital accumulation. The econometric evidence based on time series data of the USA and the UK for the period 1974-2002 lends support to the Minskian hypotheses.

Finally, there are three papers that deal with economic development and policy issues. Persefoni Tsaliki presents and critically evaluates the premises of the sustainable development literature. On the basis of the notion of 'capitalist mode of production', she suggests that an alternative economic analysis should allow the political element to play a decisive role by creating the necessary institutions that may regulate economic life to desired directions, where the profit motive not only will reproduce capital but also contribute to a cleaner environment. Richard Westra's paper is based on the Uno's school approach and deals with issues related to the state/market debate in the newly industrialized countries (NIC). Furthermore, he makes an effort to periodize capitalism and concludes with some comments on the potential held out by the capitalist market and capitalist state for development in Japan and Korea in the era of neoliberalism. Constantinos Alexiou pursues a theoretical exploration of the new liberal thinking in an effort to unveil the rationale of the macroeconomic policies in the European Union region. The analysis focuses on issues relating to industrial capacity and manufacturing, the role of the financial system and that of effective demand, and concludes that the austere economic conditions experienced by the EU population over the last decades have been the result of tight economic policies implemented by the proponents of the free-market orthodoxy.

Theodore Mariolis & Lefteris Tsoulfidis

LABOUR VALUE AND EQUALISATION OF PROFIT RATES: A MULTI-COUNTRY STUDY

Dave Zachariah*

This study investigates the empirical strength of the labour theory of value and its relation to profit rate equalisation. It replicates tests from previous studies, using input-output data from 18 countries spanning from year 1968 to 2000. The results are broadly consistent; labour values and production prices of industry outputs are highly correlated with its market price. The predictive power is compared to alternative value bases. Furthermore, the empirical support for profit rate equalisation, as assumed by the theory of production prices, is weak.

INTRODUCTION

The labour theory of value (LTV) states that the market prices of commodities tend to be proportional to the labour necessary to produce them. The scientific status of the theory depends on what it can say, theoretically and empirically, about reality. The LTV can generate interesting predictions regarding price-formation, the decreasing labour content of commodities, real exchange rates, the determination of the average profit rate etc. More importantly it is potentially a powerful analytical tool for understanding how market economies regulate social labour, a special case of a general economic problem. It is essential in order to understand the mechanism of extraction of surplus labour under capitalism which, of course, was a central concern of Marx.

Labour value is an attractor to market price, or to put it in a different way, as Valle Baeza (1997) argues; market price can be interpreted as a measure of labour value and random price-value deviations as signals to which the market, as a control system, regulates production.

But the time and effort spent investigating what merits the LTV may have in real capitalist economies pales in significance to that spent on the so-called 'transformation problem'—the problem of reconciling the LTV with the theory of production prices (TPP) within a deterministic framework. TPP states that prices are formed to ensure equal profit rates across the economy. The problem is that if there was a common profit-wage ratio, the LTV would predict that firms with higher capital-wage ratios would earn lower rates of profit, and vice versa, making it systematically in error. The problem rests on the assumptions

* School of Electrical Engineering, Royal Institute of Technology, Stockholm, Sweden, e-mail: davez@kthe.sc. I would like to thank Paul Cockshott for helpful comments.

of (i) a common profit-wage ratio and (ii) an equalisation of profit rates: (i) does not necessarily follow from the LTV, but as we will see it is certainly consistent with it; and (ii) is the central assumption of the TPP.

Farjoun and Machover's *Laws of Chaos* (1983) is a bold attempt to break with the deterministic framework of the transformation problem. To deal with chaotic market phenomena one must apply appropriate probabilistic concepts. If the regulation of social labour in capitalism operates in the way stated above we should understand market prices to be determined by labour values, not through a deterministic (as in classical mechanics) but stochastic process. Indeed, using arguments from statistical mechanics they formulate a powerful critique of the theoretical status of an equalisation of profit rates. The purpose of this article is to contribute to the empirical research on the labour theory of value and its relation to profit rate equalisation. Using the approach outlined in *Laws of Chaos*, it will replicate tests done for the economies of the United States, United Kingdom and Greece (Cockshott and Cottrell (1998, 2003), Shaikh (1998), Tsoulfidis and Maniatis (2002)) with data from 18 countries.

THEORY

Value bases and the peculiarity of labour

Let us denote the market price of a commodity as P and the direct plus indirect labour time necessary to produce it, under existing standard conditions of production, as Λ which we shall call 'labour value'. From the standpoint of *economic reproduction* it is clear that the choice of value base is not limited to labour. Λ can be substituted for any commodity-type that enters directly or indirectly into every other commodity, for example oil or steel. The 'steel value' of a commodity is the total quantity of steel necessary to produce it. However as a concept of *economic value* any value base other than labour runs into theoretical problems; if 1 ton of steel requires 0.5 tons of steel in its production then its steel value is not unity as the concept requires. On the other hand if the steel value of one unit of steel remained exactly one there would be no net production of steel.

Social labour is special in this respect. It is a direct and indirect input to every commodity and assumes the commodity form as labour power is bought and sold but it is not produced as a commodity. There is no direct analogy between the reproduction of one ton of steel and one person hour of labour so there is no non-unity problem here. The concept of abstract labour is also applicable to all types of economies with a social division of labour throughout history, not merely when goods and services assume the commodity form. It is 'abstract' precisely because of the general human capacity to acquire skills and perform all kinds of concrete tasks.

Labour is a universal but scarce resource. During any given period of time there is a limited amount of person hours available in production which constrains the feasible consumption pattern. This imposes a practical necessity to allocate it in various branches of production in order to meet changing social demands. Thus determining demand in terms of labour becomes functionally useful in order to organize and allocate labour with some degree of efficiency. In economies governed by market exchange, a large number of producers are integrated indirectly via purchases and sales. These economies face the same problematic of organizing and allocating social labour but have to solve it by the mechanisms of market exchange.

If we interpret the market price of a good or service as a stochastic signal, the LTV suggests that its labour value is a deterministic component underlying the noise. This implies a control mechanism in that deviations between market prices and prices proportional to labour values, caused by supply and demand discrepancies, will lead to counter-acting adjustments in output.

Distribution of Price-Value Ratios

A more rigorous claim was made by Farjoun and Machover: Suppose we record for each transaction i during a period of the ratio of market price to labour value of the commodity exchanged, Ψ_i. Each transaction differs in economic weight, i.e. there is a quantitative difference between the purchase of a cup of coffee and a jumbo jet, so each ratio is given a probability weight p_i proportional to the commodity's labour value. The period should be short enough for structural changes in the economy to be negligible but long enough for the number of recorded price-value ratios to be sufficiently large to apply probabilistic concepts. The expected characteristics of the distribution of price-value ratios are derived on very general statistical considerations.

The price P of any commodity can be decomposed into its costs of production inputs C, labour costs V and gross profits S. However, C is itself a price that can be decomposed into its input costs, labour costs and gross profits. This decomposition of production inputs can be repeated so that in the limit the price P of any commodity is made up the sum of its direct and indirect (or vertically integrated) labour costs $V^* = \Sigma V_l$ and gross profits $S^* = \Sigma S_l$, which was a fundamental insight of classical political economy.

$$P = C + V + S = S^* + V^* \qquad (1)$$

If we treat $\psi = P/\Lambda$ as a random variable, where each recorded ratio ψ_i during the transaction period is assigned a probability weight proportional to its labour value $p_i = \Lambda_i/\Sigma\Lambda_j$, we can use (1) to write the mean as

$$\begin{aligned} E(\psi) &= E(V^*/\Lambda) + E(S^*/\Lambda) \\ &= E(V^*/\Lambda)\,.\,[1+e^*] \end{aligned} \qquad (2)$$

where $E(V^*/\Lambda) = \Sigma V^*_i/\Sigma\Lambda_j$ and $e^* = \Sigma S^*_i/\Sigma V^*_i$ in (2) are likely to be close to the average wage rate and profit-wage ratio in the economy, respectively.[1] Due to the highly integrated nature of modern economies $\psi = P/\Lambda$ is made up by the sum of a large number of random variables; each of which is small relative to the whole sum and assumed to be independent. By a generalization of the Central Limit Theorem we would expect $\psi = P/\Lambda$ to be approximated by a continuous normal distribution, with a mean value $E(\psi)$ and standard deviation σ_ψ. This result was derived by Farjoun and Machover (1983, chap. 5), reproduced here in a condensed form of course, who further estimated the standard deviation σ_ψ

on the hypothesis that there is a small probability, less than 1/1000, that the market price is insufficient to pay the total labour-power required, at the average wage rate.

The integral □$f(\psi)d\psi$ in interval [a,b] would give the fraction of the total product measured in labour value exchanging for a price-value ratio ψ between a and b, where $f(\psi)$ is the probability density function. This information is sufficient to describe the entire distribution of price-value ratios. If the labour theory of value holds empirically, then what is the rationale that enforces price-setting agents, obviously unaware of this 'law of value', to adapt to it? We can approach this question in a slightly different manner.

Relative Prices and Labour Values

Following Shaikh and Antonopoulos (1998), relative unit prices strongly depend on relative unit costs—which is to say relative vertically integrated labour costs. For simplicity, denote the vertically integrated profit-wage ratio S^*/V^* as β and the direct profit-wage ratio S/V as α. Then re-write (1) as $P = V^*(1+\beta)$. Now let us investigate under what conditions relative prices between two arbitrary commodities i and j are approximately equal to their relative labour values: $P_i/P_j \approx \Lambda_i/\Lambda_j$.

Using our notation $P_i/P_j = (V^*_i/V^*_j) \cdot [(1+\beta_i)/(1+\beta_j)]$, i.e. relative prices are made up by relative vertically integrated labour costs multiplied by relative vertically integrated profit-wage ratios. The vertically integrated profit-wage ratio β of each producer is a convex combination or weighted average of the direct profit-wage ratios α of several other producers who enter directly or indirectly in its output:

$$\beta = w_1\alpha_1 + \dots + w_n\alpha_n = \Sigma\, w_k\alpha_k \qquad (3)$$

The weights are $w_k = V_k/\Sigma V_l$, i.e. the relative contribution of integrated labour costs. Again, given the level of interconnection of modern economies we would expect the sum in (3) to contain a large number of terms so that vertically integrated profit-wage ratios β across all producers will be more similar than their direct profit-wage ratios α. If β has a relatively small dispersion, $[(1+\beta_i)/(1+\beta_j)]$ can be viewed as a disturbance term so that relative prices strongly depend on relative vertically integrated labour costs V^*_i/V^*_j. Furthermore, if the distribution of wage rates is reasonably narrow then this ratio will not be far away from relative labour values Λ_i/Λ_j. Thus we can say that: it is the need for companies to meet the wage-bill that forces market prices to gravitate around prices proportional to labour values. We also see that the assumption of a common profit-wage ratio α is compatible with the LTV since it implies that there is no disturbance arising from differentials in vertically integrated profit-wage ratios β.

Equalisation of Profit Rates

The classical political economists also held the view that capital flows from low return to high return sectors. Supply drops and prices rise in less profitable ones and vice versa. Although this mechanism, which would appear to even out the profit rates, arguably exists, the question is on what time-scale does it operate? How does it affect the distribution of profit rates and price formation? Will the distribution narrow over time and/or remain narrow in relation to other distributions, such as price-value ratios?

In theoretical models it is assumed to be a spike, i.e. all profit rates are equal so there is no variation, but no one expects to find that in reality. In the TPP equalisation affects price formation so that market prices gravitate around 'production prices' that would ensure all producers an equal profit rate. The premise is that equalisation operates in such way to make profit rates statistically independent of capital-wage ratios and similar compositions of capital (Cockshott and Cottrell (2003, p. 749)). Holding a common profit-wage ratio across industry sectors, the premise contradicts the LTV which predicts profit rates to be systematically lower for sectors with high capital-wage ratios.

DATA AND METHOD

The rest of this paper will test 1. The hypothesis that labour value is an attractor to market price. 2. Production price is a competing attractor which will make more accurate predictions, rendering labour value as a 'first approximation' or simply redundant. 3. The premise of this theory; the equalisation of profit rates.

Data was taken from Statistics Bureau of Japan, Statistics Sweden and OECD's symmetric input-output tables, in producers or basic prices, which record monetary flows across industries. The Japanese and Swedish data contain more sectors than the OECD data, which summarizes the original information at a higher level of aggregation, so the results from the former are more significant than from the latter. The Swedish tables also contain supplementary data on fixed capital stocks and labour inputs measured in 1000 persons.

Estimation of Matrix of Technical Coefficients and Labour Time

The computation of labour values requires a matrix of technical coefficients that describes the technical conditions of production. The degree of accuracy of the estimated matrix will depend on the level of aggregation of national accounting data. To construct a matrix of technical coefficients using monetary data might at first seem to 'contaminate' the estimated labour values with price data but it has been shown, by Cockshott and Cottrell (1997, Sec. 3), that this is not the case. The fact that the matrix's elements represent a yen's worth of input from sector i required to produce a yen's worth of output in sector j does not invalidate the estimation of technical coefficients.

Sectors lacking either output or labour input figures were excluded from the analysis. 'Finance', 'real estate services', 'public administration, defence and social security' were treated as unproductive expenses which form a part of the gross profits.[2] Sectors such as education and health work services may contain a large fraction of non-marketed output but were nonetheless included despite the bias.

For simplicity all units of labour input for the Swedish data was treated as of same skill and intensity so that each unit adds equally to the labour value of a commodity. This introduces an error since we are estimating the labour time *necessary* to produce it at existing standard conditions of production. However, this error decreases as data is aggregated to industry level. For the other countries labour costs were used as a proxy for labour input as is common in the literature.

Discrete Observations

For each sector a discrete observation was obtained: output price P, production inputs C, labour costs V, gross profits[3] S, labour value of output Λ and production price of output Π. When data on depreciation of fixed capital was available it was treated as a part of C which causes some inconsistency with the computed labour values and production prices since there was insufficient information to estimate the depreciation coefficients. For the Swedish data fixed capital was taken as capital stock K.

Labour values and production prices were estimated following Shaikh and Tonak (1994, chap. 4) and Cockshott and Cottrell (1997a, sec. 2). Labour value Λ for each sector was computed by first obtaining the vector of embodied labour-output ratios $\lambda = (I-A)^{-1}l$, where I is the identity matrix, A is the matrix of input-output coefficients[4] and l is the vector of direct labour-output ratios. Labour value for sector i is then its embodied labour-output ratio λ_i multiplied by its output P_i.

Production price Π_i for each sector was computed by first obtaining the vector of production price-output ratios $p = (I-(1+r_G)A)^{-1}w$, where w is the vector of wage-output ratios. r_G is the 'general rate of profit', which was taken as the mean of the distribution of profit rates on a flow basis, $r = S / (C+V)$. Production price for sector i is then its production price-output ratio p_i multiplied by its output P_i. These prices are consistent with the equalisation of profit rates on the flow of outlays on current inputs. In Section 4.4.3 we will return to the issue of the impact of our estimated general rate of profit.

A more sophisticated study should include matrices of estimated depreciation and fixed capital stock coefficients and calculate production prices consistent with the equalisation of profit rates on a stock basis, $r^*=S/K$.

Probability Distributions

In Section 4.2 we will investigate distributions of the following variables:

1. ratio of market prices to labour content $\psi = P/\Lambda$
2. ratio of market prices to production prices $\pi = P/\Pi$
3. gross profit rate in flow terms $r = S/(C+V)$
4. gross profit share $s = S/(S+V)$
5. composition of output $o = C/(S+V)$

What we would want is to have data on these variables at firm and commodity level. To test Farjoun and Machover's hypothesis of the distribution of price-value ratios would require data for each transaction during, say, a month. However, the available data is for industry sectors so products as polyvinyl chloride will have to merge into 'rubber and plastic products'.

The OECD data was treated as discrete distributions where each sectoral observation was given a weight w_i. For the distribution of $\psi = P/\Lambda$ this was $w_i = \Lambda i/\Sigma\Lambda j$, for $\pi = P/\Pi$ it was $w_i = \Pi_i/\Sigma\Pi_j$ and for the remaining distributions the weights were $w_i = (C_i+V_i)/\Sigma(C_j+V_j)$. For Japan and Sweden continuous distributions were estimated following Cockshott and Cottrell (1998); each observation was treated as the mean of a normal distribution since it represents the aggregation of many firms and products.[5] The probability density function (pdf) for variable x is then defined as $f(x) = \Sigma\, w_i\, N_{\mu i,\sigma}(x)$ where $N_{\mu i,\sigma}(x)$ is the normal pdf with mean μ_i (the observation of sector i) and standard deviation σ (which was set to one fifth of the standard deviation of the whole convolving function).

The integral □$f(r)dr$ in interval [a,b] gives the fraction of the total social capital earning a profit rate r between a and b. □$f(\pi)d\pi$ in interval [a,b] gives the fraction of the total product measured in production price exchanging for a ratio π between a and b. An analogous interpretation can be held for the remaining probability density functions.

RESULTS

Deviation between Market Prices, Labour values and Production Prices

One way to quantify the relation between market prices, labour values and production prices is to measure the size of industry outputs in terms of price, labour value and production price and compute how well the measures correlate with each other.[6] Pearson's correlation coefficient ñ quantifies the linear co-variation between two sets of data. Expressing the set of prices and labour values relative to that of any specific sector will of course not affect the measure. Another measure used in the literature is the weighted average of relative deviations, MAWD, using two data sets represented as vectors x and y. MAWD $= \Sigma\, w_i |y_i - x_i| / \Sigma\, w_i\, x_i$. It has however the drawback that it is affected by the normalization of the data but allows a comparison with other studies. Following Shaikh (1998) prices are rescaled so that the sum of prices equals the sum of labour values or production prices. Weights are set proportional to output size in labour value or production price. A final measure is to treat the deviation between vectors as a geometric property; as the angle θ, in degrees, between vectors x and y.[7] The results are summarized in Tables 1 and 2 which also includes the correlation between labour values and production prices. Production prices in Shaikh (1998) and Tsoulfidis and Maniatis (2002) are computed on the assumption of equalisation of profit rates on a stock basis.

In terms of predicting output price the LTV and the TPP are approximately equal, both Λ and Π are highly correlated with P. In 52 out of 55 data sets the obtained correlation coefficients were above 0.900. The exceptions for labour values were Greece 1994, Norway 1997 and Poland 1995, for production prices the two first countries and West Germany 1978. More detailed national data is required to analyse the causes of this deviation. One can see the effects of aggregation of data between the national and OECD data for Japan 1995, and of methodological differences between Cockshott and Cottrell's study (1998) and the OECD data for Britain 1984.

The results are broadly consistent with the results from previous studies summarized in Table 1. It is also notable that Λ and Π are in terms of correlation close to each other and in several cases closer than either is to *P*.

Table 1
Summary of Measures of Deviation. # Denotes Number of Samples. Results from Previous Studies: USA 1947 to 1972 from Shaikh (1998); USA 1987 and GBR 1984 from Cockshott and Cottrell (1997b, 2003), correlations on logs of data; GRC 1970 from Tsoulfidis and Maniatis (2002), adjusted ρ^2

			LTV			*TPP*			
		#	ρ	*MAWD*	θ	ρ	*MAWD*	θ	$\rho(\Lambda, \Pi)$
JPN	1995	85	0.986	0.131	8.88	0.984	0.098	8.71	0.992
JPN	2000	95	0.983	0.141	9.52	0.983	0.088	8.88	0.995
SWE	1995	48	0.956	0.200	14.06	0.984	0.103	7.95	0.975
SWE	2000	48	0.960	0.184	13.21	0.988	0.091	7.03	0.972
USA	1947	71	n.a.	0.105	n.a.	n.a.	0.114	n.a.	n.a.
USA	1958	71	n.a.	0.090	n.a.	n.a.	0.075	n.a.	n.a.
USA	1963	71	n.a.	0.092	n.a.	n.a.	0.076	n.a.	n.a.
USA	1967	71	n.a.	0.102	n.a.	n.a.	0.084	n.a.	n.a.
USA	1972	71	n.a.	0.071	n.a.	n.a.	0.063	n.a.	n.a.
USA	1987	47	0.971	n.a.	n.a.	0.968	n.a.	n.a.	0.936
GRC	1970	35	0.942	0.216	n.a.	0.939	0.154	n.a.	0.950
GBR	1984	101	0.955	n.a.	n.a.	n.a.	n.a.	n.a.	n.a.

Table 2
Summary of Measures of Deviation OECD data

			LTV			*TPP*			
		#	ρ	*MAWD*	θ	ρ	*MAWD*	θ	$\rho(\Lambda, \Pi)$
AUS	1968	30	0.968	0.108	10.72	0.966	0.134	10.95	0.991
AUS	1974	30	0.982	0.081	8.32	0.976	0.118	9.47	0.994
AUS	1986	30	0.955	0.196	14.09	0.970	0.155	10.64	0.979
AUS	1989	30	0.948	0.218	15.68	0.971	0.161	10.47	0.983
CAN	1971	31	0.977	0.132	9.27	0.974	0.124	9.59	0.988
CAN	1976	31	0.966	0.154	11.46	0.966	0.117	10.99	0.987
CAN	1981	31	0.950	0.179	13.48	0.957	0.131	12.03	0.984
CAN	1986	31	0.974	0.136	9.86	0.963	0.128	11.11	0.972
CAN	1990	31	0.978	0.139	9.52	0.967	0.126	10.84	0.978
CAN	1997	32	0.967	0.130	10.08	0.957	0.136	10.91	0.954
DEU	1978	29	0.942	0.160	11.72	0.882	0.226	16.80	0.951
DEU	1986	29	0.961	0.118	9.53	0.945	0.156	11.12	0.976
DEU	1988	29	0.965	0.113	9.09	0.950	0.153	10.73	0.979

contd.

			LTV			TPP			
		#	ρ	*MAWD*	θ	ρ	*MAWD*	θ	$\rho(\Lambda,\Pi)$
DEU	1990	29	0.968	0.110	8.85	0.952	0.156	10.71	0.981
DEU	1995	33	0.965	0.102	9.89	0.949	0.143	11.83	0.989
DNK	1972	28	0.976	0.109	9.82	0.977	0.120	9.64	0.980
DNK	1977	28	0.974	0.118	10.11	0.982	0.116	8.59	0.976
DNK	1980	28	0.978	0.115	9.17	0.987	0.091	7.06	0.974
DNK	1985	28	0.967	0.134	10.77	0.976	0.133	9.29	0.978
DNK	1990	28	0.974	0.123	9.55	0.976	0.135	9.30	0.981
DNK	1997	36	0.957	0.159	13.03	0.964	0.142	11.62	0.991
FRA	1980	31	0.958	0.120	11.12	0.953	0.182	12.11	0.961
FRA	1985	31	0.959	0.127	10.96	0.952	0.173	12.10	0.952
FRA	1990	31	0.972	0.108	9.34	0.960	0.167	11.47	0.957
FRA	1995	37	0.976	0.078	8.31	0.977	0.122	8.26	0.981
GBR	1968	31	0.990	0.076	5.20	0.980	0.093	7.31	0.985
GBR	1979	31	0.980	0.078	7.49	0.977	0.099	7.92	0.987
GBR	1984	31	0.941	0.128	12.93	0.947	0.127	12.24	0.981
GBR	1990	31	0.952	0.183	13.17	0.953	0.146	13.24	0.985
GBR	1998	37	0.977	0.121	8.88	0.977	0.133	8.91	0.996
JPN	1970	32	0.965	0.145	11.72	0.954	0.167	11.95	0.968
JPN	1975	32	0.960	0.125	11.30	0.967	0.123	10.13	0.982
JPN	1980	32	0.967	0.138	10.50	0.974	0.111	8.91	0.987
JPN	1985	32	0.966	0.152	10.78	0.978	0.100	8.13	0.982
JPN	1990	32	0.984	0.116	8.18	0.986	0.071	6.84	0.983
JPN	1995	37	0.986	0.113	7.80	0.977	0.123	8.99	0.982
JPN	1996	37	0.986	0.115	7.95	0.977	0.125	8.93	0.982
JPN	1997	37	0.985	0.114	8.04	0.975	0.124	9.07	0.980
NLD	1995	35	0.965	0.138	11.34	0.975	0.115	9.36	0.985
NLD	1996	35	0.964	0.139	11.56	0.973	0.115	9.78	0.985
NLD	1997	35	0.966	0.139	11.18	0.975	0.115	9.35	0.985
NLD	1998	35	0.970	0.130	10.50	0.977	0.120	9.03	0.986
CHN	1997	35	0.965	0.212	13.32	0.991	0.105	6.36	0.986
CZE	1995	37	0.986	0.075	6.55	0.984	0.099	7.09	0.987
ESP	1995	36	0.948	0.188	13.18	0.948	0.188	13.21	0.974
GRC	1994	33	0.837	0.384	25.60	0.891	0.318	20.99	0.914
HUN	1998	33	0.982	0.081	7.18	0.977	0.127	8.08	0.969
ITA	1992	35	0.907	0.238	16.74	0.904	0.232	16.99	0.973
KOR	1995	36	0.933	0.171	13.76	0.940	0.174	13.06	0.955
NOR	1997	37	0.863	0.244	23.73	0.872	0.222	22.89	0.983
POL	1995	33	0.888	0.305	20.46	0.913	0.233	18.18	0.969

Empirical distributions

The mean values of the distributions are summarized in Tables 3 and 5. For the Swedish data $\psi = P/\Lambda$ was measured in units of the average wage rate (the ratio of aggregate wages to labour). When using labour costs as a proxy this rate equals 1 by definition. It is notable that the mean values $E(\psi)$ across countries and time are quite close to each other. This follows from the yet unexplained fact that the aggregate ratio of gross profits to wages, estimated as e_0 in the tables[8], is quite stable and tends to be in the same order of magnitude across industrialized countries.

Under the conditions outlined in Section 2.2, Farjoun and Machover predict $E(\psi) \approx 1+e_0$. In our data this tends to be an underestimate in most cases, on the other hand it is given for one year under which an economy surely undergoes structural change. They suggest further that $Pr(\psi<1)$, i.e. the probability that the market price is insufficient to pay the total labour-power required, at the average wage rate, is low. A guesstimate is that $\psi=1$ is three standard deviations from the mean on a normal distribution. Figure 1 illustrates this prediction. Sectors with very low price-value ratios are typically health care and education services and similar non-marketed outputs. The outliers in the high ratio region are tobacco and mainly a category of products presumably exhibiting high rent effects such as crude petroleum, natural gas and petroleum refinery products.

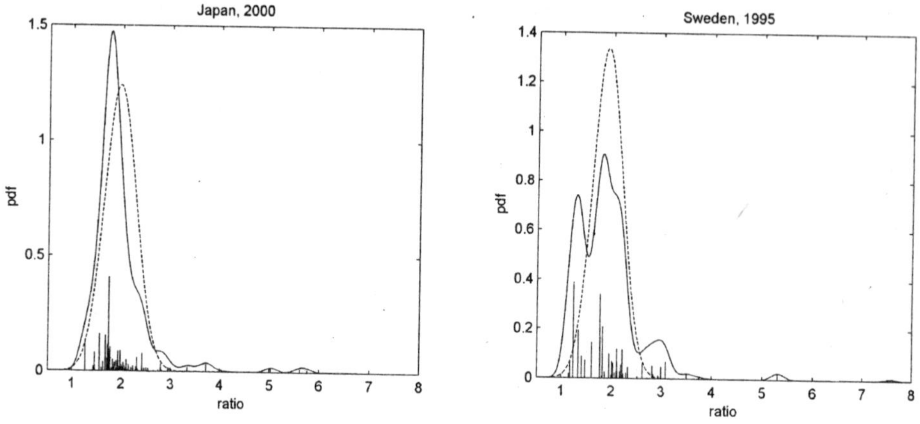

Figure 1: Empirical Distributions of price-value ratios. Dashed line represents normal Distribution with standard deviation $\sigma_\psi = (E(\psi)-1)^3$

Figure 1 shows that the predicted normal distribution is a good approximation of the core of capitalist sectors.

The coefficient of variation (c.v.) measures the dispersion of a random variable as the standard deviation divided by the mean. The results are summarized in Tables 4 and 6. The distributions of $\psi = P/\Lambda$ and $\pi = P/\Pi$ remain fairly narrow and narrower than of the other variables. Note that the Japanese and Swedish data excludes two and one oil related sectors respectively while the OECD data makes no such adjustments. The dispersion of the composition of output, $o = C/(S+V)$, tends to be of a certain order, a fact that is typically ignored in theoretical models which can make them quite unrealistic. The tables also show that the distribution of profit rates $r = S/(C+V)$ is wide and shows no consistent tendency to narrow over time. The limited data from Sweden of the distribution of profit rates on a stock basis $r^* = S/K$ does not contradict this conclusion. This is illustrated in Figure 2.

Table 3
Mean Values of Empirical Distributions. Oil Industry Excluded
GBR 1984 from Cockshott and Cottrell (1998)

		#	ψ	π	r	s	o	e_0
JPN	1995	83	1.973	1.644	0.206	0.357	1.553	0.816
JPN	2000	93	1.946	1.640	0.195	0.345	1.622	0.800
SWE	1995	47	1.884	1.538	0.188	0.338	1.484	0.708
SWE	2000	47	1.807	1.500	0.156	0.299	1.681	0.636
GBR	1984	96	n.a.	n.a.	0.211	0.315	0.846	n.a.

Table 4
Coefficients of Variation of Empirical Distributions. Oil industry excluded
GBR 1984 from Cockshott and Cottrell (1998) GRC 1970 from Tsoulfidis and Maniatis (2002) does not exclude oil industry

		#	ψ	π	r	s	o
JPN	1995	83	0.303	0.276	0.889	0.454	0.735
JPN	2000	93	0.295	0.275	0.900	0.491	0.820
SWE	1995	47	0.321	0.238	0.911	0.432	0.627
SWE	2000	47	0.276	0.194	0.828	0.450	0.725
GRC	1970	35	0.291	0.211	1.262	n.a.	1.417
GBR	1984	96	0.104	0.114	0.608	0.423	0.752

Table 5
Mean Values of Empirical Distributions OECD Data

		#	ψ	π	r	s	o	e_0
AUS	1968	30	1.995	1.352	0.330	0.447	1.331	0.951
AUS	1974	30	1.707	1.261	0.272	0.358	1.292	0.683
AUS	1986	30	2.177	1.400	0.438	0.502	0.909	1.049
AUS	1989	30	2.408	1.560	0.489	0.552	0.885	1.238
CAN	1971	31	2.083	1.642	0.322	0.416	1.190	0.812
CAN	1976	31	2.115	1.652	0.329	0.495	1.051	0.829
CAN	1981	31	2.243	1.708	0.328	0.437	1.795	0.901
CAN	1986	31	2.240	1.670	0.364	0.465	1.248	0.953
CAN	1990	31	2.190	1.655	0.362	0.451	1.352	0.913
CAN	1997	32	1.899	1.353	0.317	0.439	1.365	0.791
DEU	1978	29	1.827	1.339	0.217	0.346	1.769	0.633

Contd.

		#	ψ	π	r	s	o	e_0
DEU	1986	29	1.847	1.402	0.222	0.375	1.461	0.629
DEU	1988	29	1.847	1.402	0.234	0.378	1.364	0.646
DEU	1990	29	1.887	1.413	0.252	0.393	1.298	0.697
DEU	1995	33	1.757	1.348	0.284	0.360	1.107	0.674
DNK	1972	28	1.861	1.266	0.327	0.405	1.410	0.850
DNK	1977	28	1.844	1.265	0.291	0.419	1.510	0.794
DNK	1980	28	1.759	1.188	0.260	0.419	1.575	0.733
DNK	1985	28	2.076	1.430	0.308	0.455	1.658	0.908
DNK	1990	28	1.997	1.399	0.347	0.449	1.153	0.905
DNK	1997	36	1.833	1.476	0.253	0.362	1.286	0.613
FRA	1980	31	1.945	1.231	0.356	0.473	1.188	0.959
FRA	1985	31	2.061	1.282	0.399	0.493	1.086	1.057
FRA	1990	31	2.297	1.388	0.512	0.552	0.856	1.299
FRA	1995	37	1.741	1.234	0.274	0.410	1.263	0.711
GBR	1968	31	1.619	1.212	0.233	0.382	1.360	0.616
GBR	1979	31	1.688	1.264	0.222	0.387	1.558	0.649
GBR	1984	31	1.974	1.353	0.314	0.450	1.451	0.896
GBR	1990	31	2.091	1.328	0.413	0.481	0.969	1.125
GBR	1998	37	1.743	1.294	0.265	0.398	1.122	0.702
JPN	1970	32	2.760	1.931	0.272	0.524	2.093	1.174
JPN	1975	32	2.285	1.772	0.223	0.439	2.079	0.787
JPN	1980	32	2.347	1.824	0.214	0.451	2.097	0.788
JPN	1985	32	2.282	1.754	0.235	0.465	1.741	0.797
JPN	1990	32	2.189	1.642	0.262	0.469	1.545	0.824
JPN	1995	37	1.811	1.358	0.302	0.410	1.078	0.717
JPN	1996	37	1.832	1.367	0.313	0.417	1.034	0.734
JPN	1997	37	1.810	1.355	0.305	0.410	1.041	0.713
NLD	1995	35	1.936	1.402	0.285	0.429	1.449	0.798
NLD	1996	35	1.929	1.399	0.276	0.429	1.527	0.787
NLD	1997	35	1.923	1.391	0.273	0.432	1.574	0.786
NLD	1998	35	1.887	1.366	0.271	0.428	1.438	0.769
CHN	1997	35	1.992	1.305	0.217	0.488	1.939	0.873
CZE	1995	37	2.212	1.313	0.230	0.505	2.150	1.052
ESP	1995	36	2.025	1.326	0.334	0.454	1.393	0.958
GRC	1994	33	3.153	1.381	0.670	0.619	1.235	2.152
HUN	1998	33	2.225	1.482	0.271	0.504	1.830	0.990
ITA	1992	35	2.315	1.451	0.407	0.495	1.195	1.217
KOR	1995	36	2.519	1.448	0.340	0.558	1.648	1.293
NOR	1997	37	2.037	1.400	0.324	0.377	1.463	0.899
POL	1995	33	2.531	1.461	0.327	0.512	2.013	1.318

Table 6
Coefficients of Variation of Empirical Distributions. OECD data

		#	ψ	π	r	s	o
AUS	1968	30	0.235	0.229	0.811	0.307	0.691
AUS	1974	30	0.222	0.233	0.900	0.398	0.902
AUS	1986	30	0.255	0.222	0.600	0.324	0.746
AUS	1989	30	0.285	0.209	0.537	0.289	0.685
CAN	1971	31	0.218	0.227	0.795	0.284	0.796
CAN	1976	31	0.279	0.271	0.998	0.810	0.764
CAN	1981	31	0.308	0.287	1.027	0.306	1.402
CAN	1986	31	0.242	0.262	0.862	0.263	0.834
CAN	1990	31	0.241	0.261	0.794	0.256	1.294
CAN	1997	32	0.222	0.223	0.783	0.301	1.225
DEU	1978	29	0.235	0.273	0.800	0.630	1.107
DEU	1986	29	0.196	0.201	0.631	0.441	0.764
DEU	1988	29	0.189	0.200	0.612	0.475	0.697
DEU	1990	29	0.188	0.201	0.612	0.490	0.617
DEU	1995	33	0.293	0.316	0.937	0.411	0.776
DNK	1972	28	0.232	0.208	0.774	0.411	0.932
DNK	1977	28	0.220	0.174	0.700	0.372	0.982
DNK	1980	28	0.191	0.146	0.627	0.394	0.855
DNK	1985	28	0.279	0.219	0.774	0.331	1.234
DNK	1990	28	0.277	0.260	0.779	0.303	0.793
DNK	1997	36	0.317	0.292	0.904	0.432	1.401
FRA	1980	31	0.236	0.238	0.647	0.369	0.683
FRA	1985	31	0.232	0.238	0.622	0.332	0.625
FRA	1990	31	0.217	0.227	0.511	0.202	0.584
FRA	1995	37	0.190	0.185	0.608	0.323	0.693
GBR	1968	31	0.106	0.123	0.572	0.303	0.714
GBR	1979	31	0.190	0.185	0.789	0.416	0.657
GBR	1984	31	0.343	0.305	1.098	0.359	1.078
GBR	1990	31	0.251	0.245	0.711	0.529	0.477
GBR	1998	37	0.193	0.178	0.591	0.348	0.505
JPN	1970	32	0.260	0.261	0.780	0.281	0.591
JPN	1975	32	0.259	0.233	0.805	0.386	0.724
JPN	1980	32	0.248	0.212	0.670	0.377	0.648
JPN	1985	32	0.234	0.192	0.506	0.343	0.609
JPN	1990	32	0.201	0.173	0.431	0.261	0.628
JPN	1995	37	0.240	0.226	0.766	0.349	0.717
JPN	1996	37	0.237	0.221	0.739	0.344	0.705
JPN	1997	37	0.242	0.225	0.754	0.349	0.715
NLD	1995	35	0.336	0.285	0.967	0.309	0.814
NLD	1996	35	0.362	0.312	1.046	0.373	0.859
NLD	1997	35	0.345	0.294	1.025	0.357	0.895
NLD	1998	35	0.311	0.265	0.912	0.364	0.677
CHN	1997	35	0.203	0.125	0.580	0.399	0.465
CZE	1995	37	0.143	0.147	0.556	0.298	0.504
ESP	1995	36	0.252	0.245	0.833	0.359	0.689
GRC	1994	33	0.528	0.432	0.860	0.309	0.916
HUN	1998	33	0.157	0.155	0.528	0.277	0.690
ITA	1992	35	0.332	0.341	0.849	0.364	0.580
KOR	1995	36	0.292	0.284	0.810	0.286	0.557
NOR	1997	37	0.537	0.520	1.942	0.505	0.788
POL	1995	33	0.362	0.311	1.068	0.406	0.738

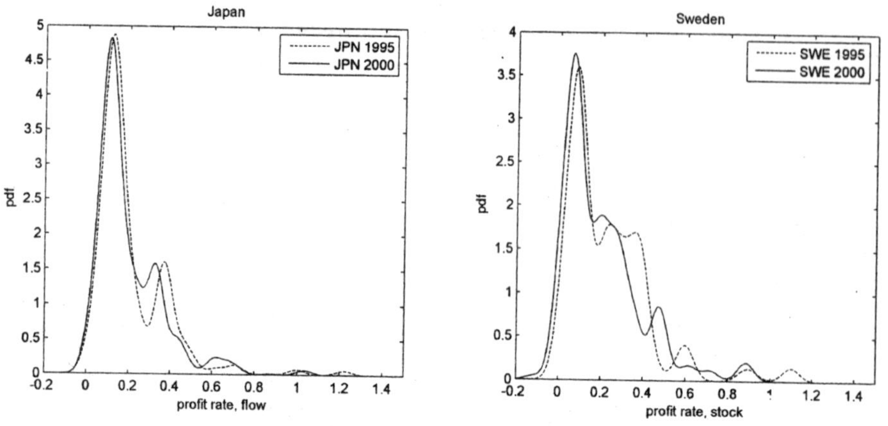

Figure 2: The distribution of profit rates. Coefficient of variation: Japan 0.919 and 0.907; Sweden 0.912 and 0.951, for years 1995 and 2000 respectively

Alternative Value Bases: the Empirical Evidence

In this Section we will address the significance of the empirical results by comparison to alternative value bases. In Section 2.1 it was argued that any value base produced as a good would be problematic to use on theoretical grounds. Value bases, such as energy, fuel, chemicals, and products of agriculture, can nonetheless be empirically tested as predictors of market prices.[9] The alternative values of industry outputs were calculated the same way as labour values (see Section 3.2) but the direct labour inputs were substituted by the alternative direct inputs. From a theoretical point of view it is worth noting that e.g. to produce 1 unit of fuel requires total 0.069 units of fuel. The results are summarized in Table 7. The alternatives clearly fall short in the presence of labour which indicates that its empirical strength is not a statistical artefact.

Table 7
Measures of Deviation from Market Prices, 48 Samples. Sweden, 1995

	ρ	θ	*C.V.*
Agriculture	0.192	73.29	2.085
Chemical	0.471	46.58	0.815
Fuel	0.541	40.81	0.833
Energy	0.722	31.83	0.540
Labour	0.956	14.06	0.343

Kliman (2005) argues that this is not a significant result since it follows from the close correlation between prices and costs. Indeed this was shown in Section 2.3. But the objection has it backwards, for what are costs if not prices? Surely, a labour theory of value cannot fall short to something as tautological as a cost theory of value.

Some Theoretical Considerations

Equalisation of profit rates

There is no evidence that the dispersion of profit rates is small or that it tends to decrease over time. As pointed out in Section 2.4, however, the TPP rests on the idea that the equalisation renders profit rates statistically independent of capital-wage ratios, and similar compositions of capital.[10] Tables 8 and 9 show that this is not the case. In most data sets there is a significant negative correlation between profit rates in flow terms $r = S/(C+V)$ and compositions of output $o = C/(S+V)$, and also between profit rates in stock terms $r^* = S/K$ and capital-wage ratios $o^* = K/V$.

Cockshott and Cottrell (1998) also find a positive correlation between composition of output and profit shares. This mechanism would indeed push profit rates closer to each other as a fraction of firms with high compositions would be 'compensated' with higher profit shares. It appears to be more of a British, rather than universal, feature of capitalism as there is no consistent tendency in the data and few correlations are statistically significant.

Table 8

Correlations between variables. Correlations in panel (b) weighted by K. Figures with* indicate p > 0.05. GBR 1984 and USA 1987 from Cockshott and Cottrell (1998, 2003)

(a)		#	$\rho(r,o)$	$\rho(r,1/o)$	$\rho(o,s)$
JPN	1995	85	-0.333	0.533	0.147*
JPN	2000	95	-0.332	0.550	0.156*
SWE	1995	48	-0.304	0.735	-0.078*
SWE	2000	48	-0.361	0.645	-0.117*
GBR	1984	96	-0.288	n.a.	0.369
(a)		#	$\bar{\rho}(r,o)$	$\rho(r,1/o)$	$\rho(o,s)$
SWE	1995	48	-0.478	0.758	0.538
SWE	2000	48	-0.520	0.758	0.438
USA	1987	47	-0.454	0.780	n.a.

Table 9

Correlations between variables. OECD data. * indicates p > 0.05

		#	$\rho(r,o)$	$\rho(r,1/o)$	$\rho(o,s)$
AUS	1968	30	-0.456	0.716	0.159*
AUS	1974	30	-0.366	0.454	0.076*
AUS	1986	30	-0.550	0.598	0.153*
AUS	1989	30	-0.566	0.557	0.322*
CAN	1971	31	-0.473	0.786	-0.142*
CAN	1976	31	0.123	0.670	-0.922*
CAN	1981	31	-0.325	0.718	0.020*
CAN	1986	31	-0.473	0.854	-0.062*

contd.

		#	$\rho(r,o)$	$\rho(r,1/o)$	$\rho(o,s)$
CAN	1990	31	-0.390	0.773	-0.116*
CAN	1997	32	-0.346	0.633	0.034*
DEU	1978	29	-0.359*	0.427	-0.368
DEU	1986	29	-0.377	0.308*	-0.116*
DEU	1988	29	-0.462	0.344*	-0.195*
DEU	1990	29	-0.475	0.376	-0.188*
DEU	1995	33	-0.369	0.486	-0.112*
DNK	1972	28	-0.483	0.678	-0.112*
DNK	1977	28	-0.408	0.640	0.188*
DNK	1980	28	-0.376	0.559	0.358*
DNK	1985	28	-0.284*	0.623	0.251*
DNK	1990	28	-0.327*	0.820	0.013*
DNK	1997	36	-0.213*	0.556	-0.070*
FRA	1980	31	-0.529	0.642	-0.007*
FRA	1985	31	-0.650	0.698	-0.188*
FRA	1990	31	-0.697	0.646	-0.216*
FRA	1995	37	-0.565	0.362	-0.160*
GBR	1968	31	-0.405	0.442	0.437
GBR	1979	31	-0.348*	0.577	0.392
GBR	1984	31	-0.244*	0.651	0.383
GBR	1990	31	-0.460	0.560	-0.023*
GBR	1998	37	-0.476	0.490	-0.125*
JPN	1970	32	-0.522	0.428	0.113*
JPN	1975	32	-0.353	0.421	0.358
JPN	1980	32	-0.419	0.549	0.420
JPN	1985	32	-0.393	0.368	0.416
JPN	1990	32	-0.476	0.369	0.252*
JPN	1995	37	-0.443	0.419	-0.012*
JPN	1996	37	-0.431	0.441	0.041*
JPN	1997	37	-0.425	0.411	0.031*
NLD	1995	35	-0.374	0.450	-0.407
NLD	1996	35	-0.354	0.471	-0.105*
NLD	1997	35	-0.341	0.458	-0.014*
NLD	1998	35	-0.438	0.406	-0.043*
CHN	1997	35	-0.522	0.538	0.298*
CZE	1995	37	-0.628	0.638	-0.214*
ESP	1995	36	-0.574	0.381	-0.034*
GRC	1994	33	-0.555	0.253*	-0.155*
HUN	1998	33	-0.539	0.553	0.230*
ITA	1992	35	-0.659	0.261*	-0.539
KOR	1995	36	-0.553	0.390	0.180*
NOR	1997	37	-0.315*	0.694	0.138*
POL	1995	33	-0.415	0.380	0.156*

The Assumptions of the Transformation Problem

We can also address the two extreme assumptions of the transformation problem: (i) a common profit-wage ratio, the 'ideal case' for labour values; and (ii) equalised profit rates, the 'ideal case' for production prices. If the profit rate $r^* = S/K$ is re-written as $r^* = s^*/o^*$, where $s^* = S/V$ and $o^* = K/V$, it is clear that the assumptions predict two different sets of profit rates:

1. $r_1 = e_0/o^*$, where e_0 is the average profit-wage ratio.
2. $r_2 = \mathrm{E}(r^*)$, which is the mean profit rate.[11]

Both sets are compared to the empirical profit rates in Figure 3. Empirical data does not fall neatly into either of these predicted profit rates, but it is clear that assumption (i) is better in accounts with reality than (ii). This is further implied by the positive linear correlation between profit rates and the inverse capital-wage ratio in Table 8.

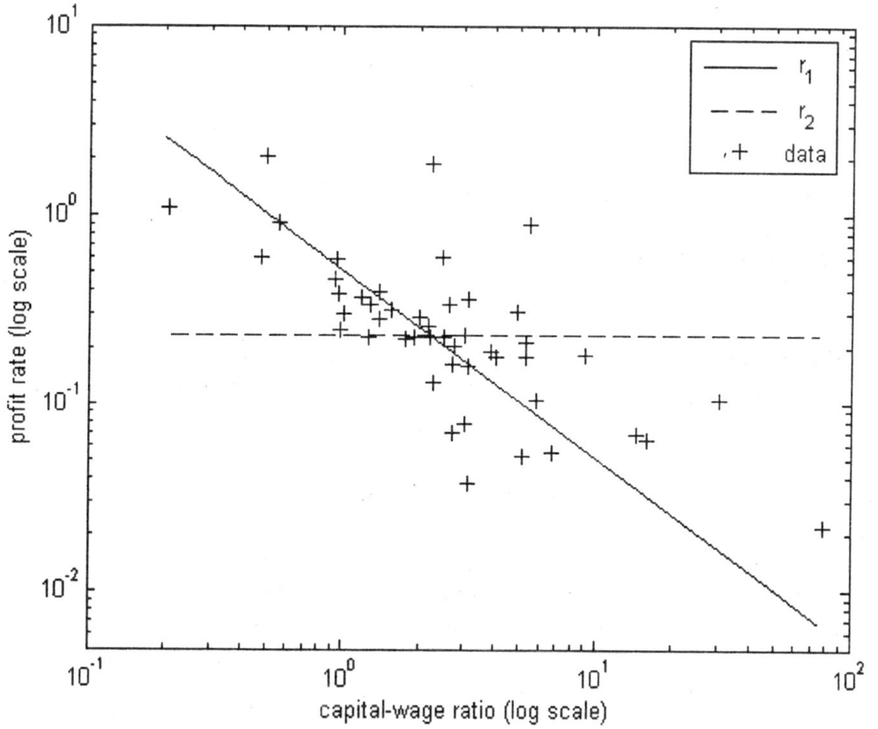

Figure 3: Profit rates versus capital-wage ratios, in log-log scale, 47 samples (negative data excluded). Sweden 1995

Production Prices and the General Rate of Profit

Production prices Π were computed from $p = (I-(1+r_G)A)^{-1}w$, where r_G is the general rate of profit towards which profit rates are thought to gravitate. If $r_G = 0$ production prices are proportional to labour values, when abstracting from wage-rate differentials across industries. How will an increase in this parameter affect the deviation of production prices to market prices? To answer this r_G was set to 501 equally spaced values in the interval [0,0.50], resulting in 501 different sets of production prices. For each set the correlation coefficient $\rho(P, \Pi)$ was calculated. The result is shown in Figure 4 where $\rho(P, \Pi)$ is plotted against r_G.

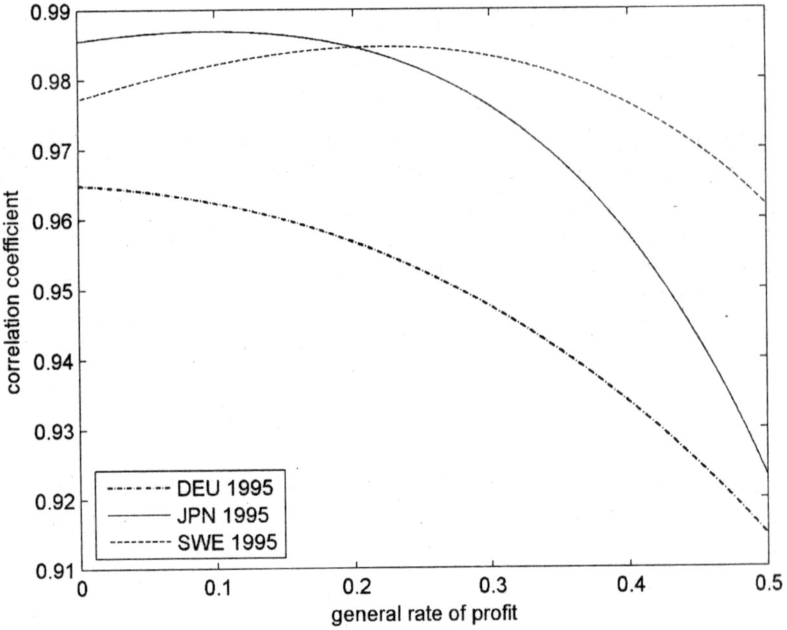

Figure 4: Correlation coefficient $\rho(P,\Pi)$ versus general rate of profit r_G. Note that r_G was set to 0.284 (Germany), 0.212 (Japan) and 0.186 (Sweden) respectively, for 1995

Increasing r_G, which pushes production prices further apart from labour values, does lead to a slight improvement in predictive power for Sweden but marginally for Japan and negatively for Germany, acting only as a disturbance on the matrix of technical coefficients. It is notable that when it is set to 0.50, roughly two times greater than the empirical estimate, correlation coefficients are still above 0.9. This could help explain the puzzling fact that despite the anomalies for the TPP its predictive power is approximately equal to the LTV.

CONCLUSION

We have found that market prices and labour value of industry outputs are highly correlated for a fairly broad sample of economies covering different sizes, levels of development and institutional structures. The results are in line with similar studies done for the US, Britain, Greece, Italy, former Yugoslavia and Mexico. (See Tsoulfidis and Maniatis (2002).) The distribution of price-value ratios remains narrow in relation to the distribution of profit rates and alternative value bases and is broadly consistent with the prediction Farjoun and Machover made some twenty years ago. The results for the alternatives indicate that the empirical strength of labour is not a statistical artefact.

Production price is not found to be a superior predictor of market price and indeed deviates little from labour values. The equalisation of profit rates does not appear to operate in the way assumed by the theory of production prices: The distributions of profit rates were wide and showed no consistent sign of narrowing over time. Whatever forces pushing profit rates closer, they are always checked by counter-forces so profit rates should instead be thought to conform to some statistical distribution when the economy is in a stable condition. The profitability mechanism that pushes firms to move from low to high return industry sectors is likely to operate on a longer time-scale than the more immediate constraints imposed by the need to pay the wage-bill and by technical conditions represented by the production matrix. Reducing the scale of production in one sector while building up capital stocks in another is by its nature a relatively slow process. These constraints explain why the simple labour theory of value is better in accounts with empirical data than the theory of production prices.

Further research must explain why the disturbance between labour values and market prices, arising from variations in the vertically integrated profit-wage ratio, is relatively low. For each firm this ratio is the weighted average of the direct profit-wage ratios of all producers that enter directly and indirectly in its output. Part of the explanation lies in the level of interconnection in modern economies but the question that remains is what restricts the dispersion of direct profit-wage ratios?

The results suggest that labour value is an attractor to market price. This could be interpreted as a practical way for market economies, capitalist or socialist, to regulate social labour, a special case of a general economic problem. Market prices are then a measure of labour value and, according to measurement theory, they will be subject to (1) random errors caused by supply-demand discrepancies which are necessary for the market to regulate social labour, (2) systematic errors caused by profit rate equalising mechanisms and rent effects. From this perspective the preoccupation with the 'transformation problem' appears to be a mistake, drawing time and effort away from useful theoretical and empirical research aimed at uncovering the processes of economies governed by market exchange.

NOTES

1. 'Average' meaning the aggregate ratio of wages to labour-time and profits to wages.
2. A deeper analysis and elaboration is not pursued here but a rational definition of productive activities could be proposed, analogous to the Sraffian basic commodities (Sraffa (1983, § 6)), that every activity that directly or indirectly enters into the wage-bundle, and thus reproduces the economy, is productive. (See forthcoming article, 'Hunting Productive Work', in *Science and Society* by Cockshott and Zachariah.)
3. Basically gross value added plus unproductive costs less wages. Less depreciation of fixed capital if data was available. For consistency between i/o tables cast in

producer and basic prices, 'net taxes on products' proportional to the productive inputs were treated as a part of C.

4. Matrix element a_{ij} represents the input of j required to produce a unit of i.
5. There is no significant difference of the summary statistics between the discrete distribution and the continuous approximations.
6. Hence it would be inappropriate to deflate industry outputs by size, as suggested in Kliman (2005, sec.4), in order to address any spurious correlation arising from aggregation. This should rather be done by using less aggregated data or comparing results to alternative predictors as in Section 4.3.
7. The angle θ is defined by the dot product between the vectors: $x.y = |x|\,|y|\cos\theta$. Note that the unit is degrees. Cockshott (2005), however, suggests that the appropriate measures are for vectors in a 'commodity amplitude space'.
8. Lacking depreciation coefficients, depreciation was included in gross profits for estimates of e_0.
9. The direct and indirect input of 'Electrical energy, gas, steam and hot water' (energy), 'Coke, refined petroleum products, nuclear fuels' (fuel), 'Chemicals, chemical products and man-made fibres' (chemical) and 'Products of agriculture, hunting and related services' (agriculture).
10. Such as $o = C/(S+V)$ to be consistent with the methodology in Cockshott and Cottrell (1998).
11. Since r^* is weighted by K, $E(r^*)$ is equivalent to the theoretical 'general rate of profit' on a stock basis.

REFERENCES

Cockshott, W.P. and Cottrell, A. (1997a), The Scientific Status of the Labour Theory of Value. Paper presented at the IWGVT conference at the Eastern Economic Association meeting, in April 1997. Available at: http://www.wfu.edu/~cottrell/

Cockshott, W.P. and Cottrell, A. (1997b), Labour time versus Alternative value bases: a Research note, *Cambridge Journal of Economics*, 21, 545-9.

Cockshott, W.P. and Cottrell, A. (1998), Does Marx Need to Transform?, in R. Bellofiore (ed.), *Marxian Economics: A Reappraisal,* vol. 2, Basingstoke, Macmillan/St Martin's Press.

Cockshott, W.P. and Cottrell, A. (2003), A Note on the Organic Composition of Capital and Profit Rates, *Cambridge Journal of Economics*, 27, 749-54.

Cockshott, W.P. and Cottrell, A. (2005), Robust Correlations between Prices and Labour values: a Comment, *Cambridge Journal of Economics*, 29, 309-16.

Cockshott, P. (2005), Symmetries and Exchange Relations, *Politica y Cultura*, 23, 3-32.

Farjoun, E. and Machover, M. (1983), *The Laws of Chaos*, London, Verso.

Foley, D. (2000), Recent Developments in the Labour theory of Value. Paper Presented at the IWGVT Conference at the Eastern Economic Association meeting, in April 1997. Available at: *http://www.iwgvt.org*. Published in *Review of Radical Political Economics*, 32, 1-39.

Kliman, A. (2005), Reply to Cockshott and Cottrell, *Cambridge Journal of Economics*, 29, 317-23.

OECD (2002), Input-Output tables, 1995 and 2002 editions. Available at: http://www.oecd.org

Shaikh, A. (1998), The Empirical Strength of the Labour Theory of Value, in R. Bellofiore (Ed.), *Marxian Economics: A Reappraisal*, vol. 2, Basingstoke, Macmillan/St Martin's Press.

Shaikh, A. and Antonopoulos, R. (1998), Explaining Long Term Exchange Rate Behavior in the United States and Japan, Working Paper No. 250, The Jerome Levy Economic Institute. Available at: http://www.levy.org

Shaikh, A. and Tonak, A. (1994), *Measuring the Wealth of Nations*, Cambridge, Cambridge University Press.

Sraffa, P. (1983), *Produktion av varor medelst varor*, Röda Bokförlaget AB. [*Production of Commodities by Means of Commodities*. Cambridge University Press, 1960.]

Statistics Bureau of Japan (2004), Transaction Tables. Available at: http://www.stat.go.jp/english/data/io/

Statistics Sweden (2004), Symmetric Input-Output tables. Available at: http://www.scb.se

Statistics Sweden, Arbetade timmar (ENS95) efter naringsgren SNI92 och tid. Available at http://www.scb.se

Tsoulfidis, L. and Maniatis, T. (2002), Values, Prices of Production and Market Prices: some more Evidence from the Greek economy, *Cambridge Journal of Economics*, 26, 359-69.

Valle Baeza, A. (1997), Prices for Regulating and Measuring Marxian Labour Values, *Research in Political Economy*, 16. Available at: http://usuarios.lycos.es/vallebaeza/

A CRITIQUE OF THE 'NEW APPROACH' TO THE TRANSFORMATION PROBLEM AND A PROPOSAL

*Theodore Mariolis**

This paper shows that the 'New Approach' to the 'problem of transforming values into prices', first, is subjected to a crucial logical inconsistency and second, is not in a position to deal with the heterogeneous labour case. Thus, the paper proposes an approach, which overcomes these problems and concludes that values of commodities are their actual prices.

INTRODUCTION

In contrast with the *traditional* approach to the so-called 'transformation problem', in the context of which the values of commodities are defined as the quantities of labour 'embodied', the 'New Approach or Interpretation'[1] (NA hereafter), which has been developed independently by Duménil (1980) and Foley (1982), does not disregard the lessons of the Sraffian theory and, at the same time, is based on the notion of *abstract social labour*. Thus, according to the NA, the value of 'labour power' and surplus product is determined by their *actual* prices and, specifically, is equal to the product of their actual price times a coefficient known as the 'value of money'.

In this paper, we shall prove the following three propositions:[2]

P_1. The NA, first, is subjected to a crucial *logical* inconsistency and second, is not in a position to deal with the *heterogeneous* labour case.

P_2. The NA can remove this inconsistency. However, even it is rid of it, then, first, it is economically insignificant and second, it is still unable to deal with the heterogeneous labour case. All this shows that in the context of the NA, the notion of abstract social labour has not been correctly formulated.

P_3. If the notion of abstract social labour is correctly formulated, then it is possible to develop a consistent and general approach to the 'transformation problem', which results in the conclusion that values of commodities are their *actual* prices.

---

* Department of Public Administration, Panteion University, Athens, Greece; e-mail: mariolis@panteion.gr I am indebted to Professors D.K. Foley, A. Freeman, d. Laibman, I. Steedman, and Associate Professors C. Lapavitsas, S. Mavroudeas, L. Tsoulfidis for helpful comments on earlier versions of this paper. The reponsibility for the views expressed rests entirely with the author.

Precisely because our proposed approach, first, takes into account the lessons of the Sraffian theory, and, at the same time, is based on the notion of abstract social labour, second, is general enough so as the NA when corrected for its inconsistencies becomes one of its infinite special cases and third, covers the heterogeneous labour case, we *may* call it the 'Completed New Approach' (CNA hereafter; an initial sketch of which is in Mariolis (1998)).

The remainder of the paper is organized as follows. Section 2 briefly presents the NA. Section 3 critically evaluates the NA. Section 4 elaborates the CNA. Section 5 determines the relationships between the CNA and the NA. Finally, Section 6 concludes.

THE NEW APPROACH

The NA does not presuppose (it is not necessary for it to presuppose), the existence of linear techniques of single production and prices of production.[3] However, in order to avoid needlessly burdening the discussion, we shall present the NA under these presuppositions (for a presentation of the NA, see also Glick and Ehbar (1987), Mohun (1994), Saad-Filho (1996), Foley, (1997)).

Consider a system of single production that uses the linear, indecomposable and *viable* technique $[A, a]$, where A denotes the $n \times n$ matrix of input coefficients and a denotes the $1 \times n$ vector of inputs of direct *homogeneous* labour, and in which the prices are *production* prices (see, e.g., Kurz and Salvadori, (1995, ch. 4)). Assume that the magnitudes $p \equiv [p_j]$, the $1 \times n$ vector of prices, w, the money wage rate, X, the $n \times 1$ vector of activity levels, are given and economically significant, whilst the composition and level of the real wage rate are unknown *a priori* (for the justification of this choice, see Duménil (1980, ch.7 and pp. 121-5), Foley (1982, p. 43) and Mohun, (1994, pp. 400-2)). On the basis of the above, we can calculate the $1 \times n$ vector $\omega \equiv [\omega_j]$ (> 0) of the quantities of labour 'embodied' in the different commodities, the $1 \times n$ vector Y of the net output, the total profits, P,[4] and the following magnitude λ_m:

$$\lambda_m \equiv (aX / pY) \equiv (\omega Y / pY) \tag{1}$$

which is called 'value of money'.[5] If, now, the unit value of 'labour power', V, is *defined* as the product of the value of money times the money wage rate, i.e.,

$$V \equiv w\lambda_m \tag{2}$$

then for the total 'surplus value', S, which, is *by definition* equal to $aX(1 - V)$, the following will hold:

$$S \equiv aX(1 - w\lambda_m) \tag{3}$$

Consequently, for the total profits, the following holds:

$$S \equiv P\lambda_m \tag{4}$$

Finally, if we rearrange (1) as follows

$$aX\,(\equiv \omega Y) \equiv pY\lambda_m \tag{1a}$$

then it is clear that (1a) and (4) express the validity of a modified (with respect to the net output) 'Marxian double equality': For all p, w, X, the value of the net output (the surplus value) is equal to the product of the value of money times the price of the net output (times the total profits).[6]

It is clear that the crucial point of the NA is the definition introduced by (2). Thus, it could possibly be considered that by virtue of (2), the following *premise* is implicitly introduced: The quantity of labour 'embodied' in the real wage equals the share of wages in national income. That is, it could be considered that although the real wage rate is unknown *a priori*, the advocates of the NA argue the following: The quantity of labour which has been 'embodied' in all those bundles of commodities, which workers can purchase with the money wage rate, equals the share of wages in national income.

If this were the case, then the NA would be correct only by way of exception, i.e., when (i) the real wages and the net output have the same composition; or (ii) the real wages and the net output are associated with each other just as the Standard commodity of Sraffa (1960, ch. 6) is associated with the Standard commodities of Miyao (1977); or (iii) the commodity prices are proportional to the quantities of labour 'embodied'; or (iv) $w = 0$; or (v) by chance, that is, for certain, perhaps, positive values of w. In reality, however, the NA is *not* founded on the aforementioned premise (see also Mohun (1994, pp. 398-9)) and, to be precise, the advocates of the NA maintain something completely different. Thus, Foley (1982, p. 42) *interprets* (2) as follows: 'The basic insight of the labor theory of value is its claim that value forms, money, commodities, and so on, are expressions of *abstract social labour*. Thus in any transaction involving value, what is changing hands is control over some part of total abstract social labor time. *The value of labor power, in this perspective, is the fraction of the total abstract social labor time claimed by workers in the form of the wage*. This is an exchange of abstract labor in the form of money for the particular labor power a worker has to offer on the market. If we follow this path, we would *interpret* the value of labor power in general as the money wage multiplied by the value of money...' [emphasis added], whilst at the same time, at other points he clarifies that: 'A unit of money [...] can be thought of as a claim to a certain amount of the abstract social labor expended in the economy [...] (p. 37). The advantage of interpreting the value of money as the ratio of aggregate labor time to aggregate money value added is that the sum of the value gained and lost by all the producers in exchange will be zero. In other words, this interpretation of the value of money corresponds to the idea that value is created in production but conserved in exchange. (p. 41). [Thus–T.M.] we retain at the global level the relation between money and embodied labor which is central to the idea that money is a form of value and that the substance of value is abstract social labor. (p. 41)'. Finally, Mohun (1994, pp. 404-5) sums up the NA as follows: 'It is an aggregative theory in which total labour performed defines the value of net output; the value of net output and aggregate value added in money terms defines the value of money; and the value of money and the money wage define the value of labour-power. *A price system is then a method of distributing aggregate labour-time expended across individual commodities*. Hence prices are always [...] representations or forms of value, of abstract labour. [...] Market processes of exchange commensurate commodities, and hence *a posteriori* commensurate the labour-times objectified in their production. Abstraction from concrete labours occurs as heterogeneous commodities are valued in units of homogeneous money. Value is then labour-time as it appears as money.' (emphasis added; see also Duménil (1984, pp. 340-3)).

From the above, we may deduce that within the framework of the NA, the following hold:

1. The magnitude $aX \equiv \omega Y$ is considered as the total quantity of *abstract social* labour that corresponds to a given system $[A, a, X]$. Consequently, the one unit of labour that has been 'embodied' in the net output, Y, is *chosen* as the *unit of measurement* of *abstract social* labour.
2. The dimension of the magnitude λ_m is not only: units of 'embodied' labour per unit of money, but also: units of abstract social labour per unit of money. For precisely this reason, λ_m is defined 'as the coefficient which enables a translation between prices into labour-times' (Mohun (1994, p. 402)), whilst its level expresses how many units of abstract social labour are represented by one unit of money (see also Foley (1982, p. 41)).
3. The magnitude V defined by (2) has the dimension: units of abstract social labour per unit of labour power expended. It is, therefore, a magnitude, which differs entirely from the unit value of labour power, as this is defined *traditionally*. In addition, the magnitude S (see (3) and (4)) has the dimension: units of abstract social labour per unit of surplus product. It is, therefore, a magnitude, which differs entirely from the quantity of labour 'embodied' in the surplus product, i.e., from the surplus value, as this is defined *traditionally*.
4. Given $[A, a]$ and X, the magnitudes V and S depend on p and w. However, the sum of the surplus value and the value of total labour power is *always* equal to the quantity of total abstract social labour.
5. The value of the net output, of labour power and of the surplus product is measured in units of abstract social labour. When $[A, a]$ and X remain constant, and p, w change (not proportionally), the value of the net output expressed in units of abstract social labour does not change (because it is equal to aX), but the value of labour power and of the surplus product change, because to the said commodities there now correspond different proportions of the total abstract social labour of the system ('The amount of labour time expended in a given period is the value of a given bundle of commodities. *A price system expresses the reallocation of these hours of productive labor time to this bundle of commodities*. The total amount of labor time expended in a period being the value of the net output of the period, this quantity of labor must be reallocated to this net output. Thus, Marx's first equalities (sum of value = sum of prices), must be defined for the *net output of the period* and not the gross output as in the old solution.' (Duménil (1984, pp. 341-2); see also Mohun (2000)).

It is precisely these points, which constitute the core of the NA and what remains is to check its consistency and significance.[7]

CRITIQUE OF THE NEW APPROACH

We have so far shown that the NA is founded on the notion of abstract social labour, which means that in principle it transcends all the well-known critical evaluations that have been made of the *traditional* approach. We shall now show, however, that the NA is neither consistent (1) nor general (2):[8]

1. Within the framework of the NA, the values of three, and only three, commodities (i.e., the value of the net output, of labour power and of the surplus product) are defined/expressed in units of abstract social labour, whilst the values of all the other commodities are defined/expressed in units of 'embodied' labour.[9] In other words, the NA (and moreover, without explaining why) defines one and the same magnitude, value, in disagreement (in the case of the aforementioned 'special' commodities) and, at the same time, in agreement (in the case of any other commodity) with the *traditional* conception. This contradiction is of course not without repercussions, for the question: 'to what is the value of the surplus product equal?' accepts, in the context of the NA, two mutually excluding answers: (i) Because the surplus product consists of n kinds of different commodities, it follows that its value is equal to the aggregate of quantities of labour that have been 'embodied' in those commodities. (ii) Because the total abstract social labour is equal to aX and because the value of total labour power is equal to $w\lambda_m aX$, it follows that the value of the surplus product is equal to $aX(1\text{-}w\lambda_m)$. So, at this point there is a crucial logical inconsistency in the NA.

2. The NA identifies total abstract social labour with the quantity aX. Subsequently, it considers that this quantity, on the one hand *appears* as pY and, on the other hand, is *redistributed* among the commodity labour power and the surplus product according to the ratio of the price of each of these commodities to the price of the net output of the system (i.e., $V \equiv (w/pY)aX$, $S \equiv (P/pY)aX$). A 'rule' of redistribution, which apparently entails the validity of the following relation:

$$VaX + S \equiv aX \tag{5}$$

So, in accordance with the NA, it must be said that this relation expresses a 'conservation principle'[10], which governs the *conversion* of labour from 'embodied' to abstract social (a conversion which takes place in the framework of the exchange of commodities mediated by money).[11]

If, however, commodities are produced by means of m (> 1) types of labour, then, as is well known, the quantities of 'embodied' labours are determined by

$$\Omega \equiv L[I - A]^{-1} \tag{6}$$

where L denotes the $m \times n$ matrix of labour input coefficients and Ω the $m \times n$ matrix of 'embodied' labours.[12] Consequently, the total quantity of direct labours is represented by an $m \times 1$ vector and, thus, each attempt to find a 'conservation principle' (i.e., any connection whatsoever between the multidimensional magnitude LX and the total quantity of abstract social labour, which corresponds to the given system $[A, L, X]$ and which is by definition a scalar) proves to be devoid of any economic meaning and content.[13]

We shall therefore show below that in the framework of the NA, the notion of abstract social labour has not, in reality, been correctly formulated.

THE COMPLETED NEW APPROACH

As is well known, Marx tried to show that in a society of independent producers, in which 'labour power' is a commodity ('capitalist mode of production'), the products of *labour*[14] necessarily appear, and consequently, are exchanged, as products of the various *capitals*. This entails that in the capitalist mode of production, first, the social division/combination of labour is mediated both by exchange[15] and the aim to maximize the individual money rates of profit and second, the commodity prices systematically deviate from the quantities of labour 'embodied' (see also Foley (1982, pp. 39-40)).

But when prices deviate from the quantities of labour 'embodied', the following occurs: By virtue of the *exchange* defined by the ratio (p_g/p_j) $(\neq (\omega_g/\omega_j))$, $g, j = 1, 2, \ldots, n, g \neq j$, the ω_g units of homogeneous labour 'embodied' in one unit of commodity g are *equated with* the $(p_g/p_j)\omega_j$ units of homogeneous labour 'embodied' in (p_g/p_j) units of commodity j, and thus constitute equal quantities of a – completely different to their own, and consequently–'*new*' quality: *abstract social labour*.[16] They constitute, that is, B (*by convention*, where B denotes a positive real number) units of abstract social labour.[17] Because, according to Marx,[18] abstract social labour constitutes the substance of value and consequently value is measured in units of abstract social labour, it follows that the unit *value*, ω_g^*, of the commodity g is B units of abstract social labour and the unit *value*, ω_j^*, of the commodity j is $(p_j/p_g)B$ units of abstract social labour. Alternatively, we could choose (*arbitrarily*), as a *unit of measurement* of abstract social labour, the C units of labour that have been 'embodied' in a produced commodity u, where u denotes an $n \times 1$ *semi-positive* vector. In this case, which exists *only* when labour is homogeneous, we would have:

$$\omega^* u = \omega u/C \tag{7}$$

$$\omega_j^* = p_j[(\omega u/C)/pu], j = 1, 2, \ldots, n \tag{7a}$$

$$V^* = w[(\omega u/C)/pu] \tag{7b}$$

$$S^* = P[(\omega u/C)/pu] \tag{7c}$$

where ω^* denotes the $1 \times n$ vector of unit *values*, V^* the unit *value* of 'labour power', and S^* the *surplus value*.

Consequently, we conclude that the values of the commodities are always proportional to their actual prices. However, the arbitrary choice of the measure of values and the unit of measurement of abstract social labour is an unnecessary and meaningless act, because this act has 'already' been performed within the economic reality *itself*: Exchange is mediated by money and consequently money constitutes the measure of value, whilst the unit of money constitutes the unit of measurement of abstract social labour. Therefore, values are always equal to the actual prices, that is[19]

$$\omega^* \equiv p \tag{8}$$

$$V^* \equiv w \tag{8a}$$

$$S^* \equiv P \tag{8b}$$

Evidently, it is not money that transforms the products of labour into commensurate magnitudes. Exactly the opposite holds: Exchanged in proportions which express in the main *all* the features of the constituted society, the products of labour become commensurate and can be measured in terms of some homogeneous extensive thing.[20] In this way, the said thing (which is not necessarily a commodity) is transformed into a common measure of the value of commodities or money. Money (the price) constitutes, therefore, the necessary form of existence of 'embodied' labour (of the quantity of 'embodied' labour), which has 'first' been transformed into abstract social labour (into a quantity of abstract social labour). When commodities are exchanged as products of labour, i.e., $(p_g/p_j) = (\omega_g/\omega_j), g, j = 1, 2, \ldots, n$, prices express, from a qualitative viewpoint, the corresponding quantities of 'embodied' labour in a distorted manner. Although the vectors p, ω are collinear, the element p_j has the dimension: units of money per unit of commodity j, and the element Hu_j has the dimension: units of 'embodied' labour per unit of commodity j. In this case, therefore, there is an intrinsic-immanent ('embodied' labour) and an extrinsic (money) measure of value. When commodities are not exchanged as products of labour, the prices express, both from a qualitative and a quantitative viewpoint, the corresponding quantities of 'embodied' labour in a distorted manner. In this case, therefore, there is one and only one measure of value: money. Precisely for this reason, in the *capitalist* mode of production the quantities of 'embodied' labour cease to have any *valid* significance for the economic subjects: *For example*, each individual capitalist realizes that both that part of the total profits of the system, which he can acquire, and the very existence of a positive, for him, profit, are exclusively dependent (are completely independent) on the money prices of commodities (of labour, i.e., the only factor that, according to Marx, creates the net output and consequently the surplus product).[21,22] However, it is a situation, which, on the one hand, was created by the subjects themselves, within the framework of which, on the other, their aforesaid realization is not contradicted but rather verified and therefore constitutes a valid condition of their action.[23]

THE RELATIONSHIPS BETWEEN THE COMPLETED NEW APPROACH AND THE NEW APPROACH

The CNA is expressed first of all through the relations (7)-(7c). So, if we choose $u = Y$ and $C = 1$, then we will get the NA without the logical inconsistency that we highlighted in Section 3 (1). Consequently, it could be said that the NA constitutes a special case (among the infinite cases) of the CNA, because it follows from it by virtue of an appropriate choice of the measure of value and the unit of measurement of abstract social labour.[24] Nevertheless, the following should be noted (in relation to what was said in Sections 3 and 4):

1. The choice of the measure of values and the unit of measurement of abstract social labour is an unnecessary and meaningless act, because this act has 'already' been performed in economic reality itself: Exchange is mediated by money and consequently money constitutes the measure of value, whilst the unit of money constitutes the unit of measurement of abstract social labour.

2. As we have already seen, the followers of the NA justify their view as follows: 'The advantage of interpreting the value of money as the ratio of aggregate labor time to aggregate money value added is that the value gained and lost by all the producers in exchange will be zero. In other words, this interpretation of the value of money corresponds to the idea that value is created in production but conserved in exchange' (Foley (1982, p. 41); see also Duménil (1984, pp. 346-7) and Mohun (1994, pp. 402-3)). However, 'value' in terms of 'embodied' labour is something *quite different* (as we have showed in Section 4) from value in terms of abstract social labour. Thus, the premise for the existence of any connection whatsoever between these magnitudes (i.e., not only $\omega^{*}Y = \omega Y$, which according to the NA expresses a 'conservation principle') has no economic meaning and, consequently, is not logically consistent. Furthermore, it is by no means necessary to introduce the 'conservation principle' $\omega^{*}Y = \omega Y$, in order to express 'the idea that value is created in production but conserved in exchange', because, according to Marx, exchange always presupposes exchange of equivalent things, i.e., exchange of equal values and consequently 'profit' and 'loss' never arise within the framework of each separate exchange (which, supposedly, cancel each other out when one takes into consideration the entirety of exchanges performed). For one to assert that when one unit of commodity g is exchanged for p_g/p_j units of commodity j, profit and loss arise because $(p_g/p_j) \neq (\omega_g/\omega_j)$, has exactly the same economic significance as the assertion that profit and loss arise because the quantities that are exchanged do not have the same weight or the same mass.[25]
3. To be precise, the choice of the measure of values is not only an unnecessary and meaningless act, but also leads to 'perverse' situations (in the general case). For example, if we choose $u = Y$, then in order for $\omega^{*} > 0$ to result, it is necessary and sufficient for $pY > 0$ to hold (see (7a)). In reality, of course, nothing prevents *a priori* the validity of, $pY \leq 0$.[26] Furthermore, when this latter relation holds, nothing prevents us from choosing a different u and converting the indeterminate or negative values of single commodities into positive ones.[27]
4. Even if we for a moment ignore all the preceding issues, the case of heterogeneous labour (see Section 3 (2)), in the context of which each syllogism based on the existence of any kind of 'conservation principle' collapses, shows conclusively that the NA erroneously sets forth the issue of abstract social labour.

In view of all the above, it therefore follows that in the best case the NA constitutes one of all those infinite special cases of the CNA, which are economically insignificant and unrealistic, and it is clear that all the various problems presented by the NA stem from the fact that it has not correctly formulated the notion that is fundamental to it, namely the notion of abstract social labour. For, in the opposite case, it would be both logically consistent and in a position to deal with the case of the existence of heterogeneous labour.

CONCLUDING REMARKS

In accordance with the Marxian theory, the notion of the capitalist mode of production presupposes the interpretation of profit, the determination of its source. But because profit is the money price of a particular commodity, i.e., of the surplus product, it follows that the Marxian notion of the capitalist mode of production presupposes the *interpretation* of commodity, price and money.

The 'New Approach or Interpretation' was different to the *traditional* approach precisely because it turned its attention to the fundamental issue of abstract social labour, that is, to the analysis of the so-called 'forms of value'. However, quite paradoxically, it did not manage to put together a coherent and complete formulation of the said issue. Most likely because, at the same time, it displayed an (un)justifiable focus on the validity of 'Marxian double equality'. As a consequence, it managed to reach, let us put it this way, only the halfway point of the distance it should have covered.

The approach that has been elaborated here has covered (we wish to believe) the 'remaining distance', and should not be judged only on the basis of its final conclusion (relations (8)–(8b)), a conclusion which shows, *inter alia*, that each theoretical and empirical effort to find an economically significant, quantitative relationship of any kind between prices and quantities of private and concrete labours is pointless, but primarily on the basis, first, of the logical course followed in order to reach this conclusion, second, the degree to which it sets out and, subsequently, reconstructs in a logically consistent manner the core of Marxian theory and third, its contribution to the attainment of theoretical targets which Marxian theory has set for itself.

NOTES

1. We prefer, as being more precise, these terms to the term: 'New Solution'. In this respect, see Saad-Filho (1996, pp. 116-8) and Foley (1997, p. 45).
2. For brevity's sake, we shall not deal here either with the *traditional* approach (our positions are set out in Mariolis (1998, 2002b, 2003)) or the other more recent approaches / interpretations.
3. Steedman (1992) proved that in the joint production case more than one profit rate can be associated with an exogenously given value of the share of wages in national income. Consequently, the *realistic* case of joint production creates insurmountable problems for the NA (see also the subsequent discussion between Mohun (1993a,b) and Steedman (1993); moreover, see Steedman (2002, pp. 2-4)). It should be clarified that we do not consider an exogenously given wage share as a basic element of the NA *in the sense* that one can present the NA without using this element (see below).
4. As is well known, the following hold:

$$\omega \equiv a[I-A]^{-1}$$
$$Y \equiv [I-A]X$$
$$\omega Y \equiv \alpha X$$
$$P \equiv pY - waX$$

where I denotes the $n \times n$ identity matrix and $(I\ X)$ the $n \times 1$ vector of the gross output.

5. It should be noted that the NA does *not* premise the (semi-)positiveness of the net output. But when prices deviate from the production prices, it demands that $pY > 0$ (obviously, when prices equal the production prices, and the production technique is indecomposable, the validity of this relation is *always* given), because it considers that in the opposite case 'the idea of a 'transformation problem' becomes self-contradictory' (Duménil (1984, p. 347)).
6. If the absolute price level is not given, then we can introduce the normalization equation $pY = aX$. Thus, we will get the following: $S \equiv P$.
7. We do not consider the criticism of the NA set forth by Roemer (1990, p. 1728), Shaikh and Tonak (1994, p. 179), Sotirchos and Stamatis (1998), Stamatis (1998-99), Febrero Pãnos (2000) and Mavroudeas (2001), to be 'fair', because within the framework of this criticism, the NA is not set out faithfully (see also Mohun (2000)). We believe, however, that it is precisely the issues that we present below (Section 3) which prevent the comprehension, and consequently the faithful impression of the NA.
8. As the reader will ascertain, these two issues are to begin with independent of each other. However, it will subsequently be shown (Section 5) that they are related.
9. '[I]t is clear that in general the price of any commodity multiplied by the value of money as defined here will not be equal to the labor value of the commodity. [...] The price of a commodity in this interpretation is the amount of money for which it exchanges on the market, an amount of money which may represent more or less social labor than is embodied in the commodity itself and which determines its labor value' (Foley (1982, p. 43 and 44)). For an argument that is similar to ours, see Sinha (1997, p. 52).
10. See the excerpts from p. 41 of Foley (1982), which we have already presented here (Section 2), as well as Duménil (1984, pp. 346-7) and Mohun (1994, pp. 402-3).
11. Precisely for this reason, the NA has no choice but to assert that when the price of the net output is not positive, 'then the idea of a 'transformation problem' becomes self-contradictory' (Duménil (1984, p. 347)).
12. For a critique of each attempt to 'reduce' one type of labour to another, see Steedman (1977, ch. 7, 1980, 1985, 1990) and Mariolis (2002a, pp. 208-9).
13. It should be noted that Foley (1997, p. 45) does not deal with this problem directly, but places it on an empirical level: 'There are also issues of measurement of [...] the living labor expended. In principle it is necessary to adjust total hours worked for the skill levels of workers. A variety of method, some based on relative wage weights, and others on more direct measures of skill, have been proposed to make this adjustment. [...] In the rest of this paper I will assume (contrary to reality) that some agreement has been made on these measurement issues...'.
14. It is clear that if the expression 'the products of labour' is to have any meaning, it must be assumed (contrary to what applies in the real world) that labour is homogeneous. This assumption is introduced solely because it facilitates not only the exposition of the CNA but also the determination of the relationships between the CNA and the NA.
15. Through the exchange of products, exchange that is defined quantitatively by the actual prices and mediated by money, the quantities of corresponding ('embodied' in the various products) *private* and *concrete labours* are also exchanged. Thus, through this process and without it being the aim of the producers or even being realized by them, the products of labour are transformed into commodities, labour

and production are socialized, the set of independent producers is formed into a society, and the aforementioned quantities of private and concrete labours are transformed into quantities of social and abstract labour, respectively, and are represented as different, commensurate quantities of one and the same thing: money.

16. Because the exchange of commodities presupposes their production and their production presupposes exchange that took place in an earlier period of time, we are not talking about a 'new' quality from the point of view of time, but about a 'new' quality from the point of view of logic. It is for this reason that the word 'new' appears in inverted commas.

17. If, as we assume here, the quantities of private, concrete labours are homogeneous, then the exchange creates a 'new' measure of equivalence of commodities: abstract social labour, which cancels (as we shall see later) the 'initial' measure of their equivalence: 'embodied' labour. If the quantities of private, concrete labours are heterogeneous, then there is no 'initial' measure of equivalence of commodities. Only as percentages of overall abstract social labour are commodities equivalent.

18. This does not mean that the position maintained here is in agreement with what Marx wrote (and especially with the chapters on the 'Transformation Problem' in Volume III of 'Capital'; see also Steedman, (1977, 1985, 1991) and Mariolis (2000, 2002a, 2005)). We believe, however, that it is in agreement with the core of Marxian theory. Finally, it should be stressed that this position is based on Rubin ([1927] 1978, [1928] 1994) and Goldmann (1959) (despite their various differences and in spite of the existence of certain contradictions and uncompleted analyses in their writings) and that it is very close (as was pointed out to me by Professor D.K. Foley, when he read one of the previous versions of this paper) to the position advocated by Reuten and Williams (1989, Parts 1-2).

19. It goes without saying that this conclusion is independent of the assumption of the existence of homogeneous labour (and/or: single production, one, and only one, linear technique, only reproduced inputs, 'stationary' prices, a closed economy, etc.). Thus, in the case where labour is heterogeneous (see (6)), the only thing that varies is the relation (8a), which is written as follows:

$$V_k^* \equiv w_k,\ k = 1,2,\ldots, m \tag{8aa}$$

where V_k^* and w_k denote the unit value and the unit price of type k 'labour power', respectively. Finally, it must be emphasized that Krause (1980, pp. 124-7), who begins with the notion of abstract labour, arrives at the relations (7)-(7c), with $u = Y$ and $C = 1$, but not at this conclusion (which seems paradox to us; see also Krause (1998, p. 8)). Therefore, in order to deal with the heterogeneous labour case, he constructs a 'reduction' operator of concrete labours to abstract labour (see Krause (1980, pp. 127-31)). However, the proposed 'reduction' is economically unrealistic and not always economically significant, that is, the 'reduction' coefficients are not always strictly positive (though it is useful from a formal point of view; see Krause (1981) and Fujimori (1982, pp. 111-3)).

20. Consider the textbook 'Ricardian' model of foreign trade, in which two commodities are produced by means of unassisted labours alone (see, e.g., Krugman and Obstfeld (2000, ch. 2)). In equilibrium, the relative price of commodities is determined as a function of the available quantities of 'labour powers', the quality of 'labour powers' and the consumer preferences in the two 'countries'-producers (see also Simpson (1975, ch. 14)). So, the *totality* of features of the constituted 'international' society is summed up by the ratio of exchange of commodities, and it could not be different. It should be noted, finally, that because it is not out of the question for a certain

commodity to be produced by both 'countries', it is perfectly possible for the quantities of labour 'embodied' in the separate units of that one and the same commodity to be heterogeneous. Therefore, it is not only the various commodities that become commensurate, but, in the general case, also the various units of that one and the same commodity.

21. For other 'examples', see Steedman (1977, 1979, Essays 8-11, 1991, 1999a, 2002), Steedman and Metcalfe (1981), Kurz and Salvadori (1995, chs 4-8 and 11), Bidard (1997) and Mariolis (2004) (and take into account Steedman (1999b, 2000) and Steedman and Tomkins (1998)). Moreover, it should be noted that according to the CNA the surplus value $S^{*}(\equiv P)$ is positive iff the 'new value' produced by the expenditure of one unit of 'labour power', pY/aX, is greater than the value of one unit of 'labour power', w, a condition which neither presupposes nor entails (when prices deviate from the production prices) that the quantity of labour 'embodied' in the surplus product is positive (see Mariolis (2000, 2002a, 2005)).

22. What was said in note 17 is therefore correct: The 'new' measure of equivalence of commodities cancels the 'initial' measure. These measures of equivalence can co-exist only in the mind, a fact that leads certain Marxists to believe in the existence of 'unequal exchange', and, therefore, a 'transfer of value (or surplus value)'.

23. At this point, we could quite clearly go into issues of 'reification' and 'commodity fetishism'. This is, however, not necessary for the purposes of this paper.

24. It is worth noting that Laibman (1998a,b, 2002) arrives at the relations (7)-(7c), with $u = Y$ and $C = 1$. As far as we can judge, however, the process of working out these relations is not based on the formulation of the notion of abstract social labour and is therefore not adequately founded. But even if we do an injustice to him on this point, we consider that all the other points of our critique of the NA are valid also with respect to Laibman's proposal.

25. See also note 22.

26. As is well known, it is possible for the net output to contain also negative elements. In that case at least one process is reproduced on a lower scale (unless the system disposes stocks; see also Mariolis (2000, 2002a)).

27. It therefore follows that the relevant position of Duménil (see notes 5 and 11) should be considered erroneous.

REFERENCES

Bidard, C. (1997), Pure Joint Production, *Cambridge Journal of Economics*, 21, 685-701.

Duménil, G. (1980), *De la Valeur aux Prix de Production*, Paris, Economica.

Duménil, G. (1984), The so-called 'Transformation Problem' Revisited: A Brief Comment, *Journal of Economic Theory*, 33, 340-48.

Febrero Pãnos, E. (2000), A Re(in)statement of the Labour Theory of Value: A comment, *Cambridge Journal of Economics*, 24, 107-11.

Foley, D.K. (1982), The Value of Money, the Value of Labor Power and the Marxian Transformation Problem, *Review of Radical Political Economics*, 14, 37-47.

Foley, D.K. (1997), Recent developments in the Labor Theory of Value, *International Working Group on Value Theory*, Mini-Conference, USA 3-6 April 1997, Working Papers, 38-51.

Fujimori, Y. (1982), *Modern Analysis of Value Theory*, Berlin, Springer-Verlag.

Glick, M. and Ehrbar, H. (1987), The Transformation Problem: An obituary, *Australian Economic Papers*, 26, 294-317.

Goldmann, L. (1959), La Réification, in L. Goldmann, *Recherches Dialectiques*, Paris, Gallimard.

Krause, U. (1980), Abstract Labour in General Joint Systems, *Metroeconomica*, 32, 115-35.

Krause, U. (1981), Heterogeneous Labour and the Fundamental Marxian Theorem, *Review of Economic Studies*, 68, 173-8.

Krause, U. (1998), Abstract Labour and Money, in H.D. Kurz and N. Salvadori (eds), *The Elgar Companion to Classical Economics*, vol. 1, Cheltenham, Edward Elgar.

Krugman, P. and Obstfeld, M. (2000), *International Economics. Theory and Practice*, New York, Addison Wesley Longman.

Kurz, H.D. and Salvadori, N. (1995), *Theory of Production. A Long-Period Analysis*, Cambridge, Cambridge University Press.

Laibman, D. (1998a), Recent Controversies in Marxian Value Theory, in H.D. Kurz and N. Salvadori (eds), *The Elgar Companion to Classical Economics*, vol. 2, Cheltenham, Edward Elgar.

Laibman, D. (1998b), Value Theory: Beyond Gridlock, *Utopia* (in Greek), 28, 29-47.

Laibman, D. (2002), Value and the Quest for the Core of Capitalism, *Review of Radical Political Economics*, 34, 159-78.

Mariolis, T. (1998), The so-called Problem of Transforming Values into Prices, *Utopia* (in Greek), 28, 205-15 (English translation in *Political Economy. Review of Political Economy and Social Sciences,* 5(1999), 45-58).

Mariolis, T. (2000), The insignificant and the incorrect aspects of the so-called Fundamental Marxian Theorem: Positive (Non-Positive) Surplus Value with Non-Positive (Positive) Profits (in Greek), *Political Economy. Review of Political Economy and Social Sciences,* 7, 81-126.

Mariolis, T. (2002a), On the Lack of Correspondence between Surplus Value and Profit, in A. Kalafatis, P. Livas and T. Skountzos (eds). (2003), *Essays in Honour of Professor Apostolos Lazaris*, vol. 1, Piraeus, University of Piraeus.

Mariolis, T. (2002b), The Correct Approach-Solution and the so-called 'New Approach-Solution' to the Problem of Transforming Values into Prices (in Greek), *Political Economy. Review of Political Economy and Social Sciences*, 10, 73-105.

Mariolis, T. (2003), Controllability, Observability, Regularity, and the so-called Problem of Transforming Values into Prices of Production, *Asian-African Journal of Economics and Econometrics*, 3, 113-27.

Mariolis, T. (2004), Pure Joint Production and International Trade: A note, *Cambridge Journal of Economics*, 28, 449-56.

Mariolis, T. (2005), A Critical Note on Marx's Theory of Profits, *Asian-African Journal of Economics and Econometrics* (forthcoming).

Mavroudeas, S. (2001), The Monetary Equivalent of Labour and certain Issues regarding Money and the Value of Labour-Power, *Economie Appliquée*, 54, 37-74.

Miyao, T. (1977), A Generalization of Sraffa's Standard Commodity and its Complete Characterization, *International Economic Review*, 18, 151-62.

Mohun, S. (1993a), A note on Steedman's 'Joint Production and the 'New Solution' to the Transformation Problem', *Indian Economic Review*, 28, 241-6.

Mohun, S. (1993b), Response to Steedman's Reply, *Indian Economic Review*, 28, 248-50.

Mohun, S. (1994), A Re(in)statement of the Labour Theory of Value, *Cambridge Journal of Economics*, 18, 391-412.

Mohun, S. (2000), New solution or Re(in) Statement? A reply, *Cambridge Journal of Economics*, 24, 113-7.

Reuten, G. and Williams, M. (1989), *Value-Form and the State*, London and New York, Routledge.

Roemer, J.E. (1990), Review of Duncan K. Foley, *Understanding Capital, Journal of Economic Literature*, 28, 1727-30.

Rubin, I.I. ([1927] 1994), Abstract Labour and Value in Marx's System, in S. Mohun (ed.), *Debates in Value Theory*, Basingstoke, MacMillan.

Rubin, I.I. ([1928] 1972), *Essays on Marx's Theory of Value*, Detroit, Black and Red Books.

Saad-Filho, A. (1996), The Value of Money, the Value of Labour Power and the Net Product: An Appraisal of the 'New Approach' to the Transformation Problem, in A. Freeman and G. Carchedi (eds), *Marx and Non-Equilibrium Economics*, Brookfield, Edward Elgar.

Shaikh, A.M. and Tonak, E.A. (1994), *Measuring the Wealth of Nations*, Cambridge, Cambridge University Press.

Simpson, D. (1975), *General Equilibrium Analysis*, Oxford, Basil Blackwell.

Sinha, A. (1997), The Transformation Problem: A Critique of the 'New Solution', *Review of Radical Political Economics*, 29, 51-8.

Sotirchos, G. and Stamatis, G. (1998), A note on Foley's Article 'The Value of Money, the Value of Labour Power and the Marxian Transformation Problem', *Political Economy. Review of Political Economy and Social Sciences,* 3, 35-40.

Sraffa, P. (1960), *Production of Commodities by means of Commodities*, Cambridge, Cambridge University Press.

Stamatis, G. (1998-99), On the 'New Solution', *International Journal of Political Economy,* 28, 23-46.

Steedman, I. (1977), *Marx after Sraffa*, London, New Left Books.

Steedman, I. (ed.) (1979), *Fundamental Issues in Trade Theory*, London, Macmillan.

Steedman, I. (1980), Heterogeneous Labour and 'Classical' Theory, *Metroeconomica*, 3, 39-59.

Steedman, I. (1985), Heterogeneous Labour, Money Wages and Marx's Theory, *History of Political Economy*, 17, 551-74.

Steedman, I. (1990), Comment (on Suzanne de Brunhoff: 'Reflections on Marx and Sraffa') in K. Bharadwaj and B. Schefold (eds), *Essays on Pierro Sraffa*, London, Unwin Hyman.

Steedman, I. (1991), The Irrelevance of Marxian Values, in G.A. Caravale (ed.), *Marx and Modern Economic Analysis*, vol. 1, Aldershot, Edward Elgar.

Steedman, I. (1992), Joint Production and the 'New Solution' to the Transformation Problem, *Indian Economic Review*, Special Number in memory of Sukhamoy Chakravarty, 27, 123-7.

Steedman, I. (1993), A Reaction to Simon Mohun on the 'New Solution', *Indian Economic Review*, 28, 247.

Steedman, I. (1999a), Production of Commodities by means of Commodities and the Open Economy, *Metroeconomica*, 50, 260-76.

Steedman, I. (1999b), Vertical Integration and 'reduction to dated quantities of labour', in G. Mongiovi and F. Petri (eds), *Value Distribution and Capital. Essays in Honour of Pierangelo Garegnani*, London, Routledge.

Steedman, I. (2000), Income Distribution, Foreign Trade and the Value-Added Vector, *Economic Systems Research*, 12, 221-30.

Steedman, I. (2002), Marx After Sraffa and the Open Economy (Some Notes), mimeo.

Steedman, I. and Metcalfe, J.S. (1981), On Duality and Basic Commodities in an Open Economy, *Australian Economic Papers*, 20, 133-41.

Steedman, I. and Tomkins, J. (1998), On Measuring the Deviation of Prices from Labour Values, *Cambridge Journal of Economics*, 22, 379-85.

DEMOGRAPHY AND THE FALLING RATE OF PROFIT

Allin Cottrell[*] *& Paul Cockshott*[**]

We discuss the original formulation of the theory of the falling rate of profit by Marx and the criticisms of the theory's micro-foundations by Roemer. We then counterpose to this an alternative macroeconomic interpretation in which the falling rate of profit is driven by demographic factors. We follow this up with an examination of why the assumptions made in Roemer's analysis are empirically unjustified. In particular we criticize his use of the average rate of profit rather than the monetary interest rate as the regulator of investment decisions. We conclude with an examination of the social implications of a declining rate of profit.

'...the difficulty which has hitherto troubled the economists, namely to explain the falling rate of profit...' (Marx, Capital, *vol. III, p. 230).*

INTRODUCTION

The concept of a tendency for the rate of profit to fall was a common theme in classical political economy. Smith, Ricardo and Marx all held such a theory. However, their grounds for believing in this tendency were quite various. Smith thought in terms of accumulation leading to an increase in competition between capitals, hence driving down prices and profits. Ricardo dismissed this as confusion–competition between capitalists influenced the distribution of profit, not its overall amount–and held a theory whose motor lay in the confrontation between rising population and diminishing returns in agriculture. Marx's theory was in a sense more akin to Smith's–at least insofar as it had nothing to do with diminishing returns–but it was quite distinct.

We distinguish three elements in Marx's writings that are particularly relevant to our topic. The first we call the 'main argument': this is the argument Marx set out at length (and which appears in Capital I, his notebooks of the 1860s, and Capital III) to the effect that the rate of profit must tend to fall due to an increase in the organic composition of capital, an increase itself driven by the search for maximum profit on the part of capitalists. The second is a brief coda to the main argument (appearing towards the end of Chapter XV of Capital III) but worthy of mention in its own right in view of its relevance to later discussions of the TRPF. We call it the 'micro-macro bridge'. The third element

* Department of Economics, Wake Forest University, USA.

** Department of Computing Science, University of Glasgow, UK.

is what Marx calls 'absolute overproduction of capital': this element forms the basis for the revised TRPF theory that we defend below.

In outline, our argument is as follows. First, Marx's 'main argument' is flawed, and vulnerable to the Okishio critique. Specifically, Marx's micro-macro bridge is invalid. Nonetheless, the Okishio critique is questionable on various grounds and we explore some of these. Second, it is possible to construct a revised version of the TRPF theory, which is not vulnerable to the Okishio critique, on the basis of Marx's concept of absolute overproduction of capital, that is, accumulation of capital in excess of the growth rate of the workforce. And this construction is worthwhile, because the underlying concept is now more relevant than in Marx's day and promises to become increasingly relevant over the 21st century. Our simulations below address the consequences of continued accumulation of capital when the employable workforce, on a global scale, ceases to expand due to the movement of people from pre-capitalist forms of production into the capitalistic labour-market and becomes limited by natural population growth.

We begin by sketching Marx's main argument, for reference. The argument may be expressed thus:

1. It is an inherent, intrinsic feature of capitalism that capitalists are driven to seek maximum profits.
2. While profits can be gained in many ways, the most fundamental means of augmenting profit in developed capitalism is via increases in the productivity of labour.
3. The enhancement of the productivity of labour involves workers working with an increased 'mass' of machinery or means of labour, and working up a larger quantity of materials per unit time.
4. Although the value of the means of labour, materials, etc (in Marx's terminology, constant capital) will not generally increase in full proportion to the 'mass', it will nonetheless increase, and faster than the variable capital. The organic composition of capital tends to rise.
5. A rise in the organic composition of capital lowers the rate of profit, other things equal.
6. Other things cannot be expected to remain equal. The same increase in the productivity of labour, driven by profit-seeking, that expresses itself in a rising organic composition, also expresses itself in a rise in the rate of exploitation, which by itself raises the rate of profit.
7. Nonetheless, as a long-run tendency, the increase in organic composition must outweigh the increase in the rate of exploitation, in its effects on the rate of profit.

Most critics of Marx's main argument have not questioned points 1 or 2 above, and neither will we.

Point 3 is perhaps more questionable. Certainly there are many examples of technological change that conform to this pattern: the switch from fluvial transport to railways, or from handlooms to machine ones, but there are also counterexamples. Sometimes, as for instance in the move from metal casting to plastic moulding for many uses, the more advanced process accomplishes its results more cheaply while deploying a lesser 'mass' of means of production. But let's accept point 3 as broadly correct, at least for the sake of argument (strengthen this statement?). Similarly for point 4: this may not always be true, but it is at least plausible and we will not question it here.

Points 5 and 6 are certainly correct within Marx's conceptual framework.

That leaves point 7, the primary locus of controversy. To expose the issue here, it may be useful to write down the relevant equations. Marx's rate of profit (here denoted by r) is the ratio of surplus value, s, to the sum of constant capital, c, and variable capital, v:

$$r = s / (c + v)$$

The organic composition of capital is the ratio c/v and the rate of exploitation is the ratio s/v. Dividing both the numerator and the denominator by v, we can write

$$r = [s/v] / [(c/v) + 1]$$

which makes it plain that an increase in c/v lowers the rate of profit and an increase in s/v raises it.

If the pursuit of profit (via the pursuit of higher labour productivity) has the effect of raising both c/v and s/v, does that not leave the overall effect on the rate of profit indeterminate? Neither s/v nor c/v has any obvious theoretical upper bound. Why does Marx talk in terms of a basic tendency for the rate of profit to fall due to rising c/v, and treat rising s/v as merely an 'offsetting factor'? Why not a tendency for the rate of profit to rise due to rising s/v, with the increase in c/v treated as an offsetting factor? (Or no 'basic tendency' at all, just an indeterminate outcome.)

Marx clearly had an ideological investment in the idea that the falling rate of profit was primary. This proposition licensed the conclusion that 'the real barrier of capitalist production is capital itself' (*Capital*, vol. III, p. 248). The very process that constituted capitalism's historical 'justification'–namely, its development of the productivity of social labour to an unprecedented level–was at the same time the source of a falling rate of profit, which places a roadblock in the way of further development.

If the only reason Marx had for asserting the primacy of the tendency of the rate of profit to fall was that it fit well with his ideological agenda, one could accuse him of intellectual dishonesty. That is too harsh. It seems clear that he had a strong theoretical hunch or intuition that the rise in c/v must outweigh the rise in s/v. A further manipulation of the rate of profit may help here. In relation to the original definition of the rate of profit as s/(c+v), divide both the numerator and the denominator by (s+v) to give:

$$r = [s/(s+v)] / [c/(s+v) + v/(s+v)]$$

The ratio s/(s+v) is not exactly Marx's rate of surplus value, but it is a closely related magnitude with an upper bound of 1.0, namely the fraction of the total social working time during which workers perform surplus labour, or generate profits for their employers. Similarly, c/(s+v) is not exactly Marx's organic composition, but it is a closely related quantity which seems to have no upper bound, namely the ratio of the value of constant capital to the total 'living labour'. Looking at this variant of the rate of profit equation it becomes easier to share Marx's intuition. Suppose the ratio s/(s+v) is driven to its maximum (wages are effectively zero; the workers 'live on air', as Marx puts it). In that case the second element in the denominator, v/(s+v), goes to zero, and then any rise in the ratio of constant capital to current labour is bound to lower the rate of profit. It then seems plausible that as s/(s+v) gets closer to 1.0 it will become increasingly difficult to find an offset on this account for an ongoing rise in c/(s+v), or in other words a rising rate of exploitation can't keep capitalism out of trouble for ever.

The relevant question though is whether capitalists seeking to maximize their rate of profit would act so as to raise c/(s+v) sufficiently to lower the overall rate of profit. Okishio (1961) and Roemer (1981) have argued that they would not. Roemer lays considerable emphasis on the need for a sound microeconomic foundation for discussions of the rate of profit. The falling rate of profit is a macro-economic phenomenon, but it derives, he argues from the decisions of individual capitalists unaware of the macroeconomic consequences of decisions that they make. From this he argues that we have to examine what are plausible decision-making criteria for individual capitalists when making investment decisions. The thrust of his analysis is that if capitalists take the current set of prices and profit rates as givens, then, any decisions that they make on technical changes which are more profitable to them personally, will also be more profitable to the capitalist class as a whole and, in consequence, will tend to raise the aggregate rate of profit for the whole economy. This theoretical project amounts to the search for an adequate microfoundation for the theory of accumulation.

Our approach comes from the opposite direction. We shall start from certain propositions about macro-economic magnitudes - population growth, the share of profits going as accumulation, the rate of technical change - and then draw conclusions about the trajectory of profit rates.

THE MACROECONOMIC ARGUMENT

When discussing the rate of profit in value terms we are dividing a quantity of profit by a stock of capital. Profit can be thought of as a flow of value and as such its dimension its units are person hours/annum, which in dimensional terms is just persons since the hours/annum just give us a scalar. Thus the annual flow of profit when measured in value terms corresponds to a certain number of people-the number of people whose direct and indirect output is materialised in the goods purchased out of profits.

We divide this by a stock of capital whose units are person hours, thus the dimension of the annual value rate of profit is given *as persons / (persons x time)*, which cancels out to $time^{-1}$. As such it expresses the potential expansion rate per year of a sum of capital. Obviously an analogous dimensional reduction could be achieved if we used Euros as our unit rather than person hours. Again we would come up with a dimension of $time^{-1}$.

This dimensional issue is obscured in the classical discourse which talks in terms of a 'production cycle'. In this the components of capital, c+v, are treated as sums of value as is the profit, and the time dimension is abstracted from, since every thing is thought of as taking place over a single cycle. Capital is advanced on wages and means of production at the start of the cycle; at the end of the cycle the means of production and labour power have been used up and we are left with a product whose value replaces the advanced capital with a profit. Since there is only one production cycle the rate of surplus value, s/v, and the rate of profit, s/(c+v), appear dimensionally identical as simple scalars.

The whole debate in Okishio and Roemer is cast within the context of a choice over techniques, and whether any rational choice of techniques by a capitalist will result in techniques being chosen that will lower the rate of profit. This is a fundamentally mistaken starting point, although there are interesting issues raised by them and we will return to these later in our argument. Instead one should focus on what the rate of profit tells us. It tells us something about the potential rate of expansion of capital stocks. It sets an upper limit on the rate of expansion that can be achieved out of internal funding-the rate of capital growth that will be achieved if all profit is reinvested.

The focus of the analysis should be on how this rate of expansion will change over time if capital actually is reinvested. If we answer this question we can then go on to look at the circumstances under which capital might be reinvested and also look at the consequences of capital not being reinvested.

If we approach the time evolution of the rate of profit from the standpoint of capital accumulation, then the issue becomes simpler. Initially we will assume that all measurements are performed either in labour hours, or what amounts to the same thing in a monetary unit of account whose labour hour equivalent does not change from year to year. Let us further assume that all profits are reinvested. Thus a 5% rate of profit will imply a 5% growth per annum of the capital stock. Let us also assume at first that the division of value added between wages and profit remains unchanged over time.

This means that total profit per year will be a constant multiple of total wages per year. Under these circumstances it is clear that the rate of profit will fall over time if the rate of growth of wage income is less than the rate of profit, and the rate of profit will rise if the rate of growth of wage income is higher than the rate of profit.

We then focus on the determinants of the rate of growth of wage income, measured in labour hours per annum. The dimensions give it away, since wage income in these terms corresponds to a number of people the number of people whose direct and indirect labour supports the employed population. The rate of growth of wage income comes down to the rate of growth of the working population (given the assumption of a constant rate of surplus value). The appropriate focus for analysis of the falling rate of profit is not technological choice but historical demography.

Once the argument is on this terrain one has to ask what determines the rate of growth of the working population. There are clearly two components that are important:

1. The natural rate of population growth.
2. The fraction of the total population that is employed as wage labourers under capitalist relations of production.

Economies undergoing transition from peasant farming to capitalist industry typically have a rapid rate of growth of the working population from both factors. The birth rate tends to be high and infant mortality falls during the transition from peasant agriculture to capitalist industrial economy. This gives a rapid rate of natural population increase. At the same time the fraction of the population employed as wage labourers rises to give a high compounded rate of growth of the employed population.

In a mature capitalist economy things are different, although infant mortality continues to fall, this is offset by a falling birth rate, which in many advanced capitalist economies falls below replacement level. At the same time the share of capitalistically employed wage labour in the population tends either to plateau or even to fall. The result is a relatively stagnant or declining capitalistically employed population.

Our initial model has the following variables: C denotes capital stock; W denotes working population; and P denotes profit.

The rate of profit r=P/C. We assume that all profit is reinvested so that $C_{t+1} = C_t + P_t$. Profit itself we assume to be set by 0.5, or in other words we assume that one worker in every two is producing commodities which will be purchased out of surplus value, so that the rate of surplus value is 100%. The working

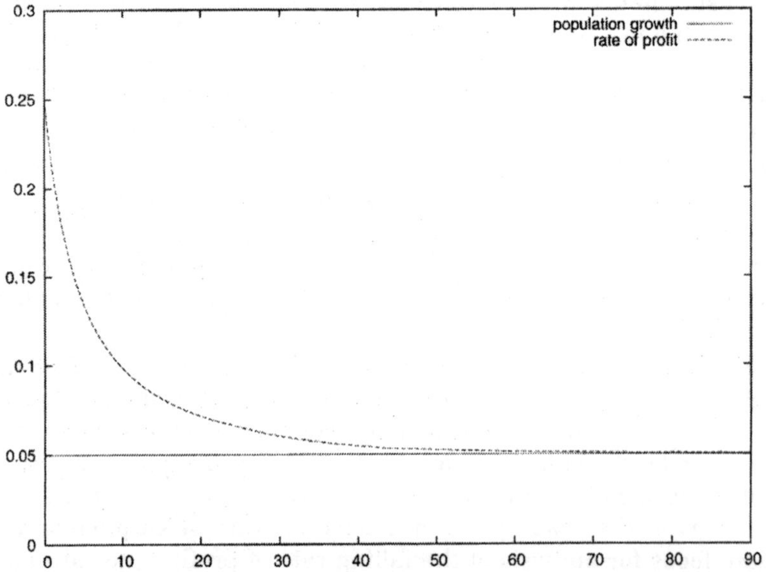

Figure: Profit rate under constant population growth

population is assumed to grow such that $W_{t+1} = (1+g)W_t$, with g being the rate of working population growth.

If we assume that the rate of growth of the employed population is fixed then the effect is that the actual rate of profit tends towards the rate of growth of the employed population:

In the graph above we start out with an initial rate of profit of 25% and have the population growing at 5%. All profits are reinvested so the rate of profit on capital tends towards 5% as well as this is the only rate at which the rate of growth of the capital stock will equal the rate of growth of the population.

If we take a more realistic model as shown in Figure 2, where the rate of growth of the population declines with time, then the rate of profit chases the rate of population growth downwards.

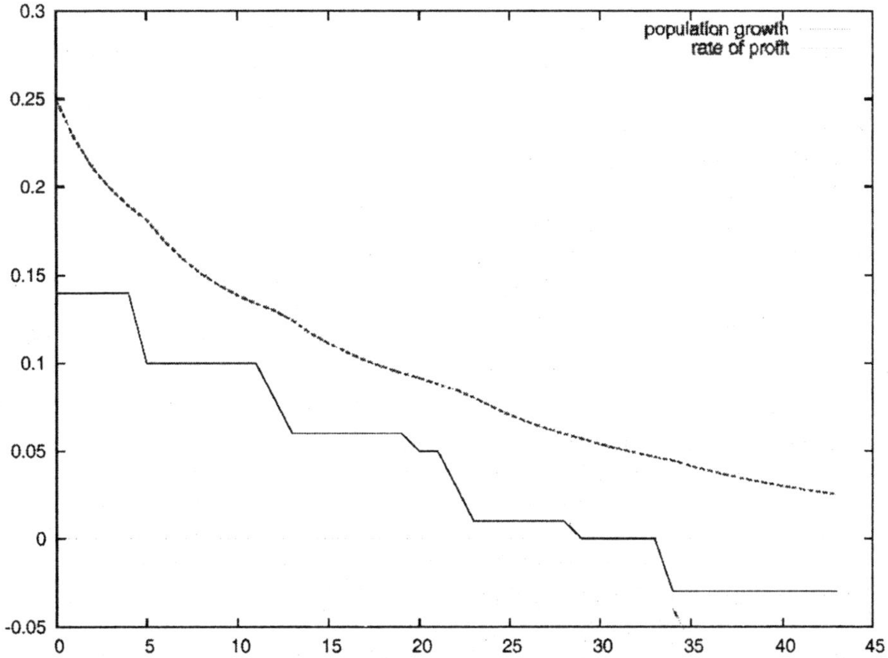

Figure 2: Profit rate under declining population growth

These cases have used an assumption of fixed proportions of wages and profits. What will be the case if we assume that wages fall relative to profits with time?

We again simulate the effect of profits being reinvested with a constant 5% growth of the employed population but this time with a 5% decline in the value of the real wage each year. Thus we assume that $P_t = (1-L_t)W_t$, where L_t represents the proportion of the working year required to reproduce the value of labour power. We model the decline in the value of labour power by $L_{t+1} = 0.95\ L_t$.

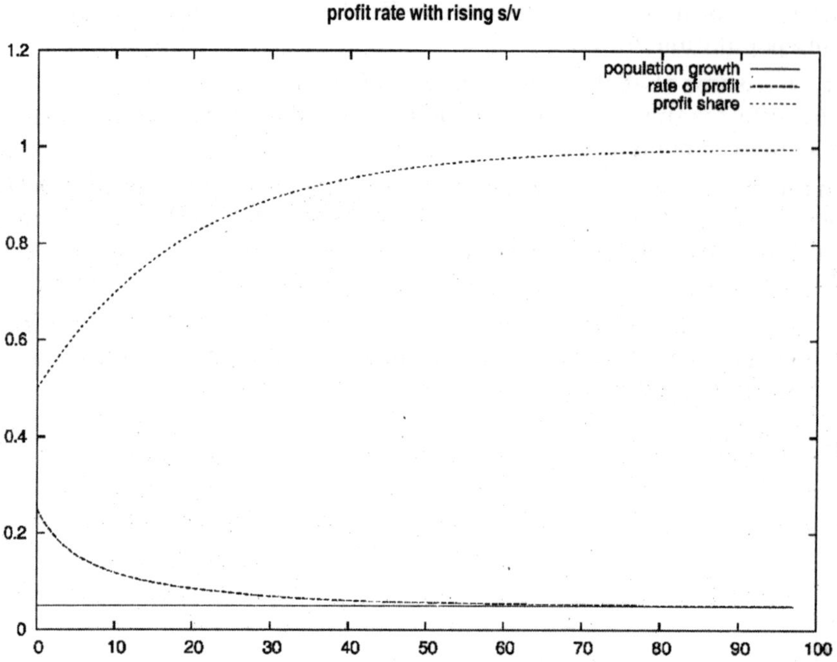

Figure 3: Effect of a Rising Profit Share

We see that the profit share in net value added heads towards unity, but that this only serves to delay the equilibration of the profit rate at 5%. Again we find that the rate of population growth is the ultimate determinant of the long run rate of profit.

Up to now we have assumed that all profits are accumulated. What happens if a smaller portion of profits is accumulated?

What if population grew at 5% a year and half of all profits were accumulated?

As the graph above shows, the result would be that the profit rate would tend towards 10% instead of 5%, because this is the rate of profit that would keep capital stock and working population growing at the same rate. In the example above the profit share in net value added is held constant. In general we can conclude that the equilibrium profit rate will be given by g/i where g is the rate of employed population growth and i is the investment share of profit. In dynamic equilibrium $(P_t/C_t) = (P_{t+1}/C_{t+1})$ so the rate of growth of profit and of capital must be the same. The rate of growth of profit in units of persons $(P_{t+1}/P_t) = 1 + g$ (assuming a constant rate of surplus value). The rate of growth of C, is $1 + (iP_t/C) = 1 + ir$. Since in equilibrium growth the rate of growth of profit must equal the rate of growth of capital we have, $1 + g = 1 + ir$ so the rate of profit has to be g/i. However if the employed population is static or declining, then for any positive i, the equilibrium rate of profit will be zero. In the above we are implicitly assuming that the remaining 50% of profits are used to fund capitalists personal expenditure rather than investment.

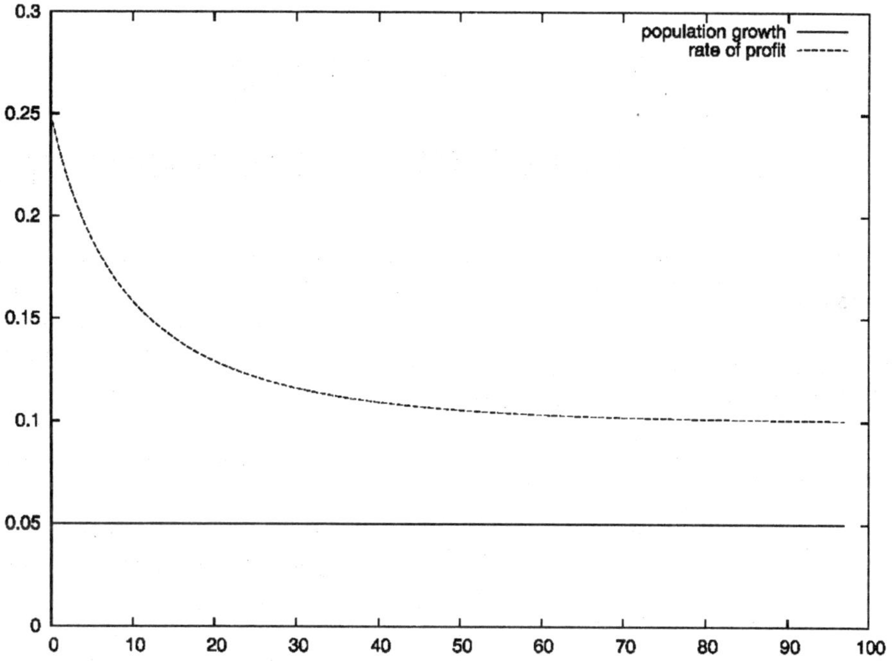

Figure 4: Effect of lower accumulation rates, 50% in this case

COUNTERVAILING FACTORS

Technical change

Investment in new plant and equipment can be expected to improve production techniques and reduce the prices of capital goods. Under these circumstances the value of the stock of invested capital will depreciate. This will tend to slow the growth of the capital stock. At the same time, it will result in losses on the capital account to firms whose assets have depreciated. If we take these points into consideration when calculating profits we find two opposite effects. The depreciation of capital stocks slows down the growth of stocks, which tends to mitigate any decline in profit rates. Conversely, the losses on the capital account tend to directly reduce profits.

We simulate this in the following example where we assume that all net profits are invested. Population grows 5% a year for the first 30 years before gradually falling below replacement rate. For the first 50 years productivity grows 3% a year leading to a 3% depreciation per annum of the capital stock. Then for a period of 20 years the rate of technical change accelerates to 7% a year before falling back to 2% a year.

When technical change accelerates, the net rate of profit declines sharply as the losses on capital account kick in, followed by a period during which profits rates recover. The recovery occurs because the organic composition of capital

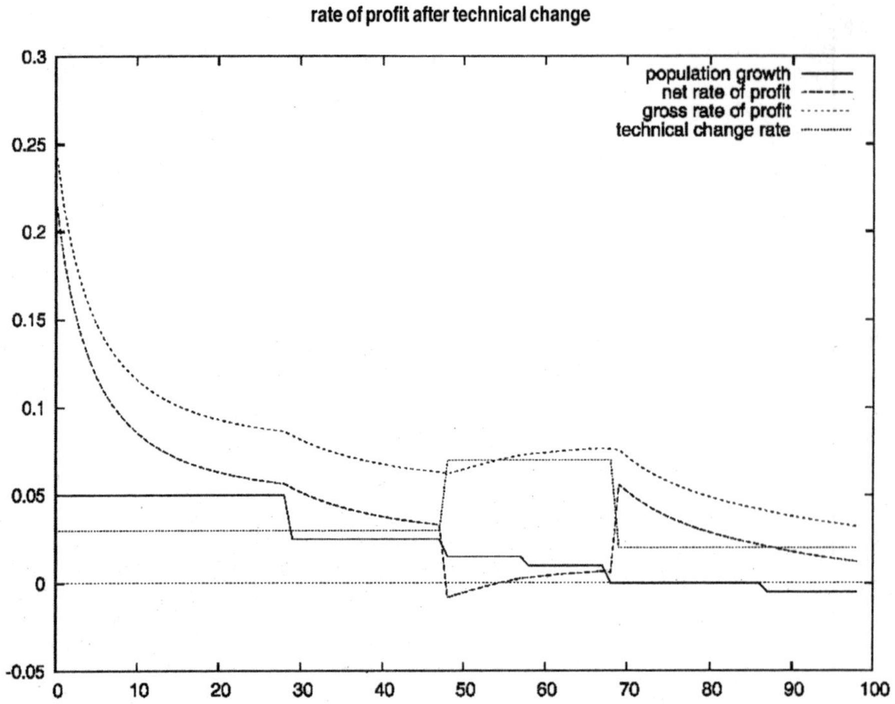

Figure 5: Effect of technical depreciation

falls when the net rate of investment is insufficient to keep up with the growth of the working population. A slowdown in technical change allows net profit rates to rise for a period before tending back towards equilibrium. In the presence of technical change, it is still the rate of growth of the working population that governs the long run rate of net profit.

Falling Investment

Let us now look at the effect of a fall in investment on realization and thus on profit rates, using Kaleckian arguments. Up to now we have only looked at the effect of varying the share of investment in total profits, keeping total profits unchanged under such a change. However we know from Kalecki (1971) that total profits are casually determined by the sum of current capitalist consumption plus net investment. If workers neither borrow nor save, then the sum of investment expenditure and capitalist consumption limits the sum of realizable profit.

To analyse this in more detail let us assume that capitalist consumption is given by some fraction of the average profits over the last few years. Thus capitalists are assumed to adjust their expenditure to their long run income, their savings buffering them from short-term income falls.

In dimensional terms, capitalist consumption as flow of value, has dimension person hours / hour = persons. In value terms it represents the number of people directly and indirectly meeting the needs of capitalist consumption. If we assume that the rate of surplus value is 100% then for each person employed producing goods and services for capitalist consumption, a further person will be employed producing wage goods. Similarly for each person employed making net investment goods, a total of two people will be employed, one of who will be making wage goods. Thus total employment will be 2 x (*capitalist consumption* + *investment*). This total will be limited by the employable workforce, whose growth we have been modelling up to now, but it can fall short of the employable workforce if investment and capitalist consumption are too small. Let us construct a new simulation in which we allow for the possibility of unemployment.

In this model we assume that the labour force grows, stabilizes and then finally falls. We assume that accumulation is driven by the following rules:

1. If the rate of profit is below the rate of interest then accumulation is reduced, in this case by 3%.
2. If the rate of profit is greater than the rate of interest then accumulation grows by 6% relative to last year's rate of accumulation.
3. If, as a result of rule 2, the total employed workforce would be greater than the available labour force, then realized accumulation is constrained to be no more than would achieve full employment.

We assume that the interest rate is regulated by a central bank (CB) which attempts to stabilize employment levels. If employment approaches 100% the CB will raise interest rates, but if unemployment rises too high the CB lowers interest rates.

Figure 6 plots the evolution of the population and of the employed population. The most striking feature is that in the initial 25 years the employed workforce rises rapidly, then accumulation suddenly falls off producing a consequent fall in employment. Looking at the evolution of profit and interest rates (Figure 7), the reason for this becomes evident.

In year 25 because of the rise in the capital stock relative to the employed population, the rate of profit falls below the rate of interest. This produces a decline in accumulation, which in turn reduces the mass of profit as well as the rate of profit. The bank eventually responds by cutting interest rates sufficiently to restart accumulation. A long period of low interest rates allows accumulation to resume until labour shortages eventually force the bank to raise interest rates. During the last 30 years of the simulation the simulated economy oscillates between full employment and periods of recession. During this period the trend of both rates of profit and real interest rates is downwards.

We think that this is a reasonably realistic portrait of what tends to happen to a closed capitalist economy in the long run. Obviously actual economies are not closed so that accumulation can rise higher than could be supported by the domestic workforce. Similarly, an individual economy may offset a decline in the labour force by immigration. However if we consider the global economy, this sort of mechanism could operate, provided that there was some international coordination of interest rates.

Figure 6

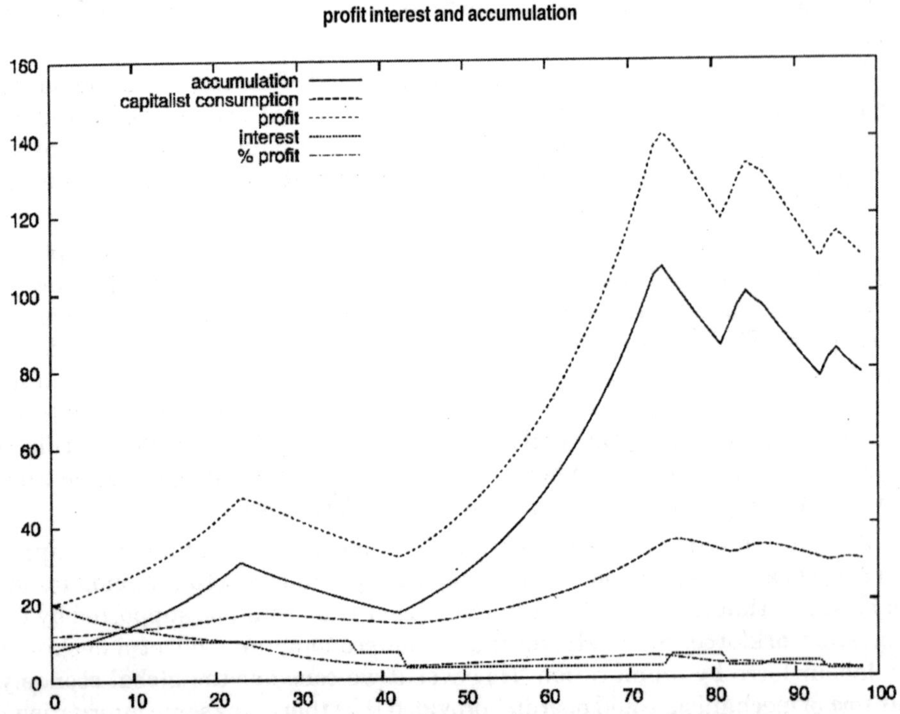

Figure 7

CONDITIONS OF ACCUMULATION

If there is a conflict between what the macroeconomic equations tell us and the conclusions of Roemer's microeconomic argument, then one of the arguments must be wrong. Either: (i) One of us has a logical flaw in our deductive arguments; or (ii) The initial assumptions made in one or other of the arguments are incompatible.

Let us allow, for now, that each argument is logically well founded and follows from its initial premises. Roemer's argument has shown that capitalists will not carry out investments in new production technologies if the result of these would reduce the average profit rate in the whole economy, and we show that any net accumulation greater than the rate of growth of the working population will tend to reduce profit rates in the long run.

One conclusion from this might be that there will never be any accumulation faster than the rate of population growth. It is possible that microeconomic factor set limits to the maximal rate of accumulation that macroeconomy can exhibit. Another possibility is that some of Roemer's microassumptions are invalid and should be dropped. In the end, as with all scientific hypotheses, the criterion has to be their ability to predict what actually happens.

We believe that there is evidence that over periods of decades in individual economies the rate of accumulation has exceeded the rate of population growth and that as a consequence the organic composition of capital has risen (Cockshott, Cottrell, and Michaelson (1995), Edvinsson (2003)). Since this should not occur on the basis of the microeconomic arguments put forward by Roemer, this predisposes us to believe that there must be some premises in his argument that are not an accurate reflection of the way capitalist economies actually work.

Assumption of Profit Equalisation

Although Roemer's argument is intended to provide microeconomic foundations for a discussion of the falling rate of profit it is not microeconomic in the neoclassical sense. Instead the micro-foundations are laid upon what amounts to a macroeconomic bedrock in the form of input-output analysis. The prices and profit rates that firms are supposed to be responding are deduced as the solution to a set of linear i/o equations applying to the whole economy. There is obviously a fairly long tradition of Marxist economists analysing capitalist economies this way, most obviously in Sraffa (1960) and others such as Samuelson (1973) and Steedman (1981). The price theory that results is macroeconomic in the sense that its solutions depend upon knowledge of input-output relationships across the whole economy. It also makes certain very strong assumptions about profit rates. It assumes that the rate of profit is the same for all industries and that it is independent of the organic compositions of capital in these industries. The existence of a tendency for profit rates to equalise across different industries was recognised by the classical economists and by Marx, and it was the attempt to reconcile this tendency with the labour theory of value that gave rise to the famous transformation problem; however, an assumption of fully equalised profit rates in all industries is neither realistic nor appropriate when the problem under consideration is the evolution of profit rates over time.

Capitalist economies are inherently chaotic (that is, subject to continuous buffeting from changes in the available set of production techniques and changes in the pattern of consumer demand, both of which impulses are at least in part endogenous) and one would therefore expect an equilibrium condition to be characterised not by a single profit rate, but by a stable probability density function describing the distribution of profit rates. This observation is due to Farjoun and Machover (1983). This spread of profit rates will occur both within individual industries and across sectors of the economy. The distribution of profit rates turns out, moreover, not to be simply random. Empirical data indicate a systematic inverse relationship between organic composition of capital in an industry and the mean rate of return on capital in that industry (Cockshott and Cottrell (2003)). We will argue below that the presence of such a distribution of profit rates undermines the arguments that Roemer deploys against a tendency for the rate of profit to fall.

Even in the absence of such empirical data, the assumption of equal equilibrium profit rates within and across industries is inherently implausible in the context of a discussion of the effects of technical change. The process by which equilibration of profit rates is supposed to come about was originally invoked by Ricardo in the context of comparing things like wine maturation and forestry, which had multiple year turnover times, with corn growing, which had an annual turnover period. The argument was that capital would only be invested in low turnover activities if it yielded the same return as in normal agriculture. This argument may have some plausibility when applied to activities such as agriculture and viticulture where the rate of technical change is low, and where decades or centuries can be allowed for the establishment of relative prices. It is much less clear that it can be invoked where there is rapid technical change, when the time taken to establish equilibrium could be much longer than the lifespan of the technology. This is especially true in some industries with a high capital/labour ratio, ones which are particularly relevant to the question at hand. Consider the Victorian railway booms. Here was an entirely new technology requiring huge capital investment. The lifetime of the capital in the form of bridges embankments and stations would be a century or more. The booms resulted in over capacity, which, by the early 20th century resulted in a process of line closures. But before the capital invested in railways could depreciate to a level at which the return of railway capital reached equilibrium levels, the whole technology was superseded by road transport. The sort of equilibrium that Roemer invokes in his arguments can be so long in coming that the industry has died before it is relevant. Keynes's aphorism ('In the long run we're all dead') was no joke.

Fixed type Structure of Output Vector

This points to another limit on what Roemer and Okishio have demonstrated. Their arguments address technical change in the context of a pre-existing set of products. They consider which technologies will be chosen to minimize costs in an existing industry. This says nothing about what happens when new products are invented. Consider the shift from horse vehicles to petrol cars. Even if one grants that the Okishio theorem pointed to a restraint on the organic composition of capital in the manufacture of horse drawn carts, this would place no limitation on the organic composition of capital in the manufacture of lorries. In the semi-conductor industry, successive generations of chips are different products. They have new capabilities and their physical construction is different. Typically each generation has smaller transistors. To produce the smaller transistors has required successive fabrication plants to be able to produce images with shorter and shorter wavelengths of light, moving from visible light to far ultraviolet.

This process has driven the costs of fab plants up. There is another aspect to the question of economic limits. Rock's Law (Ross 2003) states that the capital requirements rise exponentially along with chip densities. The cost of a new semiconductor fabrication plant in 1966 was US $14 million. In 1995, the typical cost of such a plant had risen to US $1500 million. The current cost of a modern fabrication plant is now approaching US $10 billion. These changes have occurred as production moves to successive generations of processor chip. Since each generation is a new product, the Okishio theorem gives us no purchase on what is happening. The example is taken from one of today's leading industries, but the same process is occurs more generally. Advances in science make sophisticated products possible. Such products often involve substantial investment in new fabrication technologies, research, prototyping etc, without which the product itself would be impossible. All of these constitute possible avenues for the absorption of new capital investment which can raise the organic composition of capital in society as a whole.

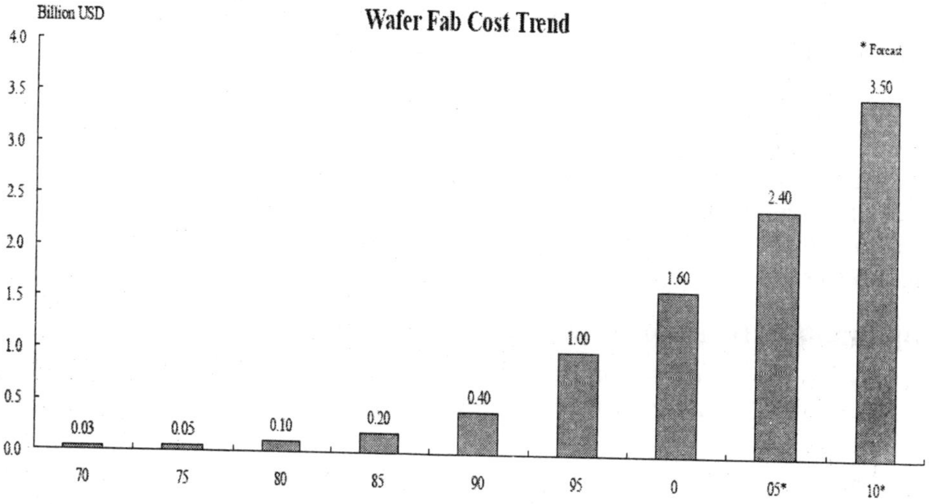

Figure 8: Rise in wafer fab costs, (IC Insights, 2002)

EXTENDED OR SIMPLE REPRODUCTION

At one level the sort of analysis involved in the Okishio theorem is macroeconomic, in that it considers the input/output matrix of the economy as a whole. But in another sense it abstracts away from some crucial details of the input/output structure. All that is used in the analysis is the technical coefficient matrix of the economy. The actual destination of the net output is not analysed in detail. We know from the technical coefficient matrix how much of gross output will be consumed as means of production in the current period, and we know from the real wage vector how much of the remaining net output will be consumed by the working class. But the analysis leaves undefined the composition of the surplus product vector.

No explicit assumption is made that the system is in a steady state of simple reproduction, so the analysis must be supposed to apply to growing economies. But for a growth path with equilibrium profit rates to be followed,

1. The firms producing new means of production must produce exactly the right amount of each product;
2. Other firms must place new investment orders for exactly these products; and
3. The capitalist class as a whole must chose to spend sufficient on unproductive consumption to exactly absorb the rest of the surplus product.

Were the total orders for investment goods and luxury consumption to fall below the level needed to fully monetise the total surplus product, then the actual rate of profit would fall short of the equilibrium rate of profit given by Roemer's linear equation model. The whole scenario of growth along an equilibrium growth path is quite counter to what we know of the history of capitalism, which has always been characterised by an economic cycle. In these cycles the level of investments and profit rates fluctuate. Steady growth along a von Neumann ray, is, if anything, an idealised presentation of the behaviour of a centrally planned economy rather than a market economy. Even if a real capitalist economy could momentarily achieve the uniform equilibrium rate of profit hypothesised in Roemer's formalism, this state would be unstable. The first investment slowdown would depress profits in means of production industries relative to others. Soon you would be back to quotidian reality with a dispersion of profit rates between industries, and between firms in individual industries.

DISPERSION OF PROFIT RATES

If we drop the unrealistic assumption of there being a single profit rate which coincides with the average rate of profit, what are the implications for Roemer's argument?

The key point is that the rate of profit no longer appears as a given value or datum to be used in calculations by individual capitalists. Insofar as an average rate of profit exists, it can only be discovered by analysis of national income statistics, it is not something immediately present to capitalist calculation. Thus decisions on what is a rational discount rate to utilise in planning future investment cannot be based on the average rate of profit.

What is present as a given datum is the rate of interest on loan capital. The rate of interest is something quite distinct from the average rate of profit, and is set by different mechanisms. While the average rate of profit in the economy can be plausibly deduced from considerations about aggregate production functions, the real wage and stocks of means of production, the interest rate is driven by monetary considerations including central bank policy.

On very general grounds we can expect the rate of interest to be below the average rate of profit for a substantial part of the business cycle. When this condition does not hold, a significant proportion of firms will be earning insufficient profit to meet their interest payments and would be threatened with insolvency. At any given time there are always some firms in this situation, but when the rate of interest rises above the rate of profit then a large fraction of all firms become insolvent. Since, under normal trading conditions, only a relatively small fraction of firms are insolvent, it follows that for most of the time interest rates are below average profits. It further follows that it would be rational for most firms to engage in investments even if the rate of return on these investments was lower than they were currently obtaining - provided that the return was higher than they could get by depositing their cash in the banks. If the discount rate used in evaluating the future profitability of fixed capital is systematically lower than the current profit rate, then there can exist a pressure to raise the organic composition of capital, with a resulting depression of the rate of profit. Of course, firms can never tell what profit they will actually obtain from investments, but Roemer's arguments are based on firms' taking current prices as given and projecting these into the future. He argues that they will not invest in fixed capital if, given current prices, the discounted rate of return on the investment would be less than the current rate of profit. This is what he terms a 'viable' investment. He then shows that such viable investments cannot depress the aggregate rate of profit. If firms actually use the current rate of interest as the discount rate, then investments which on Roemer's calculus are unviable and which tend to depress the average rate of profit, will in fact be undertaken.

It could be argued that the average rate of profit is actually available to firms in the form of the rate of return on equities. We accept that there will be feedback relations between the rate of return on equities and the rate of return on real capital. If an individual firm has a high rate of return on real capital invested, its equity price is likely to rise to reflect this. If we further assume that arbitrage operations on the stock market will tend to narrow the dispersion of rates of return on equities, then a rise in the average rate of profit, will tend, other things being equal, to increases the average rate of return on equities. But for the purposes of looking at the overall trajectory of profit rates, we cannot assume that the real rate of profit is the only factor determining the return on equities.

Suppose that we have the following situation:

1. A static working population; and
2. A rate of return on equities equal to the general rate of profit.

By the extended version of the Okishio theorem covering fixed capital, then if we have an equilibrium rate of profit there will be no viable net investment in fixed capital. Any such investment would raise the organic composition of capital and is hence excluded. This implies that there should be zero net issue of new equities. If the rentier class as a whole decides to make no net saving, then the situation is stable. But this is unlikely. If the rentiers attempt to accumulate capital by investing in shares, the net effect will be to bid up the price of equities, given that no new equities are being issued. The effect of this is to depress the rate of return on equities. This will affect the discount rate used in assessing investment projects. Previously unprofitable ones will seem profitable. New equities will be issued and the proceeds invested. Given that the population is static, this will raise the organic composition of capital and depress the real rate of profit.

The weakness in Roemer's argument stems from a fundamental failing of the entire price-of-production school of marxian economics. This school identifies the formation of a general rate of return on equities with the formation of a uniform rate of profit on real invested capital. We would argue that the tendency towards the formation of a uniform rate of profit on equities will be much stronger than the tendency towards a uniform rate of profit on capital stocks. Stocks of capital goods held by companies originated as manufactured commodities with a price and a corresponding account book-value. This book value may be written down due to depreciation, or written up due to inflation, but at heart the valuation of physical means of production remains grounded in commodity prices. In contrast the stock market valuation of a company represents, to a significant extent at least, the discounted present value of its anticipated future earnings. If the company owns readily saleable capital assets, these can set a lower bound on its share price. Below this price takeovers by asset strippers become likely. Even allowing for this constraint, share prices have great flexibility and respond rapidly to changes in reported profits. These fast changes in the nominal valuation of companies can create an illusion that the rate of profit in different industries is narrowly clustered around an average profit rate.

The mechanism required to equilibrate the return on equities is quite different from that posited by the Sraffian school to create an equal rate of return on real capital. Equity returns can be equilibrated by simply marking their prices up or down. The rate of return on invested capital in different industries can only be brought into equilibrium by real capital flows between industries. If steel production earns a lower rate of profit than natural gas extraction, then in order to equilibrate the two, capital has to be withdrawn from steel production and switched to gas drilling. This has to continue until resultant shortages of steel force steel prices up and surpluses of gas push down gas prices. The speed with which this adjustment can occur will be constrained by the depreciation rate of fixed capital in the steel industry and the time taken to explore, discover and bring on-line new gas fields. It is evident that this process must be much slower than the equilibrating processes in the equity market. So we would expect a relatively wide dispersion of profit rates on the real side and a narrow dispersion of rates of return on the equity side.

Insofar as firms have an indication of the general rate of return on capital, it comes through the intermediation of the stock market. But overall levels of equity prices such as the Dow-Jones and FTSE indices are affected by factors other than the rate of return on real capital.

1. Their traces contain broad-spectrum noise. This noisy character will alone ensure that for much of the time the apparent rate of profit is lower than the real rate of profit anticipated by companies making investment decisions.
2. The overall price of equities will be influenced inversely by the prevailing rate of interest. This in turn is influenced by state monetary policy and ultimately by political as well as economic considerations. Political pressures to keep interest rates low can make capital 'cheaper', undermining the relationship between the real rate of return and investment decisions.
3. The level of savings, by companies, rentiers and wage earners can influence stock market conditions, raising or depressing the benchmark rate of return.

For these reasons we consider Roemer's theoretical demonstration that investment decisions bounded by the real rate of profit cannot lead to falls in the general rate of profit to be inapplicable to the real world.

IMPLICATIONS OF FALLING PROFIT RATES

As capitalist economies mature they undergo demographic transitions with birth rates tending to fall below the reproduction level. This presages a period of stagnant or declining labour forces. This can only be partially offset by factors such as an increase in the retirement age and increased female participation in the labour force. Under these circumstances any net capital accumulation will tend to depress profit rates. Does this matter? What are the implications of a long-term decline in profitability?

One possibility is that is does not matter. If interest rates also undergo a long-term decline so that they remain below average profit rates, then accumulation and economic activity could be maintained. Suppose, however, that there exists some fixed risk premium between interest rates and industrial profits. Let us suppose that unless interest rates are 3% below anticipated profits firms will not invest. It follows that if the real rate of profit falls below 3%, there will be no positive interest rate compatible with continued accumulation. Such a configuration would imply a future of stagnating accumulation reminiscent of the recent experience of Japan.

In an economy in which pension provision is privately provided, the prospect of falling rates of return on investment has other implications. Lower returns on equities would imply that individuals would have to build up larger investments to provide for retirement. Whether this occurs voluntarily, or by the state mandating higher contributions to pension schemes, the net effect is likely to aggravate the problem of falling returns. High savings ratios will depress demand and thereby reduce investment opportunities in the consumer goods industries. The inflow of additional savings will also tend to bid up equity prices further reducing the rate of return, which will have feedback effects on the viability of pension schemes.

A falling return on capital has other social implications. The amount of capital required to yield an income for one person will rise. This would constitute a barrier to entry into the employing class, so upward class mobility would be restricted.

These effects can be offset by international mobility of capital and labour. On a world scale, population is rising as is the capitalistically employed population. To the extent that capital can flow to this population, or the people can migrate, then the average international rate of profit need not decline. China and India currently provide rapidly growing workforces able to absorb surplus capital from Europe and Japan. But the very process of urbanisation and industrialisation set in train by this brings on demographic transition. The trajectory of Japan over the last 40 years gives us a glimpse of China's future. The rapid investment undertaken to catch up with the West, will, as reserves of rural labour dry up, lead to a rising capital/labour ratio and a falling rate of profit. But unlike Japan, China will have fewer opportunities to respond to this by exporting capital, both because there will be fewer countries left, and because these will be much smaller in relation to China's future surplus capital.

We have argued that returns on capital should be understood in the context of accumulation, population dynamics and the process of expansion of capitalism at the expense of other forms of economy. A focus purely on technical change as the controlling factor of profit rates can give misleading results. When the broader view is taken, we consider that declines in profitability are likely to be a problem for the global economy in the 21st century.

REFERENCES

Cockshott, W. P. and Cottrell, A. (2003), A note on the organic composition of capital and profit rates, *Cambridge Journal of Economics*, 21, 545-9.

Cockshott, W. P., Cottrell, A. and Michaelson, G. (1995), Testing Marx: Some New Results from UK Data, *Capital and Class*, 55,103-29.

Edvinsson, R. (2003), A Tendency For the Rate of Profit to Fall, Paper presented at the economic-historical meeting in Lund, October 2003.

Farjoun, E. and Machover, M. (1983), *The Laws of Chaos*, London, Verso.

Kalecki, M. (1971), *Selected Essays on the Dynamics of the Capitalist Economy 1933-1970*, Cambridge, Cambridge University Press.

Okishio, N. (1961), Technical Changes and the Rate of Profit, *Kobe University Economic Review* 7, 85-99.

Roemer, J. (1981), *Analytical Foundations of Marxian Economic Theory*, Cambridge, Cambridge University Press.

Ross, P.E. (2003), 5 Commandments [technology laws and rules of thumb], ***Spectrum,* IEEE**, 40 (12), 30-5.

Samuelson, P. A. (1973), Reply on Marxian matters. *Journal of Economic Literature*, 11, 64-8.

Steedman, I. (1981), *Marx After Sraffa*, London, Verso.

Sraffa, P. (1960), *Production of Commodities by Means of Commodities*, Cambridge, Cambridge University Press.

WHITHER OKISHIO THEOREM?

Dong-Min Rieu★

This paper aims to shed light on the implications of the Okishio theorem, particularly with respect to its two restrictive assumptions: (1) the constancy of the real wage rate, and (2) the establishment of new production prices. Despite the apparent negation of the theorem by its own creator, Okishio's study of the relation between technical progress and the rate of profit may be understood as a consistent research program comprising two successive stages.

INTRODUCTION

The Okishio theorem (OT) is one of the most well-known critiques of Marx's law of falling rate of profit (FRP). Its basic content can be summarized as follows:

> *'The introduction of new technology, which yields a higher profit rate measured in terms of old equilibrium prices, raises the rate of profit under new equilibrium prices when the real wage basket is kept constant' (Nakatani and Hagiwara (1997, p. 39)).*

In his last paper, however, Okishio (2001) acknowledged the limitations of the theorem's two assumptions: (1) the constancy of the real wage rate, and (2) the establishment of new production prices. This study aimed to shed light on the implications of the OT, particularly with respect to these two assumptions. Despite the apparent negation of the OT by its own creator, Okishio's study of the relation between technical progress and the rate of profit may be understood as a consistent research program comprising two successive stages.

THE OKISHIO THEOREM AS A COUNTERFACTUAL THESIS

The OT has often been misunderstood. Some researchers have thought that it implies an actual increase in the rate of profit, while others have interpreted the FRP as a necessary tendency.[1] The OT negates Marx's FRP, in the sense that it claims that a profit 'fall is due to rising wages, not mechanization *per se*' (Kliman (1996, p. 208)). However, the frequently neglected implication of the OT is that the FRP can, and actually does, result from a rise in the real wage rate. Okishio examined how introducing viable technology affects the equilibrium rate of profit by developing a counterfactual argument; he compared the normal

★ Department of Economics, Chungnam National University, Taejon, Korea(S.). This work was supported by the Korea Research Foundation Grant (KRF-2003-013-B00029). The author would like to thank Hyewon Kim, Lefteris Tsoulfidis and Takeshi Nakatani for helpful comments and suggestions. The usual disclaimer applies.

state of the capitalist economy with a hypothetical state in which the real wage was constant. The rational core of the theorem, therefore, lies in its formulation of the contraposition that 'if the rate of profit falls in the long run, this must be because of a rise in the real wage rate' (Nakatani and Hagiwara (1997, p. 41)).

The following 'minimal dynamic relationship' (Laibman (1996, p. 47)) suggests a positive correlation between the rates of change of the wage share (ω) and of the ratio of labor demand (L) to labor supply (N).

$$sign\dot{\omega} = sign(\dot{L} - \dot{N})$$

This relation may be a relevant starting point for formulating the capitalist dynamics that Okishio pursued. Biased technical change, accompanied by an increase in the composition of capital, would necessarily cause $\dot{\omega}$ to be negative, as a result of the 'industrial reserve army' effect. Therefore, in reality, no effective method exists for distinguishing the results of technical progress from changes in the labor market. Under the original form of the OT, all of the advantages of technical progress go to the capitalist, as the real wage is kept constant, and this fact highlights the OT's counterfactual character. At this stage, however, it is beside the point to criticize the OT simply because it is static. Okishio separated the problem of comparative equilibria from the adjustment process to equilibrium, as follows: '...'the theorem' treats the problem of comparing the magnitudes of the equalized rates of profit between the two equilibrium states. In that case, it is not necessary to discuss the disequilibrium process between the equilibrium states. It is not necessary for proving the result.' (translated from Okishio (1994, p. 28)).

'BENCHMARK' LITERATURE: GENERALIZATION OF THE OKISHIO THEOREM

By substituting the assumption of a constant wage share for that of a constant real wage, Roemer (1981), Foley (1986), and Laibman (1997) demonstrated the necessity of the FRP as a result of the introduction of viable technology.[2] Using Laibman's (1997) simple example of one good macroeconomy, this result can be illustrated by means of the information provided in Table 1. Let K, W, P, and Y denote, respectively, the physical capital stock, the flow of wages, profits, and net output. In addition, note that the ratio K/Y is a proxy for Marx's organic composition of capital.[3] While the second row in the table reflects the OT assumption that the real wage remains constant at 300, the last row reflects an alternative assumption that the profit share P/Y is constant at .25. One may easily confirm that the profit rate, defined as P/K, decreases under this new assumption.[4]

Table 1

	K	W	+	P	=	Y	K/Y	P/Y	P/K
Initial state	800	300		100		400	2	.25	.125
OT	920	300		148		448	2.05	.33	.1609
R-F-L	920	336		112		448	2	.25	.1217

In other words, there are two benchmarks in the existing literature, namely OT's constant real wage and Roemer–Foley–Laibman's constant wage share, each of which leads to different results. Therefore, 'it is impossible to say *a priori* whether the process of technical change will raise or lower the profit rate' (Foley (1986, p. 139)). This new benchmark, however, requires a behavioral explanation. Foley (1986), in the context of his 'New Interpretation' of Marxian value theory, argued that this implied a constant value of labor power, which he defined as the product of the money wage and the 'value of money'.

The assumption of a constant value of money is, however, too restrictive and arbitrary if technical change is the focus of the analysis. Furthermore, Okishian generalization of the OT through the modification of assumption (1) into 'a non-decreasing utility level of laborers' in the case of product innovation (Okishio (1993); Nakatani and Hagiwara (1997)) brought this explanation into question. That is, introducing new products necessarily changes the 'value of money', even when the money wage is constant. If the 'value of money' decreases as a result of product innovation, Foley's value of labor power decreases with the constant money wage, which implies an increase in the rate of profit.

As a result, the procedure of holding 'the value of labor power constant by holding the money wage and the value of money constant' (Foley (1986, p. 138)) is misleading.[5] It is interesting to note in passing that a special case of a 'constant value of money' occurs when the internal composition of the wage basket is equal to that of the physical value added, which is the case when Foley's definition of the value of labor power is consistent with the conventional definition.[6]

On the other hand, Laibman (1997, p. 47) maintained that the new benchmark implied a 'class struggle neutrality' condition. Although such an interpretation is appealing, it may be unreasonable if the utility level of workers is considered to be affected by the wage share. This problem relates in part to the incompatibility between the assumption of a constant relative share and a competitive labor market (Roemer (1981, p. 136)). It also relates to inter-sectoral competition, according to the following logic, where r_i and ω_i represent the rate of profit and the wage share, respectively, in the i-th sector.

Fig. 1

$\ldots \rightarrow \omega_i \neq \omega_j \rightarrow$ *movements of labor movements of capital* ...

In other words, suppose that the wage share in a particular sector were to decline relative to those in other sectors. Then, feeling that they were being treated unfairly, workers would exert less effort or move to other sectors.[7] Either of these actions would result in a decline in the Marxian rate of exploitation. This decline, in turn, would lead to the counter-tendency of capital to pursue higher rates of profit. Therefore, the benchmark concern may be developed into a problem of competitive process.

COMPETITIVE EQUILIBRIUM: PRICES OF PRODUCTION

One of the most salient critiques of the OT may be the following challenge: 'If the economy did not move towards the new equilibrium, or if the processes that produce technical change are themselves a function of being out of equilibrium, then how does the economy change? In either case the results of comparative statics are worthless, since the equilibrium is never attained.' (Fine (1982, p. 115)).[8]

In his later work, Okishio presented the problem posed by this line of thinking and actually tried to provide some relevant results (Okishio (1996, 1999, 2001)). In particular, Okishio (2001) showed that competition among capitals makes profit vanish under certain parameter values and other initial conditions. At the heart of Okishio's simulation model lies an emphasis on the interaction between capital mobility and the labor market, even in cases without technical change. Thus, the conventional stability condition, which was employed by Nikiado (1985), is no longer valid.[9] That this is true can be shown easily through the introduction of sectoral differences in the organic composition of capital into the simulation model of Okishio (2001).[10] Figure 2 illustrates the sectoral rates of profit under the assumption that the consumption goods sector's organic composition of capital is greater than that of the capital goods sector. As the sectoral rates of profit converge to zero, Nikaido's condition does not guarantee the formation of production prices, because the real wage is assumed to be constant in Nikaido's model. This assumption implies that the equilibration process is considered to be independent of labor market characteristics.[11] The path of the real wage rate in Figure 3 clearly illustrates this point.

Okishio's simulation results cast doubt on the reality of the OT's second assumption, which seemingly leads to a negation of the theorem itself. However, Okishio's framework can be maintained if an interaction between technical change and the labor market is introduced into the competition process. This

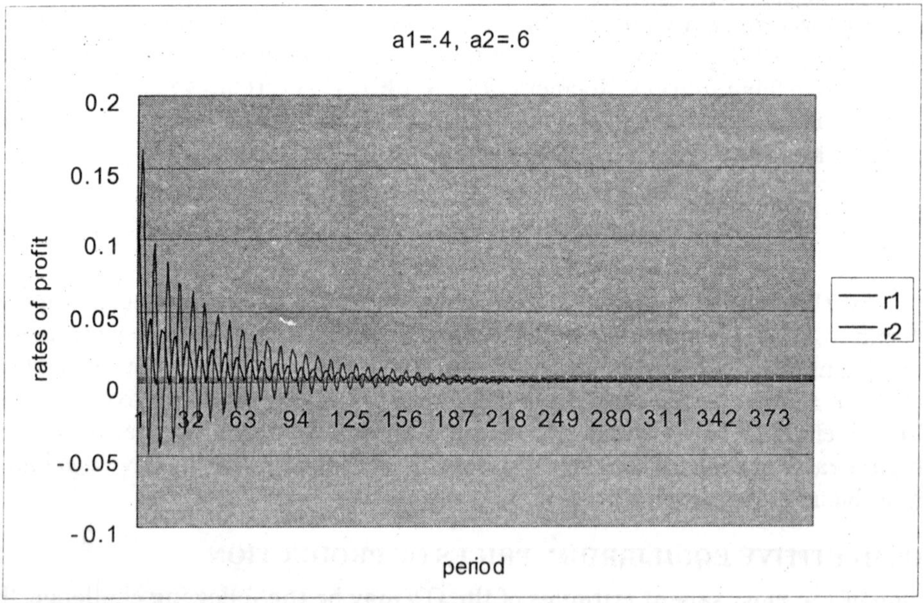

Fig.2

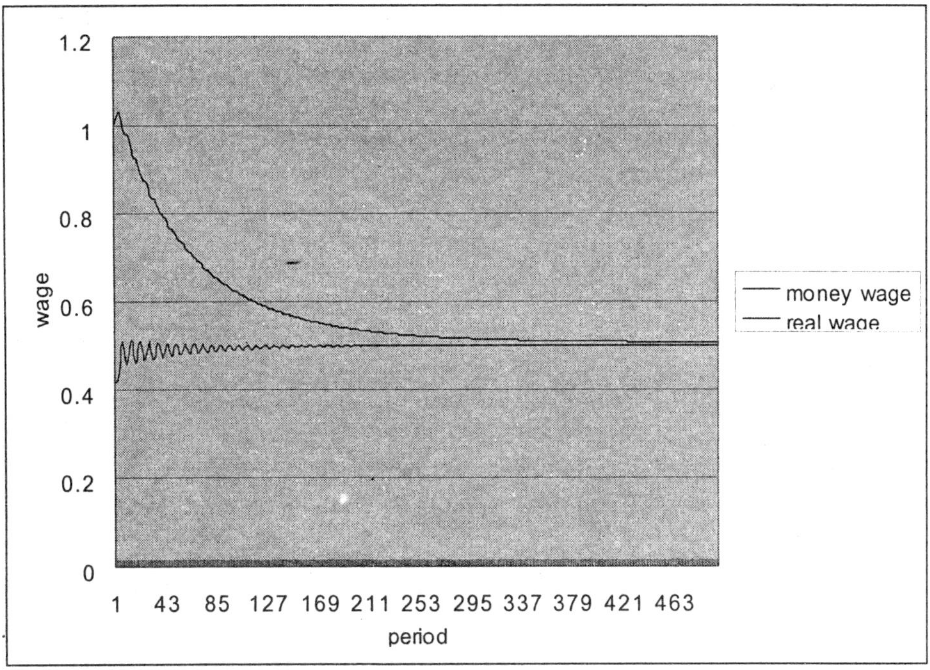

Fig.3

process has usually been conceptualized as the following cross-dual dynamics between market prices and output changes, which operate through differential profit rates (Duménil and Lévy (1993, p. 75)):

Fig. 4

... → supply ≠ demand → changes of prices → changes of profit rates → movements of capital → new supply and demand → ...

Okishio's contribution was the addition of a new level of labor market dynamics to these conventional cross-dual dynamics. At this stage, the assumption of real wage constancy was called into question. In contrast to the first stage, an exhaustion of the labor supply (and, therefore, a rise in the real wage) was explicitly introduced.

CONCLUDING REMARKS

The OT can be regarded as describing a counterfactual situation, namely the state of technical change in the context of a constant real wage. Under this interpretation, labor market dynamics concerning changes in the real wage may then be introduced during discussions of the competitive process determining production prices. In other words, Okishio tried to formulate a two-stage analysis beginning with a counterfactual argument. If one accepts this research strategy, then the OT itself cannot be refuted, except for the argument of logical inconsistency. Although the implications of the OT become limited under this interpretation, its original framework is nonetheless maintained, in the sense that the dynamic relation between technical change and the labor market is regarded as one of the most important elements of the competition process. The connection between the first and second stage stems from the observation that the generalization of the hypothetical state necessarily turns the entire problem into an equilibration process.

In a nutshell, although these two restrictive assumptions reduce the implications of the OT to being counterfactual, the OT still has meaning, given that it introduces a new dimension into the formulation of competition dynamics.

NOTES

1. For example, even in a recent paper on FRP, Okishio was regarded as taking Marx's law to be an argument that the rate of profit must fall (Petith (2005, p. 288)). This inference seems to have been partly due to Okishio's explanation of Marx's FRP as implying a decrease of the maximum rate of profit. See Okishio (1977).
2. As the OT itself is one of several comparative static results that may be derived mathematically from certain assumptions, it cannot be refuted within the given framework. Although much has been written about the OT, only the 'benchmark' literature has clearly elaborated this point. Therefore, this literature can help us to focus on the mutual relation between technical change and the labor market, rather than simply on the negation or vindication of the OT.
3. This was named the 'organic composition of production' by Okishio. One of its merits is that its magnitude does not depend upon the rate of exploitation.
4. If wages are assumed to be advanced, then the profit rate may be redefined without loss of generality.
5. Ramos (2004) first recognized this point. Ironically, however, he used his observation to refute the OT by distinguishing 'nominal' and 'labor-time' rates of profit. His 'labor-time rate of profit' was defined as the rate of profit when changes in the 'monetary expression of labor-time' are taken into account. Since he, like other temporalists, changed the definition of the profit rate itself, his inference is not a compelling challenge to the OT.
6. See the Appendix.
7. In the efficiency wage literature, whether a wage is 'fair' can affect the effort level of workers. According to Akerlof and Yellen (1990), the wage-profit ratio is one of the most important determinants of a fair wage.
8. A similar critique was recently put forward by the temporalists: '[The OT] relies crucially on the unproved assumption that the economy 'fully adjusts' to a new static equilibrium after mechanization. Under continuous mechanization, however, full adjustment will not occur and the Marxian profit rate can fall.' (Kliman (1996, p. 211)). In other words, the temporalists generally interpret FRP as a readily observable tendency, while Fine (1982) did not.
9. Nikaido's (1985) stability condition requires that the consumption goods sector's organic composition of capital be greater than that of the capital goods sector; however, this requirement contradicts the conventional wisdom of Marxian economics.
10. The same initial parameter values are used here, with the exception of the sectoral input coefficients a_1 and a_2. As Okishio (2001) presupposed that the organic

composition of capital of the 1st sector (which produces the means of production) and the 2nd sector (which produces consumption goods) were equal, he set their values to 0.5. In contrast, in order to test Nikaido's stability condition, a_1 and a_2 are here assumed to equal 0.4 and 0.6, respectively.

11. Actually, this was Okishio's (1996, p. 7) most important criticism of Nikaido's (1985) model.

REFERENCES

Akerlof, G. A. and J. L. Yellen (1990), The Fair Wage-Effort Hypotheses and Unemployment, *Quarterly Journal of Economics*, 105, 255-83.

Duménil, G. and D. Lévy (1993), *The Economics of the Profit Rate*, Edward Elgar.

Fine, B. (1982), *Theories of the Capitalist Economy*, Holmes & Meier Publishers.

Foley, D. K. (1986), *Understanding Capital: Marx's Economic Theory*, Harvard University Press.

Kliman, A. (1996), A Value-theoretic Critique of the Okishio Theorem, in A. Freeman and G. Carchedi (eds), *Marx and Non-Equilibrium Economics*, Aldershot, Edward Elgar.

Laibman, D. (1996), Technical Change, Accumulation and the Rate of Profit Revisited, *Review of Radical Political Economics*, 28-2, 33–53.

Laibman, D. (1997), *Capitalist Macrodynamics: A Systematic Introduction*, London, Macmillan.

Nakatani, T. and T. Hagiwara (1997), Product Innovation and the Rate of Profit, *Kobe University Economic Review*, 43, 39–51.

Nikaido, H. (1985), Dynamics of Growth and Capital Mobility in Marx's Scheme of Reproduction, *Zeitschrift für Nationalökonomie*, 45, 197–218.

Okishio, N. (1977), Notes on Technical Progress and Capitalist Society, *Cambridge Journal of Economics*, 1, 93-100.

Okishio, N. (1993), Introduction of New Products and the Rate of Profit (in Japanese), *Journal of Osaka University of Economics*, 44, 1–11.

Okishio, N. (1994), Reply to Critiques against the 'Okishio Theorem (in Japanese), *Journal of Osaka University of Economics*, 45, 1–32.

Okishio, N. (1996), Production Price and Competition (in Japanese), *Journal of Osaka University of Economics*, 47, 1–14.

Okishio, N. (1999), On Average Rate of Profit (in Japanese), *The Journal of Kansei Gakuin University*, 52, 1–20.

Okishio, N. (2001), Competition and Production Prices, *Cambridge Journal of Economics*, 25, 493–501.

Petith, H. (2005), Marx's Analysis of the Falling Rate of Profit in the First Version of Volume III of Capital, *Review of Political Economy*, 17, 269-90.

Ramos-Martinez, A. (2004), Labour, Money, Labour-Saving Innovation and the Falling Rate of Profit, in Freeman, A., A. Kliman, and J. Wells (eds), *The New Value Controversy and the Foundation of Economics*, Edward Elgar.

Roemer, J. (1981), *Analytical Foundations of Marxian Economic Theory*, Cambridge, Cambridge University Press.

APPENDIX

Consider the case in which all goods, including the newly introduced product (the n+1th commodity), are simultaneously used as consumption goods and production goods. According to Okishio (1993) and Nakatani and Hagiwara (1997), in order for the condition of a 'non-decreasing utility level of laborers' to be satisfied, workers must be able to purchase the new wage bundle at current equilibrium prices (p_i) and the current wage (w).

$$w = \sum_{i=1}^{n+1} b_i p_i \quad \text{(A.1)}$$

At the new equilibrium prices (q_i), the following condition must hold:

$$w = \sum_{i=1}^{n+1} b_i q_i \quad \text{(A.2)}$$

The subtraction of (A.2) from (A.1) yields

$$0 = \sum_{i=1}^{n+1} b_i (p_i - q_i) \quad \text{(A.3)}$$

On the other hand, note that Foley's 'value of money' is defined as the ratio between total labor hours and total value added. Therefore, if the 'value of money' is to be constant, then the following condition must hold, even under the simplifying assumption that total labor hours are constant. Here y_i denotes the physical value added of the i-th sector.

$$\sum_{i=1}^{n+1} (p_i - q_i) y_i = 0 \quad \text{(A.4)}$$

Taking into account equation (A.3), it can easily be confirmed that (A.4) holds in the following special case, where k is a scalar:

$$(y_1, \ldots y_{n+1}) = k(b_1, b_2 \ldots b_{n+1}) \quad \text{(A.5)}$$

Equation (A.5) implies that the internal composition of the real wage basket is equal to that of the physical value added.

HENRYK GROSSMANN' FALLING RATE OF PROFIT THEORY OF CRISIS: A PRESENTATION AND A REPLY TO CRITICS

Stavros Mavroudeas * **&**
Alexis Ioannides **

Henryk Grossmann was the first Marxist economist that proposed a theory of crisis based on the Marxian law of the falling rate of profit due to the increasing organic composition of capital. This view, while initially disappointingly minotirarian, has become very popular nowadays within Marxist Political Economy. At the same time Grossmann's theory has been severely criticised by many economists (e.g., Sweezy, Howard and King etc.*). In this essay, first, Grossmannn's theory is presented. Then it is reformulated so as to be comparable to the Harrod-Domar tradition of growth models. Third, older and newer critiques are being reviewed critically. Finally, it concludes by arguing that Grossmann's theory – despite certain deficiencies to a large extent justified by its pioneering character- has a valid methodological and analytical basis. As such it is a true founder of modern theories of the falling rate of profit theory of crisis.*

INTRODUCTION

Henryk Grossmann is renowned as the first Marxist economist who, during the mid-war era, formulated a theory of economic crisis based on the famous Marxian law of the Tendency of the Rate of Profit to Fall (TRPF) caused by the increase of the Organic Composition of Capital (OCC). This perspective, while very popular nowadays within Marxist Political Economy, had negligible support in the beginning of the 20th century when modern Marxist debates on crisis theory began. On the contrary, the other two historical theoretical perspectives (the theories of underconsumption and of disproportionality) dominated the scene.

Grossmann was born in 1881 in Cracow, coming from a rich Jewish family. He studied law and economics in Cracow and Wien with the economist Bohm-Bawerk (a leading proponent of the Austrian school) and the Marxist historian Karl Grunberg. He became active in the Left during his student years, was a founding member of the Jewish Socialdemocratic party of Galicia and, finally, in 1918, he joined the Polish Communist Party. At the same time he worked in the Central Statistical Agency and in the Free Polish University. Facing political persecutions he was forced, in 1925, to migrate to Germany. There he worked –

* Department of Economics, University of Macedonia, Thessaloniki, Greece.

** Department of Economics, University of Macedonia, Thessaloniki, Greece.

after an invitation by his former teacher Grunberg – in the famous Frankfurt Institute for Social Research where he became a professor in 1930. He left Germany in 1933 after the Nazis' ascent to power and went first to Paris and then to London. He ended up in 1937 to New York where the whole Institute for Social Research had moved. After the 2nd World War he returned to East Germany and he was inaugurated professor of Political Economy in the University of Leipzig. He died in 1950.[1]

Grossmann's magnus opus, the 'Das Akkumulations-und Zusammenbruchsgesetz des Kapitalistischen Systems' was published in 1929 (it was published in an English [regretfully] abridged version in 1992 as '*The Law of Accumulation and Breakdown of the Capitalist System*'). He also wrote 'Sismonde de Sismondi and his economic theories' in French in 1924 and the 'Evolutionary revolt against Classical Economics' in English in 1924 also. Another important work by Grossmann is the 'Die Anderung des ursprüngliche Aufbauplans des Marxschen Kapital und ihre Ursachen'('The change in the initial structure plans of Marx's Capital and their causes'), written in 1929, which studies the structure and the methodology of Marx's *Capital* a field in which followed the famous work of (the also Polish) Roman Rosdolsky (1977).

This essay studies Grossmann's theory of crisis and the macrodynamics analysis following from that. The second chapter presents Marx's analysis for the TRPF and the modern debates about it. The third chapter analyses Grossmann's contribution and focuses on two particular aspects: (a) its socio-political and theoretical background and its structure, crucial hypotheses and results and, (b) its relation to newer theories of growth stemming from Harrod's (1939, 1948) and Dommar's (1946) contributions. The fourth chapter reviews older and newer critiques and confronts certain of their arguments. The last chapter concludes by arguing that Grossmann's theory–despite certain deficiencies to a large extent justified by its pioneering character- has valid methodological and analytical basis. As such it is a true founder of modern theories of the falling rate of profit theory of crisis.

THE MARXIAN LAW OF THE TRPF AND THE MODERN CONTROVERSIES

Marx with his TRPF thesis aimed to prove that the capitalist system is inherently permeated by economic crises. In other words, economic crises in capitalism stem from organic causes. Moreover, he aimed to prove that, while the capital-labour antithesis (i.e. the wage relationship) is the fundamental one of the capitalist system, crisis tendencies are generated on its ground even when there is no active change of the class relations of power in favour of the working class. For this reason he consciously abstracted every crisis effect that can come from a change in the production process and income distribution that might favour labour. Consequently, he abstracted every factor that may lead to such effects and particularly the population constraint.[2]

The logic of the TRPF is the following. The fundamental motive in capitalism –the quest for profits–obliges every individual capital to strive (a) in the labour process against labour in order to exploit more the latter (i.e. to increase the unpaid labour-time) and, (b) in the circulation process against other individual capitals in order to realise a greater portion of surplus-value in the form of profits. In the struggle against labour the mechanisation of production is the main weapon of capital because it enhances capital's control on the labour process and its ability to change in its favour the equilibrium between necessary and surplus labour-time (and, thus, between paid and unpaid labour-time). This enhances the extraction of surplus-value predominantly through the appropriation of relative surplus-value.[3]

In intra-capitalist competition every individual capital strive to reduce its unit production costs (its unit cost prices in Marx's terms). This dictates a rapid technical change which intensifies the use of capital and economises the use of labour (i.e. capital intensive and labour saving technical change).

At this point it is necessary to distinguish between technical change that is based on a new technology and leads to a new technological model (a thorough reconfiguration of the production process) and technical change within the existing technological model. In defining the TRPF we refer to the latter, i.e. it is being posited that the overall technological model remains the same. The reason for this is that only in this case we can define the OCC as an expression of the Technical Composition of Capital (TCC) and the Value Composition of Capital (VCC) (see Fine (1989)).[4] In plain words, a wholesale change of technology (a new technological model) changes completely the structure of constant and variable capital (and, of course, their interrelationship) and makes the new configuration incomparable to the previous one. Both the structures of the capital-labour relationship (the exploitation of labour) and of the capital-capital relationship (intra-capitalist competition) are altered radically. Such changes do not happen easily nor are continuous. They rather occur in special periods (sometimes after a serious crisis) and take place in distinct waves of change (even when their elements have already emerged).

Thus, with the assumption of technical change within the dominant technological model, innovating production methods lead to more capital intensive enterprises which can take advantage of economies of scale. By increasing the quantity of fixed capital processed, under normal capacity utilisation, they manage to lower their unit production costs. Because larger-scale production enables a given number of workers to process a greater amount of product, both raw materials and output per unit of labour tend to rise. At the same time, the greater amount of fixed capital per unit output implies higher depreciation charges and auxiliary materials' costs per unit output. Consequently, for innovative production methods, the higher capital advanced per unit of output implies higher unit non-labour costs (unit constant capital) while the higher productivity implies lower unit labour costs (unit variable capital). For the innovation to be profitable, the fall in the latter must be greater than the increase of the former so that the overall effect would be the decline of unit production cost (the sum of unit constant and unit variable capital). However, under given technical conditions, existing technology and knowledge and also the ability to increase the exploitation of labour have definite limits.

When these limits are reached, subsequent increases in investment per unit output will lead to smaller reductions in unit production costs. Therefore, the more advanced individual capitals would tend to achieve a lower unit production cost at the expense of a lower rate of profit. The lower unit production cost enables them to capture a larger share of the market. At the same time, because the dominant market price is determined not by the more advanced individual capitals, but by the average conditions of production in each branch, innovating capitals supplement their profits by getting extra profits in the market. These are a net transfer of surplus-value generated under the auspices of other capitals who operate on average or below average conditions. These extra profits and the loss of market share compel other capitals to adopt the new production methods. However, this would sooner or later curtail the extra profits of advanced capitals, as their advantages would be eroded. When all production is stabilized at the new technical level, the result would be an increased rate of total constant over total variable capital and a lower general rate of profit.

The effects of the TRPF can be temporarily offset by an increase of the mass of profit, through the expansion of production. However, sooner or later, the TRPF weakens the incentive to invest leading to the stagnation of the mass of profit. This will lead to the inability to invest profitably the accumulated capital and thus *overaccumulation* takes place: the amassed capital is standing idle. For Marx, the only solution to the problem is the devalorisation (the destruction) of a significant amount of the accumulated capital. Because, in principle, the predominantly private character of the capitalist system does not facilitates a smooth (probably planned) devalorisation of capital (usually under state auspices) the devalorisation will take a wild, anarchical character; thus leading to a general crisis which affects even profitable and viable individual capitals. When devalorisation has proceeded enough then the surviving capitals will be adequately restructured and the field for profitable investment would be again expanded (with the closure of many enterprises). These will provide the necessary ground for a restart of the accumulation process.

Marx recognised that the TRPF co-exists with a number of counteracting tendencies such as (a) economies in the use of constant capital, (b) emergence of new spheres of production where the organic composition of capital (OCC–the ratio of constant to variable capital) is lower (for example, less developed countries or new branches), (c) intensification of exploitation, (d) imports of cheap inputs and depression of wages below the value of labour-power (for example, due to increases of the reserve army of labour). In actual history, whether the TRPF or its counter-tendencies will prevail is a matter of contingency. However, in principle, the TRPF is the dominant side of this contradictory unity because the counter-tendencies operate within strict constraints. For example, intra-capitalist competition induces rapid technical change, which increases the OCC, since it absorbs machinery faster than it employs workers. This relative displacement of workers by machines is met with definite limits in the ability to intensify exploitation (i.e. increase the extraction of surplus-value). This is so because, under a given technological model, capital is severely constrained by human physical limits in how much it can increase labour exploitation.

The TRPF has been at the centre of modern debates. Most of its critics refer to the Okishio (1961) theorem, which maintained that under certain assumptions (constancy of the real wage, perfect competition and so on) viable technical change raises the rate of profit. More specifically, if the real wage rate remains constant (i.e. if capitalists rip all the benefits from the improved conditions of production) then the profit rate would increase. It can only fall if workers are benefited at least partially by these new conditions of production. Hence, if capitalists choose technical change that maximizes the profit rate, then the latter is not going to fall. This thesis has been disputed from different perspectives. One route has been the questioning of Okishio's assumptions. Foley (1986) has shown that with a wage rate rising to maintain a constant wage share of output, capital-using technical change lowers the rate of profit. Fine (1989) also rejected Okishio's static equilibrium framework and argued that the TRPF law is a contradictory unity of the central tendency (translating a rising TCC to a rising OCC) and its counteracting tendencies (which affect the formation of the VCC). Another perspective accepts Okishio's assumptions but criticizes his definitions. Shaikh (1978a) distinguishes between the rate of profit estimated over total fixed and circulating capital (that is, covering the value of producer durable goods which transfer their value over a number of periods) and the margin of profits, estimated over current costs only. Capitalists introduce new techniques which-by lowering current costs-increase the profit margin but reduce the profit rate (through increased mechanization).

In a nutshell, Marx argued that it is the very success of the system (the rapid increase of accumulation) that leads to its failure (the inability to sustain the profit rate and, thus, to its fall and the subsequent crisis). This failure can, ultimately, only be surpassed through a destruction process (i.e. the devalorisation of significant portions of capital). Only this can, in the end, lead to a renewal of the accumulation process from leaner and more robust bases. This twin dialectical process of success - failure and destruction - creation is, for Marx, the crisis process.

GROSSMANN'S THEORY OF CRISIS

Grossmann's interest for the problem of economic crisis was fomented by the crisis debate within the Left in the beginning of the 20th century. To a large extent this debate was triggered by E.Bernstein's heretical thesis – representing the so-called 'neo-harmonists' - that capitalism is not destined to economically collapse and, thus, the labour movement should strive to reform it gradually. This thesis was challenged from many and different quarters. In the beginning it was confronted by K.Kautsky, the grand pope of German socialdemocracy, who in the end agreed with Bernstein's conclusions. From another perspective it was challenged by R.Luxemburg who argued that economic crisis would lead to capitalism's collapse. She attributed the cause of crisis to underconsumption (i.e. the lack of sufficient demand) and, at the same time, she explicitly rejected facets of Marx's analysis (particularly his Volume's II schemes of reproduction). In her political conclusions she argued for capitalism's revolutionary overthrow. In the same vein, Sternberg advanced an economic theory, which adopted elements by both Luxemburg and the 'neo-harmonists', but concluded with the same revolutionary call. But for Sternberg the overthrow of the system does not stem from economic necessity but from ethical requirements of a voluntarist nature.

Grossmann rejected all these views. He vehemently disagreed with Bernstein's analysis and political reformism. But at the same time he disagreed with both Luxemburg's underconsumptionism and Sternberg's voluntarism. He argued that the class struggle for the overthrow of the capitalist system is not being developed in a void but has serious objective foundations and constraints. Thus, this struggle depends upon the inherent crisis tendencies of the system that tend to lead it to economic collapse. Although he has been accused by many for adopting and economistic and crudely determinist approach, Grossmann–because of his active political engagement–never disregarded the importance of class struggle and its possibilities neither he purported that the system is going to be overthrown solely by an economic collapse and independently of class struggle. He, however, maintained that all these processes are founded and operate within objective economic constraints.

For Grossmann the cause of economic crisis does not stem from secondary facets of the capitalist economy (monopolies, international trade etc.) but from the very *essence* of capitalist accumulation. He, therefore, consciously abstracted all these secondary crisis factors that stem from these secondary facets of capitalism (e.g. disequilibria of supply and demand, problems of monetary intermediation and of the financial structure). He also abstracted the effects of working class' struggle on both the change of labour relations and income distribution. This does not imply that it does not play a significant role. But Grossmann, by 'freezing' its operation, aimed to prove that capitalism is inherently prone to crises irrespectively of working class' intervention.

From within this perspective, he proposed a general theory of economic crisis, i.e. one that analyses the general, abstract and essential causes of economic crisis irrespectively of their historical specific forms of appearance. The vehicle for his theory was the Bauer (1913) model. This model was created in order to refute Luxembourg's underconsumptionist theory of crisis and collapse. It was based on the assumptions of (a) an increasing OCC (and thus a TRPF), (b) equilibrium between supply and demand, (c) constant market prices (equal to labour values) and (d) constant value of money. Simulating this model for 4 years Bauer argued that the capitalist system is viable. Grossmann extended the simulation and proved that after several years the system is indeed going to collapse.

The Bauer–Grossmann Model

Grossmann's reformulation of the Bauer model is a two-sector model (departments of means of (a) production and (b) consumption) in the vein of Marx's reproduction schemes. He makes the following assumptions:

This is a closed economy model.

There are only capitalists and workers, i.e. there are no intermediate classes (e.g. there is no separate class of landowners and thus the complications of ground rent). Also, capitalists are pure industrial capitalists (i.e. the complications produced by the operation of merchant and money-dealing capital are being abstracted).

The rate of surplus-value is constant (at 100%).

Population's rate of increase is constant and geared to the rate of increase of variable capital.

The wage rate is constant.

Capital's turnover period is the same in all sectors (one year).

The rate of accumulation is equal in the two departments.

The rate of increase of constant capital is higher (10%) than the rate of increase of variable capital (5%), so as to exhibit the rising OCC.

The following is his own mathematical formulation of the model, slightly modified:

If c: constant capital and v: variable capital

k: capitalists' consumption share

α_c: rate of accumulation of constant capital

α_v: rate of accumulation of variable capital

s': rate of surplus-value

s: mass of surplus-value

Ω : OCC ($\Omega = c/v$)

R: rate of profit ($R = \dfrac{s}{c+v} = \dfrac{\frac{s}{v}}{\frac{c}{v}+\frac{v}{v}} = \dfrac{s'}{\Omega+1}$)

(1) $c_t = c_0 r^t$, where c_0: initial constant capital and c_t: constant capital after t periods

$$r = 1 + \left(\frac{a_c}{100}\right)$$

(2) $v_t = v_0 w^t$, where v_0: initial variable capital and v_t: variable capital after t periods

$$w = 1 + \left(\frac{a_v}{100}\right)$$

(3) $s = k + \alpha_c \frac{c}{100} + \alpha_v \frac{v}{100}$

(4) $R = \frac{k + \alpha_c \frac{c}{100} + \alpha_v \frac{v}{100}}{c + v}$

(5) Total value produced is: $AV = c + v + k + \alpha_c \frac{c}{100} + \alpha_v \frac{v}{100}$

(6) The rate of the capitalists' consumption share to the total surplus-value is k / s

(7) The rate of capitalists' investment (in constant and variable capital) to the total surplus-value is $\frac{\alpha_c \frac{c}{100} + \alpha_v \frac{v}{100}}{s}$

(8) The mass of surplus-value is derived from:

(8a) $$s = k + c_t \left(\frac{a_c}{100} \right) + v_t \left(\frac{a_v}{100} \right)$$

and

(8b) $$s = v_t \left(\frac{s'}{100} \right)$$

By equating (8a) and (8b) we get:

(9) $k = v_t \frac{(s' - a_v)}{100} - c_t \left(\frac{a_c}{100} \right)$

By substituting (1) and (2) in (9) we get:

$$k = \frac{v_0 w^t (s' - \alpha_v)}{100} - \frac{c_0 r^t \alpha_c}{100}$$

In the Bauer-Grossmann model the initial levels and the rates of growth of constant and variable capital are given. The rate of surplus-value is, also, given. Hence, the mass of surplus-value is derived. As it can easily be discerned, all the crucial factors and rhythms of the model are given except from the distribution of surplus-value between capitalists' consumption and capitalists' investment. The latter is directly determined by the (given) rates of growth of constant and variable capital. Therefore, the only variable of the model is capitalists' consumption share. However, the constant increase of accumulation –dictated by the rates of growth of constant and variable capital–require continuously increasing funds. On the other hand, the extraction of surplus-value fails to provide-to the required extent-these funds as its rate of growth (with a constant rate of surplus-value) is determined by the rate of growth of variable capital (which is by hypothesis smaller from that of constant capital). Therefore, in order for the rhythm of accumulation to be sustained, it is necessary funds to be transferred from the only available variable pool (i.e. capitalists' consumption share) to the capitalists' investment share. This gradual exsanguinations leads ultimately to the drainage of the first share and, consequently, to the collapse of the system.

In Grossmann's model when $k = 0$ then:

$$\frac{v_0 w^t (s' - \alpha_v)}{100} = \frac{c_0 r^t \alpha_c}{100} \Leftrightarrow (s' - \alpha_v) v_0 w^t = \alpha_c c_0 r^t \Leftrightarrow \left(\frac{r}{w}\right)^t = \frac{(s' - \alpha_v) v_0}{\alpha_c c_0} \Leftrightarrow \left(\frac{r}{w}\right)^t = \frac{(s' - \alpha_v)}{\alpha_c \Omega_0}$$

By taking the logarithmic form of the latter we can calculate the time of collapse of the system, which is a real number under the assumption that $s' > \alpha_v$:

$$t = \frac{\log \frac{s' - \alpha_v}{\alpha_c \Omega_0}}{\log \frac{100 + \alpha_c}{100 + \alpha_v}}$$

As it can be seen, the timing of collapse depends on (1) the initial OCC (Ω_0), (2) the rates of growth of constant (α_c) and variable capital (α_v) and, (3) the rate of surplus-value (s'). The higher the initial OCC and α_c the sooner comes the collapse. Conversely, the higher the initial α_v and s' the later comes the collapse. These relationships show the methods that can be employed in order to delay the collapse by activating appropriate countertendencies: to lower the rate of growth of or to devalorise constant capital, to lower wages or to export capitals. In these cases crises can be managed and instead of leading to collapse they will result in cyclical fluctuations (i.e. in the cyclical succession of phase of boom and down turn).

Moreover, Grossmann (1992, p.71-2) perceptively brought forward the Marxian relationship between the fall of the rate of profit and the mass of profits. He pointed out that in the initial periods the TRPF goes together with an increasing mass of profits and an increasing capitalists' consumption share. Only after the 21st year, in his simulation, the TRPF leads to a fall in the mass of profits. For Grossmann (1992, p.77), a Marxist theory of the economic cycle must be based on this changing interrelationship between the rate and the mass of profit. The increasing valorisation of capital leads to a boom even with a falling rate of profit. On the contrary, the imperfect valorisation of capital is the cause of the downturn and, ultimately, of crisis. It is very interesting how

Grossmann relates the imperfect valorisation of capital with its overaccumulation. In the boom phase, sooner or later, capital will start increasing faster than the surplus-value that can be extracted from the given population. This will cause overaccumulation and, thus, imperfect valorisation of capital. This will lead to downturn. In this phase the mass of profits would contract abruptly and, consequently, the added capital could not sustain the required rhythm of accumulation. This will result in (a) unemployment and, (b) a mass of capital that cannot be invested and remains idle; exactly as Marx has maintained. The appearance of (increasing) unemployment refutes directly Bauer's response to underconsumptionism. The latter argued that in so far as capital accumulation proceeds sufficiently fast so as to keep pace with the growth of population–with a given level of productivity–the system will create the markets it needs irrespectively of the increasing OCC. Grossmann proves that capitalism cannot sustain such a pace. Moreover, he argues that the *reserve army of labour* caused by the deficient accumulation of capital is a different process than the substitution of workers by machines. The latter is a normal tendency of capitalism, generated by intracapitalist competition and technical change and happens even in phases of boom. Contrarily, unemployment caused by deficient accumulation–which is, also, generated by the TRPF due to the increasing OCC–is a special process taking place solely in the phase of downturn.

Bauer–Grossmann and Harrod

Orzech and Groll (1983), Bronfenbrenner and Wolfson (1984) and Samuelson and Wolfson (1986) have brought forward the similarities between the Bauer–Grossmann and the Harrod model. In order to do so they have formulated single-sector models by aggregating the typical Marxian two departments of production. This is a path that Grossmann, after Bauer, had also followed in his mathematical model; although he kept in his numerical simulations the two sectors. What follows is an exposition of the Bauer–Grossmann model following Orzech and Groll.

The main assumptions are the same, of course, with those presented in the previous chapter with some notational changes.

I. Population's rate of growth is equal to the rate of growth of the workforce and, consequently, to the rate of growth of variable capital. The latter is posited as constant at a level β. Therefore, the increase of variable capital (i.e. the portion of surplus-value that goes to finance the increase of variable capital) is:

$$AV_t = \beta V_t \Rightarrow V_t = (1 + \beta)V_{t-1} \quad (1)$$

II. The rate of surplus-value is posited as constant: $s' = \mu$.

Consequently, the mass of surplus-value (M) is: $M = \mu V$.

As a result, the growth rate of surplus-value is determined by the growth rate of variable capital:

$$M_t = \mu V_t = \mu(1 + \beta)\, V_{t-1} \quad (2)$$

The mass of surplus-value finances (a) the growth of constant capital (AC),

(b) the growth of variable capital (AV) and, (c) capitalists' personal consumption share (K):

$$M = AC + AV + K$$

III. The rate of growth of constant capital is posited as constant at a level α. Therefore, the increase of constant capital is:

$$AC_t = \alpha C_t \Rightarrow C_t = (1 + \alpha)\, C_{t-1} \tag{3}$$

IV. According to the Labour Theory of Value, total income equals new value added:

$$Y_t = V_t + M_t$$

which, via (1) and (2), is transformed to:

$$Y_t = (1 + \beta)\, V_{t-1} + \mu\, (1+ \beta)\, V_{t-1} \tag{4}$$

The time expressions of all these relations are the following:

$$V_t = V_1(1 + \beta)^{t-1} \tag{1a}$$

$$C_t = C_1(1 + \alpha)^{t-1} \tag{2a}$$

$$M_t = \mu V_1\, (1 + \beta)^{t-1} \tag{3a}$$

$$Y_t = (1 + \mu)\, (1 + \beta)^{t-1}\, V_1 \tag{4a}$$

And accordingly:

$$AC_t = \alpha C_1(1+ \alpha)^{t-1} \tag{5}$$

$$AV_t = \beta V_1(1 + \beta)^{t-1} \tag{6}$$

V. Because the OCC is posited as increasing OCC, then $\alpha > \beta$.

VI. Because μ is constant and the OCC is increasing, an ever increasing rate of accumulation is required in order to secure the expanded reproduction of the system. That is, the ratio of total investment $\acute{A}_t$ (in constant and variable capital) to the total surplus-value M_t must increase more and more. This ratio is defined as:

$$\frac{A_t}{M_t} = \frac{AC_t + AV_t}{M_t} = \frac{aC_1(1+\alpha)^{t-1} + \beta V_1(1+\beta)^{t-1}}{\mu V_1(1+\beta)^{t-1}} = \frac{\alpha}{\mu}\frac{C_1}{V_1}\left(\frac{1+\alpha}{1+\beta}\right)^{t-1} + \frac{\beta}{\mu} \tag{7}$$

From this it follows that the rate of accumulation must increase in a constant relationship to α and β:

$$\frac{1+\alpha}{1+\beta}$$

VII. The rate of profit falls because of the increasing OCC:

$$R_t = \frac{M_t}{C_t + V_t} = \frac{\mu V_t}{C_t + V_t} = \mu\left(\frac{C_t - C_t + V_t}{C_t + V_t}\right) = \mu\left(\frac{C_t + V_t}{C_t + V_t} - \frac{C_t}{C_t + V_t}\right) \Rightarrow R_t = \mu\left(1 - \frac{C_t}{C_t + V_t}\right)$$

which, via (1a) and (2a), is transformed to:

$$R_t = \mu\left(1 - \frac{C_1(1+\alpha)^{t-1}}{C_1(1+\alpha)^{t-1} + V_1(1+\beta)^{t-1}}\right) \tag{8}$$

Since μ is constant, the rate of profit depends on the part of the equation within the parentheses. Because $\alpha > \beta$, the numerator increases faster than the denominator and, consequently, R_t is decreasing and tends to 0. This is proved as follows:

The limit of (8) depends on the limit of the ratio within the parenthesis which, divided by the faster increasing term, is transformed to:

$$\lim \frac{C_1(1+a)^{t-1}}{C_1(1+a)^{t-1} + V_1(1+\beta)^{t-1}} \frac{\lim \frac{C_1(1+a)^{t-1}}{C_1(1+a)^{t-1}}}{\lim \frac{C_1(1+a)^{t-1}}{C_1(1+a)^{t-1}} + \lim \frac{V_1(1+\beta)^{t-1}}{C_1(1+a)^{t-1}}} =$$

$$= \frac{1}{1 + \lim \frac{V_1(1+\beta)^{t-1}}{C_1(1+a)^{t-1}}} = \frac{1}{1 + \frac{V_1}{C_1} \lim \frac{(1+\beta)^{t-1}}{(1+a)^{t-1}}} \tag{8α}$$

Because $\alpha > \beta$, then $\frac{1+\beta}{1+\alpha} < 1$ and therefore it tends to 0. Thus, (8α) becomes

$\frac{1}{1+0} = 1$ and (8) tends to 0 as the parenthesis is nilled.

In this model the Harrodian rate of growth of net income (g_n) follows population's rate of growth:

$$g_n = \frac{Y_{t+1} - Y_t}{Y_t} = \frac{(1+\mu)(1+\beta)^t V_1 - (1+\mu)(1+\beta)^{t-1} V_1}{(1+\mu)(1+\beta)^{t-1} V_1} = \frac{(1+\mu)(1+\beta)^{t-1}\beta V_1}{(1+\mu)(1+\beta)^{t-1} V_1} = \beta$$

Respectively, the rate of growth of gross income (g_G) is:

$$g_G = \frac{(C_{t+1} + V_{t+1} + M_{t+1}) - (C_t + V_t + M_t)}{C_t + V_t + M_t} = \frac{(C_{t+1} + Y_{t+1}) - (C_t + Y_t)}{C_t + Y_t} =$$

$$= \frac{C_1(1+\alpha)^t + (1+\mu)(1+\beta)^t V_1 - C_1(1+\alpha)^{t-1} - (1+\mu)(1+\beta)^{t-1} V_1}{C_1(1+\alpha)^{t-1} + (1+\mu)(1+\beta)^{t-1} V_1}$$

$$= \frac{\alpha(1+\alpha)^{t-1} C_1 + (1+\mu)(1+\beta)^{t-1}\beta V_1}{C_1(1+\alpha)^{t-1} + (1+\mu)(1+\beta)^{t-1} V_1}$$

Because $\alpha > \beta$ and income ($V + M$) increases at the rate β (as both V and M follow this rhythm) while constant capital increases at the rate of α, then in the process of time g_G approximates asymptotically α. Consequently, there is a deviation from the balanced growth path.

The mechanism of this deviation–and, ultimately, of collapse–can be seen clearly also in the Harrodian reformulation. As it is well known, for the Harrodian knife-edge equilibrium to hold it is required that the warranted accumulation rate is equal to the actual accumulation rate and both of them equal to the population growth rate.

The warranted growth rate is:

$G_W = \Delta Y/Y = s\sigma$

where Y: income, S: savings, s: average (and marginal) propensity to save, σ: output–capital ratio, Γ: capital stock, and it holds that: $S = sY$, $\sigma = \Delta Y/\Delta\Gamma$.

The Harrodian savings (income minus consumption) is the investment in Bauer–Grossmann:

$S_t = Y_t - (V_t + AV_t + K_t) = (V_t + M_t) - (V_t + AV_t + K_t) = (V_t + AC_t + AV_t + K_t) - (V_t + AV_t + K_t) = AC_t$

As it can be seen from this relationship, for Harrod investment is only the increase of constant capital.

The Harrodian average propensity to save is the ratio of total savings to total income. In Bauer–Grossmann terms this is translated as follows:

$$s_t = S_t/Y_t = I_t/Y_t = AC_t/(V_t + M_t) = \frac{\alpha C_1(1+\alpha)^{t-1}}{(1+\mu)(1+\beta)^{t-1}V_1} \qquad (9)$$

The output – capital ratio is:

$$\sigma = \Delta Y/\Delta\Gamma = \Delta Y/AC = \frac{\beta(1+\mu)V_1(1+\beta)^{t-1}}{\alpha C_1(1+\alpha)^{t-1}} \qquad (10)$$

From (9) and (10) it is derived that:

$s_t\sigma = \beta$

That is, the Bauer–Grossmann model fulfils Harrod's balanced growth condition. However, Orzech and Groll has shown this similarity to be superficial. In the Harrod model σ and s_t are constant. Contrariwise, in the Bauer–Grossmann model s_t is increasing (as accumulation must increase continuously) whereas σ is decreasing. Simply, the changes of the one parameter are invalidated by the opposite changes of the other. From (9) it can be seen that:

$$s_t = \frac{\alpha}{(1+\mu)}\frac{C_1}{V_1}\left(\frac{1+\alpha}{1+\beta}\right)^{t-1} \qquad (11)$$

Because $[(1 + \alpha)/(1 + \beta)] > 1$ by definition, s_t increases without constraints.

Similarly, from (6) we get:

$$\sigma = \frac{\beta(1+\mu)}{\alpha}\frac{V_1}{C_1}\left(\frac{1+\beta}{1+\alpha}\right)^{t-1} \qquad (12)$$

Because $[(1 + \beta)/(1 + \alpha)] < 1$, σ decreases without constraints.

Till now there would not be any problem of reproduction despite the fact that the system is becoming more and more capital intensive and the output–capital ratio is continuously decreasing. But the Bauer–Grossmann model additionally assumes a constant rhythm of growth which requires a continuously increasing propensity to save (i.e. investment's rate of growth) so as to counterbalance the decreasing product–capital ratio. Investment (that is savings) comes from surplus-value but increase faster than the latter as its rate of growth increase while the rate of surplus-value remains constant. In order to sustain the rhythm of accumulation funds are being transferred from capitalists' consumption share. This is possible till this share is completely drained. Then the system collapses.

This process of collapse has been proved by Bronfenbrenner and Wolfson (1984). In the Bauer–Grossmann model workers do not save and capitalists save a portion from the total surplus-value. Bronfenbrenner and Wolfson (1984) argue that the Marxian equivalent of Harrod's rate of savings (s_t) is equal to the product of the propensity to save out of surplus-value (s^*_t) and the surplus-value (μV_t) divided by total income (Y_t). This distinction between the savings rate and the propensity to save out of surplus-value is necessary because surplus-value is divided between investment and capitalists' consumption share. The portion that goes for investment is further sub-divided between the part that is expended for variable capital and the part that is expended for constant capital. The former part is indirectly channelled to aggregate consumption and only the latter part constitutes–in Harrod's terms–investment. Consequently:

$$s_t = \frac{s_t^*(\mu V_t)}{Y_t} = \frac{s_t^* \mu (1+\beta)^{t-1} V_1}{(1+\mu)(1+\beta)^{t-1} V_1} = \frac{s_t^* \mu}{1+\mu} \tag{13}$$

Moreover, the propensity to save out of surplus-value has to be greater than zero (i.e. greater than some $\varepsilon > 0$). But, because capitalists expend a part of total surplus-value for their personal consumption, their exogenously determined tendency to save is smaller than unity: $0 < \varepsilon < s^*_t < 1$

From (9) and (13) it is derived that:

$$\frac{s_t^* \mu}{1+\mu} = \frac{\alpha}{1+\mu} \frac{C_1}{V_1} \left(\frac{1+\alpha}{1+\beta} \right)^{t-1} \Leftrightarrow s_t^* = \frac{\alpha}{\mu} \frac{C_1}{V_1} \left(\frac{1+\alpha}{1+\beta} \right)^{t-1} \tag{14}$$

Equation (14) shows that the propensity to save out of surplus-value depends upon a number of factors (α, β, μ and C_1/V_1, i.e the initial OCC) which are all exogenously predetermined. For the rate of accumulation to be sustained–as the increasing OCC causes the fall of the profit rate–it is required the propensity to save out of surplus-value to increase rapidly. This whittles down capitalists' consumption share till the system collapses.

GROSSMANN AND HIS CRITICS

Grossmann's theory has been severely criticised both during his days and later. Most of the critiques during his time were either disagreements in principle (usually from other crisis theoretical standpoints) or insubstantial (see Kuhn (1995, 2004)). However, a number of issues raised require particular attention.

One line of critique focused on the political aspects of his thesis and accused him of economic fatalism and having created a mechanistic theory of collapse (essentially a catastrophe theory). Grossmann has convincingly refuted this criticism (see Kuhn (1995, 2004)). This criticism has been reiterated, in a slightly different form, by Howard and King (1988) who argued that because of these Grossmann cannot see how capitalism can recover from an economic collapse. This is an unjust criticism because Grossmann was one of the first that combined a theory of crisis with a theory of cyclical fluctuations. He had very clearly clarified that crises function as a healing mechanism for the system through the devalorisation of capital that can restore viable conditions of reproduction. Cyclical fluctuations are the expression of the cyclical succession of phases of crisis and recovery and depend upon the level of the OCC, the rate of surplus-value and the growth rates of constant and variable capital.

Sweezy's (1949) critique has a special position. For quite a long time his presentation of Grossmann's theory has been its sole available exposition to the English-speaking readership. It was a presentation that did not do much justice to Grossmann. Sweezy criticized him from his own underconsumptionist perspective. His first accusation was that Grossmann neglects the realization problem (i.e. the heart of the underconsumptionist argument). This is an unjust criticism since Grossmann has, from the very beginning of his analysis, clarified that while the problem of realization exists he does not consider it as the cause of crisis but rather as a concomitant event. Thus he relegates it to a lower level of abstraction. Sweezy's second criticism is that he neglects the role of the rate of increase of population that can suspend the increase of the OCC. This is obvious but it is also well known that Marx when studying crisis abstracted from that for valid reasons (presented in the beginning of this paper). Grossmann simply followed Marx's path on this aspect. Thirdly, Sweezy attributed the increase of the OCC to the tendencies to increase the wage rate (particularly in a tight labour market). This is a completely erroneous analysis for the reasons presented in chapter 2. Finally, Sweezy argued that the rate of accumulation is the independent variable (unlike the Bauer-Grossmann hypothesis). This is true in practice but in formal modelling–as in the schemes of reproduction–it makes no sense at all. In these models the rate of accumulation depends upon the growth rates of constant and variable capital, as it has been shown in the previous section. These rates are given; therefore the rate of accumulation cannot be an independent variable.

But of all the critiques advanced two–both aired by Howard and King (1988) –are more important. First, that Grossmann implicitly adopted Say's law because supply is equated to demand (as savings are equated to investment). Second, that the rate of surplus value cannot be posited as constant because then there can be no extraction of relative surplus-value.

Grossmann and Say

Accusing Grossmann for being a crypto-Sayist is totally inaccurate and it hinges upon a misunderstanding of the Marxist dialectical method and the very purpose of the Marxian schemes of reproduction and the reproduction models in general. Shoul (1957), in a pioneering article, has shown how Marx treats Say's law. While he unambiguously rejects it as a real process and as the basis for modelling the operation of a capitalist economy he nonetheless employs not the logic of Say's law but the equation of supply and demand at certain levels of abstraction. This is not analytical inconsistency but a principled and meticulous application of his dialectical methodology of layered levels of abstraction. For Marx disequilibria of supply and demand are a normal phenomenon of the capitalist economy. Therefore its analysis cannot be based on the equation of supply and demand through some fictitious auctioneering process. Instead, its operation is based on the sophisticated process of determination of prices by labour values. In this process the sphere of production has the primary role and the sphere of circulation–to which these equilibria belong–has a subordinate role. Therefore, at the more abstract level of analysis these disequilibria are being abstracted and the equation of supply and demand is provisionally posited in order to analyse the fundamental relations of determination. Subsequently, at a lower level of abstraction, in the determination of market values these disequilibria are reintroduced as a sine qua non element of the capitalist economy and as one of the causes of deviation of actual prices from their labour value determinants.

From within this perspective Marx, in his schemes of reproduction, he posits the equation of supply and demand. Since he wanted to study the process of equilibrium and smooth reproduction of the capitalist economy he legitimately abstracted every disequilibrating process. In this vein it is equally legitimate at the higher levels of abstraction of crisis theory to leave aside mid and short-term disequilibria stemming from market fluctuations or/and changes in income distribution in order to focus on the fundamental, long-term causes of crisis. These stem from the primarily determinant sphere of production and its interaction with the most fundamental elements of intra-capitalist competition. This analysis does not consider yet actual competition which is conducted on the basis of market prices and, therefore, encompasses the interplay of supply and demand. Instead, it focuses on the long-run determinants of intra-capitalist competition, i.e. the production structure of each individual capital and its advantages and disadvantages over other individual capitals. This analysis refers to labour values and prices of production and not yet to market prices. When the fundamental crisis tendencies have been discovered then it is possible to lower the level of abstraction and encompass more concrete (i.e. more specific and at the same time of secondary importance) elements such as disequilibria of supply and demand and the formation of market prices but also the formation and the character of the general equivalent (the money), the structure of the financial system, the international economic relations and class struggle over income distribution. This, for Marxist Political Economy is not a one-way but an interactive process of determination: the more fundamental and essential processes determine the less ones but in their turn they are being influenced by them as well in the time process. Hence, a fully developed Marxist model of crisis and reproduction in the end encompasses, in a dialectical hierarchy, the most abstract fundamental and the more concrete features.

Grossmann follows exactly this analytical course and, therefore, he certainly does not lapse to Say's law.

Making the Rate of Surplus-Value Variable

The second criticism is more acute. It is logical that technical change will be accompanied by a rising rate of exploitation particularly through the extraction of relative surplus-value. Of course, in theory technical change can, under certain conditions, lead to an improvement of labour productivity without affecting the intensity of labour and the rate of exploitation. But in practice these two processes go together. Is this then a fatal error of Grossmann's model?

Marx (1981, p.318)-in the 13th chapter of *Capital* vol. III, when defining the TRPF-makes explicitly the assumption of a fixed rate of surplus-value:

> '*...then this gradual growth in the constant capital, in relation to the variable, must necessarily result in a* gradual fall in the general rate of profit, *given that the rate of surplus-value, or the level of exploitation of labour by capital, remains the same*'.

His aim was to prove that crisis is generated in capitalism because of its own inherent characteristics (and particularly the nature of technical change dictated by intra-capitalist competition) and in abstraction from workers' class struggle in production. That is the falling profit rate is not caused by a *profit squeeze* caused by increasing wages. In this way he wanted to confront Ricardo, who ascribed the falling profitability of capital in the increase of corn's relative price and, hence, to the increasing nominal wage and wage share.

Marx was fully aware that labour productivity increases are related to the rate of surplus-value. However, he argued that the law of the TRPF stands even with an increasing rate of surplus-value:

> *'The law of the falling rate of profit, as expressing the same or even a rising rate of surplus-value, means in other words: taking any particular quantity of average social capital, e.g. a capital of 100, an ever greater portion of this is represented by means of labour and an ever lesser portion by living labour. Since the total mass of living labour added to the means of production falls in relation to the value of these means of production, so too does the unpaid labour, and the portion of value in which it is represented, in relation to the value of the total capital advanced. Alternatively, an ever smaller aliquot part of the total capital laid out is converted into living labour, and hence the total capital absorbs ever less surplus labour in relation to its size, even though the ratio between the unpaid and the paid parts of the labour applied may at the same time be growing. The relative decline in the variable capital and increase in the constant capital, even while both portions grow in absolute terms, is, as we have said, simply another expression for the increased productivity of labour.'(Marx (1981, p.322)).*

Marx argued so because he maintained that the processes that increase the rate of exploitation are the same with those that displace living labour by dead labour, i.e. the processes that lead to an increasing OCC. Thus, the tendency to increase the OCC goes together with that of increasing the rate of surplus-value:

> *'However, as the same factors that increase the rate of surplus-value ... tend to reduce the amount of labour-power employed by a given capital, the same factors tend both to reduce the rate of profit and to slow down the movement in this direction.'(Marx (1981, p.342)).*

But, he argued that the tendency of the OCC to increase is stronger than that of the increase of the rate of surplus-value because the latter is possible only 'within certain definite limits' (Marx (1981), p.333). Therefore, the former is stronger and constitutes a 'law' whereas the latter is weaker and more erratic and, thus, constitutes a counter-tendency:

> *'The rise in the rate of surplus-value–particularly since it takes place under circumstances in which, as mentioned above, there is no increase in the constant capital as against the variable, or no relative increase - is a factor which contributes to the determination of the mass of surplus-value and hence also the rate of profit. This does not annul the general law. But it has the effect that this law operates more as a tendency,* i.e., *as a law whose absolute realization is held up, delayed and weakened, by counteracting factors.'(Marx (1981), p.341-2).*

Marx (1981, p.340) had also argued–contrary to Grossmann's critics–that these hold particularly in the case of relative surplus-value:

> *'It has already been shown, moreover, and this forms the real secret of the tendencial fall in the rate of profit, that the procedures for producing relative surplus-value are based, by and large, either on transforming as much as possible of a given quantity of labour into surplus-value or on spending as little as possible labour in general in relation to the capital advanced; so that the same reasons that permit the level of exploitation of labour to increase make it impossible to exploit as much labour as before with the same total capital. These are the counteracting tendencies which, while they act to bring about a rise in the rate of surplus-value, simultaneously lead to a fall in the mass of surplus-value produced by a given capital, hence a fall in the rate of profit.'*

Conversely, absolute surplus-value is much more effective in counteracting the TRPF: '...the tendency for the rate of profit to be reduced, in particular, is attenuated by the increase in the rate of absolute surplus-value that stems from the prolongation of the working-day' (Marx (1981, p.341). In this case the tendency to replace living labour with machines is weaker and capitals would prefer labour-intensive technologies in so far as they can increase the work-time without any (or an analogous) increase of the wage.

Grossmann follows faithfully Marx's logic on this issue. For this reason, immediately after the presentation of his TRPF theory, he studies four cases of counter-tendencies; the change in the rate of surplus-value being one of them. As Kuhn (1995) has accurately point out, for Grossmann the equilibrium between the TRPF and its counter-tendencies is a short-run empirical question. In the long-run the 'law' (the main tendency) will prevail over its opponents. For these reasons, although he assumed a constant rate of surplus-value, Grossmann argued that this can be rectified without compromising his approach. Bronfenbrenner and Wolfson (1984, p.179) and Samuelson and Wolfson (1986, Part ÉÉÉ)) have incorporated satisfactorily a variable rate of surplus-value in the Grossmann model. The result is not the cancellation of the breakdown tendency but simply its delay.

A variable rate of surplus-value has to follow a rule. Let us suppose that – similarly to constant and variable capital - it increases at a constant rate; for example $\tilde{a}$. This is logical since the rate of exploitation is a long-run factor depending upon certain structural features (technological paradigm, balance of power between capital and labour in the production process etc.). Thus, it does not change easily and moreover its movement cannot be very erratic. Then:

$$s_t' = s_1'(1+\gamma)^{t-1} \tag{15}$$

Accordingly, the mass of surplus-value is:

$$M_t = s_t' V_t = s_1' (1+\gamma)^{t-1} V_1 (1+\beta)^{t-1} \tag{16}$$

Substituting in (9):

$$s_t = S_t/Y_t = I_t/Y_t = AC_t/(V_t + M_t) =$$

$$= \frac{\alpha C_1 (1+\alpha)^{t-1}}{(1+\beta)^{t-1} V_1 + (1+\gamma)^{t-1} s_1' (1+\beta)^{t-1} V_1} = a\frac{C_1}{V_1}\left(\frac{(1+a)^{t-1}}{(1+\beta)^{t-1}[1+s_1'(1+\gamma)^{t-1}]}\right. \tag{17}$$

The limit to which tends the (17), dividing by the faster increasing term, is:

$$\lim s_t = \lim \frac{\alpha C_1 (1+\alpha)^{t-1}}{(1+\beta)^{t-1} V_1 + (1+\gamma)^{t-1} s_1'(1+\beta)^{t-1} V_1} =$$

$$= \frac{\lim \dfrac{\alpha C_1 (1+\alpha)^{t-1}}{(1+\alpha)^{t-1}}}{\lim \dfrac{(1+\beta)^{t-1} V_1}{(1+\alpha)^{t-1}} + \lim \dfrac{(1+\gamma)^{t-1} s_1'(1+\beta)^{t-1} V_1}{(1+\alpha)^{t-1}}} =$$

$$\frac{\alpha C_1}{0 V_1 + \lim \dfrac{(1+\gamma)^{t-1} s_1'(1+\beta)^{t-1} V_1}{(1+\alpha)^{t-1}}} =$$

$$= \frac{\alpha C_1}{s_1' V_1 \lim[\dfrac{(1+\gamma)(1+\beta)}{(1+\alpha)}]^{t-1}} = \frac{\alpha C_1}{s_1' V_1 \lim[\dfrac{1+\beta+\gamma+\beta\gamma}{1+\alpha}]^{t-1}}$$

The limit of the last equation depends upon the relation between $1+\alpha$ and $1+\beta+\gamma+\beta\gamma$ or, simplifying, between α and $\beta+\gamma+\beta\gamma$. That is s_t depends upon a complex relationship between α, β and γ. More specifically, if:

$\beta + \gamma + \beta\gamma > \alpha$ then s_t tends to nil, i.e. capitalists do not save anything.

$\beta + \gamma + \beta\gamma < \alpha$ then s_t tends to infinity, i.e. capitalists save all their income.

$\beta + \gamma + \beta\gamma = \alpha$ then s_t tends to a specific number that ensures the smooth reproduction of the system.

The first two cases are economically irrational. In the first case capitalists end up with saving nothing. In the second case they end up to save all their income. Only the third case is viable. However, there is no economic reason what so ever that can justify this specific relationship between these three rates. Thus, since the third is a very special and rare case, it is more probable that one of the other two cases will actual happen. In these cases the system breaks down again.[5]

There is another important point regarding a variable rate of surplus-value. As Yaffe (1972) argued, in order for the rate of surplus-value (s') to offset the increasing OCC its rate of increase should be unrealistically big and, thus, difficult to sustain. A simple numerical simulation can easily show that abnormally high and, thus, unsustainable rates of surplus-value are required.

Concluding, technical change based on an increasing OCC must probably lead to an increased rate of surplus-value. There is, however, a limit to the increase of the latter, imposed by humans' physical limits within a specific technological model. This limit can only be surpassed with a new technological model. If this limit is violated within the existing technological model– particularly regarding the intensification of labour then the productivity of the latter will fall instead of increasing. On the contrary, there are no such limits in the increase of constant capital. For all these reasons the increase of the rate of growth of surplus-value may counteract but it cannot cancel the TRPF.

CONCLUSIONS

Henryk Grossmann work can be justifiably characterised as a pioneering contribution in Marxist Political Economy and in macroeconomic dynamics in general.

As Bronfenbrenner and Wolfson (1984, p.180-1) argued, the 1920s generation of Marxist economists (Luxemburg, Bauer, Grossmann etc.) was the first to study–even in a primitive way–macroeconomic dynamics long before any other orthodox economist. They constructed models which, under certain rules (given rates of growth of the main variables), study if a steady growth path can be achieved. And if so whether it is stable, i.e. in the case of deviations from that whether there exist forces that can restore it. Keynesian and neo-classical economics discovered this field quite later and explored it with a rather inferior analytical toolbox. Whereas the Marxist economists followed the great tradition of both Classical Political Economy and Marx by recognising social classes and their role in the economic analysis, Neo-clasical and–to a certain extent– Keynesian theory preferred the a-social framework of marginal analysis. Furthermore, they posited economic crisis at the centre of their investigations whereas for Neo-classical economics this is completely alien since crisis is considered as something non-inherent in capitalism: if market forces operate unhindered there want be any of it. On the other hand, Keynesianism analyses crisis solely through its underconsumptionist lenses.

Grossmann's contribution distinguishes from the others of his era for a number of reasons.

First, he constructs a value-theoretic model and this continues to be an inspiration today in contrast to other radical and post-Keynesian non-value-theoretic perspectives.

Second, he places particular emphasis in Marxist dialectical methodology as a tool for his economic analysis. Although most of his generation of Marxist theorists was well acquainted with dialectics, they did not actually use it in their economic analyses. A characteristic example is its marked absence from Hilferding's influential work and its serious misunderstanding by Luxembourg in her study of Marx's schemes of reproduction. It was only after Rosdolsky's work that the importance of dialectical methodology was truly appreciated. Grossmann implements it masterfully and constructs a model through clearly defined and analytically 'legitimate' level of abstraction. He was clearly aware that their model-building was at a higher level of abstraction and not an immediate representation of the everyday working of a capitalist economy, as both Luxembourg and Bauer believed.

Third, his contribution in the Marxist theory of crisis remains seminal and provides a useful basis for contemporary theories (see Shaikh (1978b)). It is true that his model is overdetermined in the sense that his exogenous variables are more than his endogenous and because of its very assumptions it will collapse. But this is not a problem for a Marxist model of crisis since the latter is its very purpose. Furthermore, for Marxist Political Economy–contrary to orthodox economics–contradictions are not an analytical deficiency but a characteristic of real life. The capitalist system is permeated by contradictions which can only temporary be assuaged.

Fourth, his choice of capitalists' consumption share as the variable that can be manipulated is logical–contrary to later Kaleckian views (see Trigg (2004)). At the more abstract level, a capitalist is solely a 'functioning capitalist' (i.e. one geared towards accumulation of capital) and not a 'hedonist' (i.e. one geared towards a standard of living)–as in many cases it can actually be.

For all these reasons, Grossmann's work continues to be relevant today.

NOTES

1. For a more detailed biographical account see Kuhn (2004).
2. The latter is a very popular explanation of crises: a shortage in the labour market leads to higher wages and thus lower profit rates. However, Marx wanted to argue that crises erupt in capitalism even when there is no such constraint.
3. For Marx, because the extraction of relative surplus-value is more subtle and less conflictual, it pertains more to capitalism. This, however, does not mean that the extraction of absolute surplus-value becomes irrelevant. On the contrary, it is always present and, during specific periods, it can assume a very crucial role.

4. Fine (1989) points out that the concept of the OCC engulfs processes that do not necessarily move to the same direction or with the same rhythm. Marx defined the TCC as the ratio of the physical amount of the mass of means of production processed in a period to the physical amount of the mass of means of consumption consumed in the same period. As such it is an expression of the ratio of constant to variable capital but in terms of physical quantities, which do not have the same measure. The VCC expresses the same ratio but both the numerator and the denominator are in value terms, i.e. they are commensurable. Now a technical change that increases labour productivity increases also the TCC, since the same number of workers (consuming the same amount of means of production) process a greater mass means of production. The VCC would also increase since the value of the means of production would increase while the value of the means of consumption would remain constant. If the technical change is within the same technological model then these increases would be proportional. However, if this technical change leads to a different technological model, then the increase of the TCC would not necessarily correspond to an increase (or a similar increase) of the VCC. Thus, Marx (1982, p.762) argues that there is a close correlation between the VCC and the TCC and he declares that 'to express this, I call the value-composition of capital, in so far as it is determined by its technical composition and mirrors the changes in the latter, the organic composition of capital'.
5. Bronfenbrenner and Wolfson (1984, p.179) and Samuelson and Wolfson (1986, Part III) reached similar conclusions. Using exponential equations they argued that if: (1) $\alpha > \beta + \gamma$, then s_t increases without bounds. (2) $\alpha < \beta + \gamma$, then s_t tends to nil. (3) $\alpha = \beta + \gamma$, then s_t decreases till a limit that secures a constant rate of growth. But, as Samuelson and Wolfson (1986, p.76) recognize, there is nothing that can justify this particular correlation.

REFERENCES

Bauer, O. (1913), Die Akkumulation von Kapital, *Die Neue Zeit* no.31, 831-7, 862-74. Translated in *History of Political Economy*, 1986,18, 87-110.

Bronfenbrenner, M. and Wolfson, M. (1984), Marxian Macrodynamics and the Harrod Growth Model, *History of Political Economy*, 16, 175-86.

Dommar, E. (1946), Capital Expansion, Rate of Growth and Employment, *Econometrica*, 137-47.

Fine, B. (1989), *Marx's 'Capital'*, London, Macmillan.

Foley, D. Ê. (1986), *Understanding Capital*, Cambridge MA, Harvard University Press.

Grossmann, H. (1929), *Das Akkumulations–und Zusammenbruchsgesetz des Kapitalistichen Systems (Zugleich Eine Krisentheorie)*, Leipsig, Hirschfeld–abridged translation (1992), *The Law of Accumulation and Breakdown of the Capitalist System*, London, Pluto Press.

Harrod, R. (1939), An essay in dynamic theory', *Economic Journal*, 49, 14-33.

Harrod, R. (1948), *Towards a Dynamic Economics*, London, Macmillan.

Howard, M.C. and King, J.E. (1988), Henryk Grossmann and the Breakdown of Capitalism, *Science and Society*, 52, 290-309.

Kuhn, R. (1995), Capitalism's Collapse: Henryk Grossmann's Marxism, *Science and Society*, 59, 174-92.

Kuhn, R. (2004), Economic Crisis and Socialist Revolution: Henryk Grossman's *Law of Accumulation*, its First Critics and his Responses, *Research in Political Economy*, 21, 181-221.

Marx, K. (1981), *Capital*, vol. III, London, Penguin.

Marx, K. (1982), *Capital*, vol. I, London, Penguin.

Okishio, N. (1961), Technical Changes and the Rate of Profit, *Kobe University Economic Review*, 7, 85-99.

Orzech, Z. and Groll, S. (1983), Otto Bauer's Scheme of Expanded Reproduction: An Early Harrodian Growth Model, *History of Political Economy*, 15, 529-48.

Rosdolsky, R. (1977), *The Making of Marx's 'Capital'*, London, Pluto Press.

Samuelson, L. and Wolfson, M. (1986), Expository Marxism and Comparative Economic Dynamics, *History of Political Economy*, 18, 65-85.

Shaikh, A. (1978a), Political Economy and Capitalism: notes on Dobb's theory of crisis, *Cambridge Journal of Economics*, 2, 233-51.

Shaikh, A. (1978b), An Introduction to the History of Crisis Theories, in *U.S. Capitalism in Crisis*, New York, URPE.

Shoul, B. (1957), Karl Marx and Say's Law, *Quarterly Journal of Economics*, 71, 611-26.

Sweezy, P. (1949), *The Theory of capitalist development*, London, Dennis Dobson.

Trigg, Á. (2004), Kalecki and the Grossmann Model of Economic Breakdown, *Science and Society*, 68, 167-205.

Yaffe, D. (1972), The Marxian Theory of Crisis, Capital and the State', *Bulletin of the Conference of Socialist Economists*, 1, 5-58.

KONDRATIEV, MARX AND THE LONG CYCLE

Aris Papageorgiou &
Lefteris Tsoulfidis

This paper begins with a critical presentation of Kondratiev's (1926) seminal paper on the question of the existence as well as his theoretical explanation of long cyclical fluctuations of the level of economic activity. Furthermore we argue that a coherent explanation of long-run fluctuations can be based upon Marx's argument in Capital III, whereby the falling long-run tendency of the rate of profit leads to a stagnant mass of net profits, *which are associated with the onset of economic crisis. The paper concludes with a discussion of the similarities or differences and of the relative merits or weaknesses of Kondratiev's and Marx's views with respect to their visions of the long term evolution of the capitalist system.*

INTRODUCTION

Long cycles are long-run oscillations of economic conjuncture with an approximate duration of 45-55 years, whereby the phase of expansion lasts almost as long as the phase of depression. They are associated with the Russian economist Nikolai Dmitrievich Kondratiev (1892-1938) who was the first to study them thoroughly and to present rich empirical proof on their functioning. Acknowledging this fact another great scholar of economic fluctuations, Joseph Alois Schumpeter, labeled the long cycle as the Kondratiev cycle.[1] Kondratiev mentions that he arrived at the hypothesis concerning the existence of the long cycle during 1919-1921. In 1920 Kondratiev founded and became director of the Institute of Conjuncture in Moscow, an organization devoted to the study of economic fluctuations and to the submitting of policy proposals based on conjuncture forecasts. His first work specifically devoted to the subject of long cycles was the 'Long Cycles of Economic Life' (1925). It was from this article that Kondratiev became known to the western world, firstly though an *abridged* German version that appeared in the 'Archiv fur Sozialwissenschaft und Sozialpolitik' in 1926 and secondly through a translation of the *German* version in the 'Review of Economics and Statistics' in 1935.[2] In this paper Kondratiev presented his empirical findings on long cycle research, concluding by the statement that '*on the basis of the available data, the existence of long waves* (cycles) *of cyclical character is very probable*' (Kondratiev (1935, p. 115)). However

* Department of Economics, University of Macedonia, Thessaloniki, Greece.

** Department of Economics, University of Macedonia, Thessaloniki, Greece.

despite a rich exposition of statistical and historical data this paper did not contain a *theoretical* explanation of the long cycle. This drawback was amended by Kondratiev in the following year (1926) when he read an expanded version of the 1925 paper before the Institute of Economics of the Russian Association of Social Sciences Research, which included a first approximation towards a theoretical explanation of the long cycle.[3] The expanded version became available in English relatively recently (1998) and of course shed new light to Kondratiev's argument about the long cycle.

In this article we will discuss Kondratiev's paper of 1926 in connection with a long cyclic interpretation of economic life, which as shown by Shaikh (1992) can be found in the third volume of Marx's 'Capital' in Chapter 15 where Marx discusses the reflection of the law of the falling tendency of the profit rate on the movement of the mass of profit. The remainder of this article is organized as follows. In the second part we review Kondratiev's paper of 1926. In the third part we present the basic tenets of Marx's law of the tendential fall of the profit rate and discuss its association with long run fluctuations on the mass of profit. In the final section we discuss the relationship between the two interpretations of long run fluctuations and critically evaluate their main strengths and weaknesses.

KONDRATIEV'S EMPIRICAL FINDINGS AND THEORETICAL REASONING

In his 1926 paper on long cycles Kondratiev presented data on various economic series, which comprised of three groups:

(a) Value series, which included average wholesale price indices (Britain, France, USA), quotations of bond prices (England, France), nominal wages (for agricultural and cotton industry workers in England) and deposits of private savings banks (France).

(b) Real series, which included, in per capita terms, extraction of coal (England), production of cast iron (England), production of lead (England) and consumption of coal (France).

(c) Composite series, *i.e.* economic variables that are affected both by value and real factors, which included, again in per capita terms, foreign trade turnover for England and France.

With the exception of the wholesale price level series, on the unprocessed projection of which long cyclic oscillations were obvious even for the unsympathetic observer[4] the detection of long cycles on the other variables was performed through statistical processing, due to the fact that their unprocessed projection revealed secular tendencies, usually of an evolutionary nature. Kondratiev used least squares techniques to fit theoretical curves to the empirical series and then calculated the corresponding deviations between the two series sets and smoothed them using 9 year moving averages in order to eliminate the effects of medium length (Juglar) cycles, which were assumed to have a range of 7-11 years. It was on the basis of the smoothed deviations series, which reflected the alternation of acceleration and deceleration in growth of the (generally upward) trends of the variables studied, that Kondratiev was able to detect long run oscillations of economic life since the turning points of the cycles in the deviation series corresponded quite satisfactorily with those in the unprocessed price level series.

Noting that the accurate time determination of the turning points of the long cycles was impossible due to reasons such as the non-uniform movement of economic variables and the non-synchronized evolution of the main capitalist economies, Kondratiev proposed the following periodisation of the long cycles providing 5-7 year ranges for the turning points[5]:

(A) (i) Rising wave of the first cycle: from the end of 1780's-beginning of the 1790's until 1810-1817

(ii) Declining wave of the first cycle: from 1810-1817 until 1844-1851

(B) (i) Rising wave of the second cycle: from 1844-1851 until 1870-1875

(ii) Declining wave of the second cycle: from 1870-1875 until 1890-1896

(C) (i) Rising wave of the third cycle: from 1890-1896 to 1914-1920

(ii) Probable declining wave of the third cycle: from 1914-1920

Having presented empirical proof of a numerical nature for his theoretical proposition, Kondratiev proceeded by attempting to link numerical evidence with empirical data of a historical nature. He thus proposed that the two and a half long cycles, from the dawn of the Industrial Revolution to the mid 1920's were characterized by the recurrent occurrence of the following features in the socio-economic sphere that characterized the economic history of capitalism up to the first quarter of the twentieth century:

(a) Prior to the start or even at the start of a long oscillation, *i.e.* around the lower turning point of the cycle, the stagnated economic life is rejuvenated by the operation of three factors:

(i) Technical inventions are widely applied (diffused) in the depressed economy, thereby becoming clustered innovations, with far reaching effects in terms of industrial capacity and profitability trends. It is very important to note here that Kondratiev sharply distinguishes between the temporal 'sampling' distributions of technical inventions on the one hand and of the materially-economically 'useful' form they take as diffused innovations on the other. It is the latter distribution that has an economic sense. Indeed from the point of view of economic theory, even the possibility of a distribution of technical inventions is perhaps a matter of indifference. Kondratiev however stated his belief that even technical inventions were not random but they themselves depended on the requirements of practical-hence economic-activity as well as on the previous accumulation of previously accumulated scientific knowledge. What is crucial however in this aspect of the analysis is that according to Kondratiev *the economic application of technological evolution is endogenous to the rhythm of the long wave.*

(ii) World market is expanded through the deeper involvement of new countries in capitalist transactions. This expansion can occur either in a 'quantitative' sense, when new regions are absorbed by capitalism, usually because of their rich natural supplies in raw materials or in the 'qualitative' sense when an already established player assumes a strengthened and more crucial role in the world economy. Kondratiev characteristically mentions USA, which entered the world market as an independent capitalist state during the beginning of the first long cycle and assumed a strengthened and more imperative position during the 1840's just before the upswing of the second long cycle.

(iii) Production of gold increases. Kondratiev views gold as the money commodity. This means that increase in its productivity lowers its value and *may* form a prerequisite for a rise in the price level. As a commodity, albeit a special one since it is itself the embodiment of value, it has a value associated with its cost of production, a cost, which is reflected in the price level. Therefore Kondratiev notes that one should expect gold mining to rise significantly at the time when its value relative to the bulk of the other commodities increases significantly. In temporal terms this occurs around the lower turning of the long cycle when the price level is at its lowest. Indeed as it is also noted by Villar (1976, p.321) the 19th century saw a profound increase in gold mining during the lower turning points of the two long cycles associated with this century, *i.e.* in 1848-1851 with the discoveries of gold in California and Australia and in 1890-1896 with the discoveries of gold in South Africa and in the Far North of America.

(b) During the rising wave of the long cycle, social upheavals such as wars and revolutions are more numerous *relative* to the declining wave of the long cycle. While Kondratiev presented comprehensive tables of historical data ranging from USA's independence in 1776 to the end of WW1 to back his claim empirically, he also attempted to theorize his position in a profoundly Marxian manner by stating that social upheavals are a function of economic conditions, and that the economic intensity of the rising wave expressed in the form of 'economic fights for markets and raw materials' prepares the ground for social explosions. Therefore socio-political 'unrests' are not random but tend to be more densely distributed along the upswing part of the cycle.[6]

(c) The agricultural sector of the economy is particularly depressed during the declining wave of the long cycle. This depression is indicated by the steeper fall of the agricultural price level relative to the industrial price level on the one hand and by the fall in the value of ground rents on the other.

(d) Medium length cycles (Juglar cycles) are threaded on the long cycle. During the rising wave of the long cycle the upswing part of the Juglars is significantly lengthier than the downswing part and the same holds true for the downswing part of the Juglar relatively to its upswing component during the declining wave of the long cycle.

After discussing his empirical findings Kondratiev moved on to a *tentative* theoretical explanation of the long cycle. He supported the view that the wave like fluctuations of the various economic elements indicate that their movement takes place around a certain equilibrium level, which although it cannot be observed in reality it nevertheless acts as a gravitational center around which the fluctuations of economic life occur. Kondratiev also connected the relationship between the equilibrium of the economy and the oscillations around it to the oscillations of the market prices around prices of production and of individual rates of profit around average levels of profit, providing a link of his whole argument with classical and Marxist political economy. Stating that wave like fluctuations are one part of the dynamics of a capitalist economy, the other being the evolutionary nature of these dynamics, he claimed that *during* this evolutionary process the equilibrium level itself changes and is therefore movable. Taking into account the time dimension Kondratiev like a modern macroeconomist proposed that there existed three orders of equilibrium. A short run equilibrium where supply is a fixed quantity, a medium run equilibrium where the reserves of the main capital items are fixed but their production rates vary and a long run equilibrium where the reserves of main capital items themselves vary. It was around the last equilibrium level, 'third order equilibrium' as Kondratiev defined it, that long oscillations were to take place.

Kondratiev utilized Marx's argument that 'the material basis for the crises or the medium-length cycles which recur every ten years is the material deterioration, replacement and extension of the host of manufacturing tools in the form of machines with an average life of ten years' and extended the scope of the Marxian argument to cover long cycles by putting in place of 'manufacturing tools' the main fixed capital items. 'Thus it maybe asserted that the material basis for long cycles is the deterioration of, replacement and extension of the main capital goods with long production times and vast production costs. *The replacement and extension of the stock of these items is not a smooth process but a discontinuous one, which also finds expression in long cycles of conjuncture*' (Kondratiev (1998, p.56)).

This replacement and extension of fixed capital reserves, which according to Kondratiev's first empirical principle begins to occur around the lower turning point of the cycle is the starting point for his tentative explanation of the long oscillation. During the ensuing upswing the quest for raw materials necessary to support fixed capital expansion increases, while also new regions enter into the world market. On the economic level the increased investment in large scale business schemes, increases the demand for capital to such an extent that the curve of current investment gets very close to the curve of accumulation of (monetary) capital, *i.e.* savings, and eventually crosses it thus tending to raise the interest rate and making (loanable) capital more expensive. On the socio-political level the general growth of productive forces and the accompanying search for raw materials are expressed in an intensification of social upheavals in the form of wars and revolutions, causing thus a further weakening in the rate of accumulation.[7]

Eventually large-scale investment declines and as a consequence interest rate growth stops while investment schemes are abandoned. As the depression evolves the price level and the interest rate will fall, although the latter will assume a lower downward course than prices. Propensity to save will increase beginning with those population groups that have a fixed income and gain from the falling price level while also rentiers will contribute to this direction due to the slower reduction of the interest rate. The steeper fall of the agricultural price index relative to the industrial one will also facilitate savings accumulation at the hands of banks and large industrial concerns. Thus hand in hand with the upward trend of the propensity to save, loanable capital will grow. Furthermore this pool of loanable capital will be 'cheap' since the interest rate would have fallen significantly, a fall strengthened also by the increased inflow of gold, whose production accelerates due to the favorable conjuncture of a low pricing level. Although, Kondratiev is not particularly explicit, nevertheless it might be deduced that these developments, that is, the devaluation of fixed capital in combination with a falling rate of interest would be tantamount to the restoration of profitability, thereby creating the necessary preconditions for long-term capital investment and allowing the cycle to run its course anew.

MARX'S LAW OF THE FALLING TENDENCY OF THE RATE OF PROFIT AND THE THEORY OF LONG RUN CRISIS[8]

The starting point of Marx's analysis is the very nature of capitalist production, which is production aiming at the acquisition of the largest possible profit and at the expansion of productive activity as a purpose in itself. In order to achieve these goals the capitalist has to wage war in two fronts. In the first front he fights against labor in order to hold wages to the minimum level possible and to increase productivity. There is no doubt that capital tries to exhaust every possibility of lengthening the working day and of intensifying the working process, yet at every historical conjuncture there exist physical and legal limits[9] that hold back, at least to a certain extent, the social effects of capitalist greed. Given these limits therefore, the most effective way to increase profits is to reorganize the whole labor process through a more refined specialization and routinisation of the workers' functions in the production field. The subdivision of the working process decreases the wage by devaluating the worker and also creates the necessary prerequisites for the substitution of labor for machinery.

In the second front each capital competes with other capitals through the continuous reduction of the average cost and price of commodities. Those businesses that succeed in this aim are able to reduce their sales price below the average price that rules in their sector and to initially increase their market share. The ideal situation for the victorious capitals would be of course to reduce their sales price even below the average cost of the other capitals with which they compete, so as to marginalize them and ultimately lead them to bankruptcy.

This reduction of the average cost of production is achieved mainly through the mechanization and the consequent automatization of production characterized by the greater use of constant capital (buildings, machinery, raw materials) in place of variable capital (labor). In the first and third volume of *Capital* Marx clarifies that these changes in the production sphere aim at the rationalization of the productive process, the increase in the productivity of labor and consequently the reduction of the unit cost below the average unit cost of the sector in order that the realization of extra profits becomes possible and the successful capitals secure a profit rate over and above the average profit rate of the economy.

The crucial point now in Marx's argument is that the processes of mechanization and productivity increase are accompanied by the *capitalization of production*. What this means in physical terms is that the ratio of constant capital per unit of net output, K/Y, rises and this results to an increase of this ratio in its expression in value terms, C/L, where $L = v+s$ (v stands for variable capital and s for surplus value, the sum of the two terms is the Marxian value added). Marx calls the expression C/L the materialized composition of capital and its relationship to K/Y is given by the following equation:

$$\frac{C}{L}=\frac{\lambda_K}{\lambda_Y}\frac{K}{Y}$$

where λ_K is the mean unit value of the means of production and λ_Y is the mean unit value of net output. Now since technological progress, which tends to lower the unit values of commodities, is diffused throughout the entire economy the ratio λ_K/λ_Y tends to be relatively stable and thus, the movement of C/L is essentially governed by the movement of K/Y. By the equation of the rate of profit r we obtain:

$$r=\frac{s}{C}=\frac{s}{L}\frac{L}{C}=\left(\frac{s/v}{1+s/v}\right)\frac{L}{C}$$

Regardless of how fast the rate of surplus value s/v rises, the term in the parenthesis will increase at a decreasing rate since in the limit its value will approach unity as s/v approaches infinity (which means that $v \to 0$). Meanwhile the ratio L/C, which is the inverse of the materialized composition of capital, represents virtually the maximum rate of profit, which is the value that the rate of profit obtains when $v \to 0$ and when s is thus maximized. This falling tendency implies that the general rate of profit (whose size depends upon the value of v) will take values, which will lie within a range with a decreasing upper limit. Therefore the general rate of profit will eventually start to fall, for it will be pressed by the intertemporal falling tendency of the maximum rate of profit. The relationship between the maximum and the general rates of profit is depicted graphically in Figure 1.

The fall in the rate of profit does not necessarily imply economic depression as long as the rise in the mass of profit is sufficiently satisfactory. On the contrary

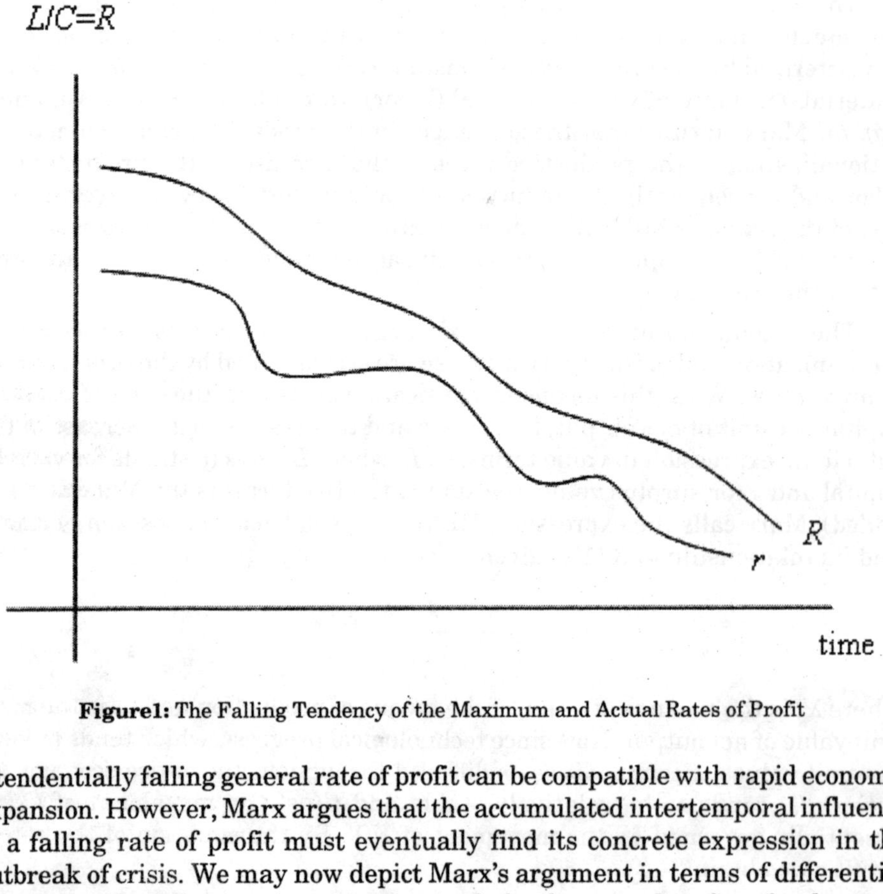

Figure1: The Falling Tendency of the Maximum and Actual Rates of Profit

a tendentially falling general rate of profit can be compatible with rapid economic expansion. However, Marx argues that the accumulated intertemporal influence of a falling rate of profit must eventually find its concrete expression in the outbreak of crisis. We may now depict Marx's argument in terms of differential calculus in the following manner. If r stands for the rate of profit, s for the mass of profit and C for total capital stock, then we have:

$$r = s/C \text{ or } s = r\,C$$

Taking the total differential of the above relationship we obtain:

$$ds = r\,dC + C\,dr$$

Dividing both parts of the equation by dC we get:

$$ds/dC = r + C(dr/dC)$$

and by factoring out the rate of profit we arrive at:

$$ds/dC = r\left(1 + \frac{dr}{dC}\frac{C}{r}\right)$$

The term ds/dC indicates the change in profits per unit of capital invested, while the term $(dr/dC)(C/r)$ is the elasticity of the profit rate, that is the percentage change of the profit rate induced by a percentage change in the capital stock. It is evident that the change in the mass of profit with regards to the change of the capital stock equals zero when the elasticity of the profit rate equals to minus one. This occurs at the point where profits are maximized, that is at the point where a percentage change of the capital stock by one unit leads to an equivalent change of profits towards the opposite direction. It is at this point, *the point of absolute overaccumulation* as Marx calls it, that the motive of capitalists for new investments weakens to the point of extinction, since the change in the rate of profit by every new investment is counterbalanced by the investment's cost. The ultimate effect of this process is stagnation in the mass of profits and the onset of crisis.

In Figure 2 below we present in a three-part graph the evolution of the relevant variables: the first depicts the evolution of the mass of real net profits, whereas the second illustrates the change of these profits *ds* which when

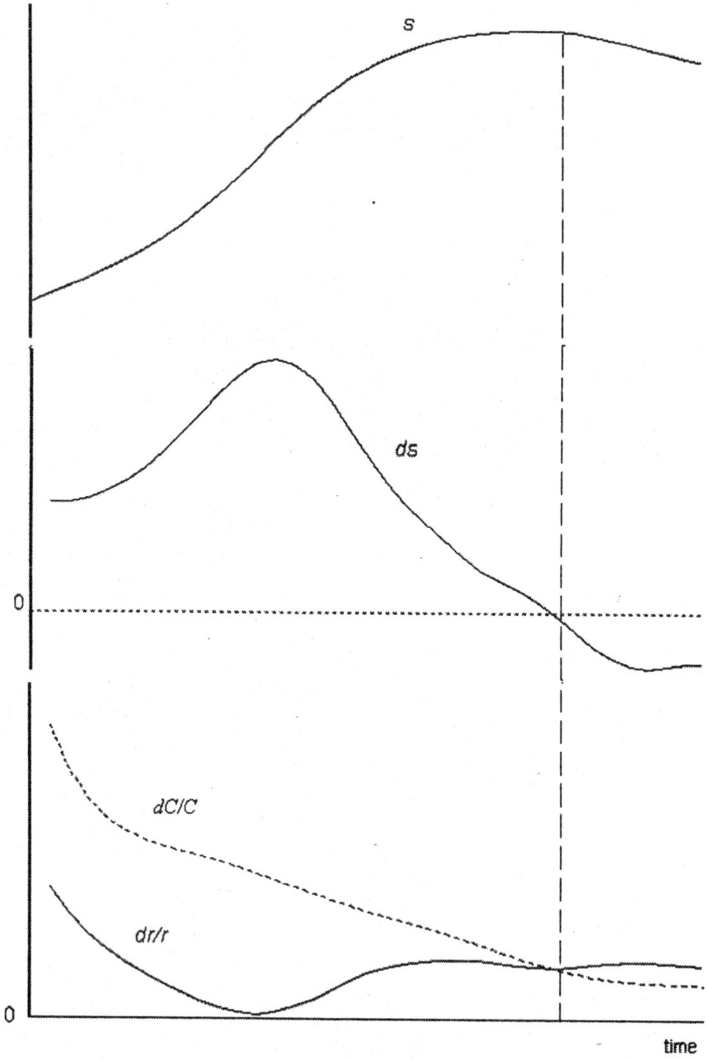

Figure 2: The Evolution of Profitability and Capital Accumulation

approximates zero the mass of profits stagnates. Finally the third part displays the growth of the rate of profit (*dr/r*) together with the growth rate of capital stock (*dC/C*) and the point of their intersection is associated with the crisis stage of the economy. It is important to point out that the graphs of Figure 2 are constructed on the basis of realistic functional forms of the mass of net real profits and real capital stock.

It is important to stress that this whole process takes place in a long run context and it reflects the accumulating and intertemporal pressure of the falling tendency of the rate of profit. According to Marx the falling tendency of the rate of profit leads to the increase in the minimum necessary scale of capital that the individual capitalist must possess in order to be able to run his business. This happens because for any given average rate of profit the mass of profit obtained by any individual capital is analogous to its size. At the point of stagnation of the mass of profits and the sharp fall in the rate of profit that accompanies it, competition would intensify. Marx notes that at times of normal capital accumulation, which in a long cycle perspective can be viewed as the time of the rising wave of conjuncture, competition does not tend to assume so fierce forms, since the capitalist class in general appropriates surplus value according to the equalization of the rate of profit and the size of the individual capitals. In short, 'competition effects an operating fraternity of the capitalist class'. However at the point of absolute overaccumulation and beyond, capitals virtually engage in a battle 'among hostile brothers' since the question is no longer one of sharing profits but one of sharing losses. It therefore follows that the first victims of the crisis would be the smaller capitals, since the 'loss share' is determined by competition and moreover by positions already held at the onset of crisis. The losses of capital in general take both a material form, in the interruption of functioning of a significant part of fixed capital which lays idle and more crucially a value form, in the devaluation of large parts of fixed capital but also of commodity capital which can only achieve its monetary transformation in the sphere of circulation at the expense of a lower price than the one it would have obtained before the crisis.

As the crisis evolves the competitive process is intensified. On the one hand small capitals are largely appropriated by larger ones, '[o]n the other hand, the fall in prices and the competitive struggle would have driven every capitalist to lower the individual value of his total product below its general value by means of new machines, new and improved working methods, new combinations, *i.e.*, to increase the productivity of a given quantity of labor, to lower the proportion of variable to constant capital, and thereby to release some laborers; in short, to create an artificial over-population. Ultimately, the depreciation of the elements of constant capital would itself tend to raise the rate of profit' (*Capital III*, p.254). This is an extremely interesting point because it illustrates that innovations, which according to Marx can be either technological or organizational or both, are mainly introduced during the crisis phase. Thus while one could suppose that innovations are a feature of normal accumulation, which is a time period when prospects of business are favorable, Marx argues that they predominantly characterize the crisis phase of the economy when the prospects of doom loom large for the individual capitals, thus forcing them to either innovate or to perish. The material preconditions for the undertaking of innovations and for their possible success lie mainly in the following processes: (i) the devaluation of fixed capital, which on the one hand tends to increase the general rate of profit and on the other hand facilitates the aggressive appropriation of smaller capitals by relatively larger ones thus promoting the centralization of capital, (ii) the increase in unemployment and the subsequent decrease of variable capital which tends to increase the rate of surplus value and the rate of profit (iii) the increase of idle monetary capital during the crisis, in the possession of credit institutions, which lowers the interest rate while waiting for available investment opportunities.[10]

Once innovations make their emphatic presence in the economic scene, the innovating capitals will be able to make extra profits by taking advantage of the difference between the individual value of their commodities and the average value that holds for their respective sectors. However as the economy starts to recover—mainly due to the action undertaken by the innovating capitals—competition will assume again the form of the equalization of the rate of profit across industries and the new methods will be diffused in the economy through their adoption by the capitalist class and thus '[...] the same vicious circle would be described once more under expanded conditions of production, with an expanded market and increased productive forces' (*Capital III*, p. 255).

CONCLUDING REMARKS

A coherent theory of the long cycle should provide adequate explanations of the transition from long run depression to long run expansion and *vice versa*, that is, of the turning points of the long cycle. It is the theoretical justification of the turning points, which highlights either the merits or the weaknesses (or both) of any long cycle argument. Turning points transition constitutes the foundation of any theoretical structure of the long cycle. Therefore it is in this connection, *i.e.* in the alternation from one wave to the other, that the movement of the *fundamental* variable (fundamental for the theorist involved), which *governs* the long cycle is more determinatively operative.

Bearing this in mind we can proceed to the detection of this fundamental variable in the respective arguments in favor of long-run oscillations presented previously. Kondratiev's theoretical model resides on long-run alterations of over-investment and under-investment in basic capital constructions the transition between which is ruled by the movement of the *interest rate.* During the upswing phase the increase in large-scale investment raises the demand for capital to a point where the interest rate rises to a prohibitive level, thus obstructing any further investment activity, while during the downswing phase the massive accumulation of 'cheap' loanable capital lowers the interest rate by such an extent that investment expectations again become favorable. Thus, although not clearly stated by Kondratiev, the evolution of investment and consequently of economic growth, is mainly governed by the movement of the interest rate.

Marx's fundamental variable on the other hand is the profit rate, which regulates the movement of the mass of profit, upon which the long run oscillations of the economy are reflected. Marx's merit in this respect is not only that he views the rate of profit as *the* main economic variable, which governs the rate of accumulation of an economy and which leads the economy to stagnation through its long run falling tendency (a point shared by many eminent economists such as Smith, Ricardo, Walras, Keynes, Schumpeter and others), but that he also theorizes the relation between this falling tendency and the outbreak of crisis. The upper turning point of the cycle is explained by the intertemporal influence of the falling tendency of the profit rate, which is expressed in the stagnation of the profit mass, while the lower turning point is explained by the material conditions which tend to raise the general rate of profit and correspondingly the mass of profits.[11]

We may say that while the movement of the interest rate is of course important as far as the rate of accumulation is concerned it nevertheless is of secondary and derived significance compared to the rate of profit, especially when the interpretation of such a large-scale economic oscillation as the long cycle is at stake. In this respect Kondratiev rather served his course poorly. Yet the main strength of his theoretical model was the endogenous interpretation of technological change in a clustered form as the carrier of economic expansion during the upswing. Kondratiev's distinction between technical inventions and their widespread application through diffusion during the upswing was also a fruitful concept, as was the idea that this process is reflected in the increased production of basic capital goods. However he did not possess in his theoretical armor an explanation of the diffusion mechanism. Marx on the other hand did and he utilized his theory of inter-industry competition to this direction by stating that the extra profits made by the innovating capitals will eventually force other capitals across industries either to adopt the innovations or to be extinguished.

Nevertheless endogeneity of technological change and its significance for economic growth remains a point of common acceptance between the two economists. The same can be also said with regards to the relationship between the price level and gold. Kondratiev's view of gold as the commodity, which represents the embodiment of value is similar to Marx's notion of gold as the money commodity. Both share an anti-quantity theory of money position. Increase in gold mining raises the price level according to Kondratiev due to the corresponding increase in the productivity of gold extraction and not due to an increase in the quantity of gold in circulation. Kondratiev's anti-quantity theory stance is even more evident when he makes the following statement while he is discussing the process of accumulation of cheap loanable capital: 'With the increasing inflow of new gold the power of the pressure of accumulating cheap capital increases significantly and finally when the obstacles are surmounted, a new long rising wave begins' (Kondratiev (1998, p.59)). Here Kondratiev associates the increase in the quantity of gold not with the increase in the general price level but with an increase in the cheapening of loanable capital thus with a decrease in the interest rate. These arguments are essentially similar to the Marxian theory of money whereby an increase in gold mining raises the price level due to the increase in productivity, since the unit value of gold falls, while an increase in the quantity of gold (beyond the needs of circulation) has a *direct* effect on the interest rate and not on the price level.

Finally another obvious relation between Kondratiev and Marx is the idea that the sociopolitical superstructure is mainly a function of economic activity. Yet Kondratiev's assertion that upheavals in the socio economic sphere are mainly located in the rising wave of the cycle due to the intensive pace of economic life is quite shaky. As it was noted before in order to allocate his historical data on the subject of social unrest between the two waves of each cycle, Kondratiev used precise turning points based on price movements. However when discussing long cycles with regards to the general economic life he gave 5-7 year ranges for the turning points. If these time ranges were to be appointed to the declining wave of the cycle then the distribution of social upheavals would be quite evenly spread between the two waves of each cycle.[12] Furthermore theoretically the deterioration of the living standards of the working classes during the long downswing could well provide sufficient reason for social unrest. A fuller discussion of these issues however lies well beyond the scope of this paper.

NOTES

1. A name often employed to describe the long cycle is the 'long wave'. However Kondratiev himself used the term cycle since he believed that long-run fluctuations are of a periodic nature and he reserved the term wave to refer to the two parts of the cycle. Therefore each cycle comprises of two waves. (Barnett (1998b)). In the remainder of the text we employ the terminology used by Kondratiev.
2. It was in the English speaking version that the term long cycle was wrongly translated as long wave (Escudier (1990)).
3. Kondratiev was removed from the directorship of the Institute of conjuncture in 1928 and was imprisoned in 1930 on unfounded allegations of him being a member of an illegal (non-existent) anti-Soviet party. One can only form hypotheses as to how his theory of the long cycle could have been evolved. For a comprehensive discussion of Kondratiev's life and works, see Barnett (1998a).
4. Indeed it was this evident, *i.e. in unprocessed form*, movement of the price level that prompted Kondratiev to study long cyclic fluctuations in the first place.
5. For a detailed discussion of the setting of turning points by Kondratiev, see Barnett (1998a).
6. Kondratiev used *precise* boundaries to allocate his historical data to the two waves of each cycle. These boundaries were based on points of inflection in the price level data. His reasoning was that price movements are the best indicators of changes in conjuncture, although he did note that they are not completely accurate.
7. Kondratiev considers wars as unproductive consumption, which has a negative effect on the social savings rate.
8. The presentation of the law of the falling tendency of the rate of profit is based on Shaikh (1992, 1978), Maniatis, Tsaliki and Tsoulfidis (1999) and Tsoulfidis (2003).
9. Legal limits have been imposed upon capital mostly through working class struggles.
10. Note that points (i) and (ii) refer to the profit rate while point (iii) to the interest rate. For Marx the crucial variable that regulates the rates of growth and

accumulation is the profit rate. The rate of interest is of secondary importance since in Marx's analysis there is no automatic link between investment and the interest rate. The benefit of a low interest rate from the point of view of an investment opportunity is that it raises the net profitability ('profit of enterprise') of this investment for any given profit rate. Yet this does not imply an automatic undertaking of this investment.

11. Note that Marx's notion of the falling rate of profit, does indeed speak about a tendency. Thus conjunctural upward departures from the dominant tendency are by no means excluded. Furthermore another point may be due here. Schumpeter had claimed that every cycle of a lower order is threaded upon the dynamics of a cycle of a higher order. Thus for example the Juglar 7-11 years cycle is threaded upon the long cycle, a point also highlighted by Kondratiev in his fourth empirical point. In respect now to the Marxian argument it can be said that the dynamics of the long cycle are threaded upon the dynamics of the falling maximum rate of profit.
12. This point was made by D.I. Oparin in the debate that took place after Kondratiev presented his paper to the Institute of Economics of the Russian Association of Social Sciences Research (Barnett (1998b)).

REFERENCES

Barnett, V. (1998a), *Kondratiev and the Dynamics of Economic Development*, New York, Palgrave Macmillan.

Barnett, V. (1998b), Dating the Long Cycle Turning Points: Kondratiev and after, in N. Makasheva and W. J. Samuels (eds), *The Works of Nikolai D. Kondratiev*, vol. I, London, Pickering and Chatto.

Escudier, J.L. (1990), Long–Term Movement of the Economy: Terminology and Theoretical Options, translated by S. Barnard in T. Vasco, R. Ayres and L. Fontvieille (eds), *Life Cycles and Long Waves*, Chapter 14, Berlin: Springer-Verlag, 239-60, republished in F. Louca and J. Reijnders (eds), *The Foundations of Long Wave Theory*, vol. II, Cheltenham, Edward Elgar.

Kondratiev, N.D. (1935), The Long Wave in Economic Life, *Review of Economics and Statistics* 17, 105-15, republished in C. Freeman (ed.) 1996, *Long Wave Theory*, Cheltenham, Edward Elgar.

Kondratiev, N.D. (1998), Long Cycles of Economic Conjuncture, in N. Makasheva and W. J.Samuels (eds), *The Works of Nikolai D. Kondratiev*, vol I, London, Pickering and Chatto.

Maniatis T., Tsaliki P., Tsoulfidis L. (1999), *Issues in Political Economy: The Case of Greece* (in Greek), Athens, Sakis Karagiorgas Foundation.

Marx, K. (1867-94), *Capital 3 vols*, New York, International Publishers (1967).

Shaikh, A. (1978), Political Economy and Capitalism: Notes on Dobb's Theory of Crisis, *Cambridge Journal of Economics*, 2, 233-51.

Shaikh, A. (1992), The Falling Rate of Profit as the Cause of Long Waves: Theory and Empirical Evidence, in A. Kleinknecht, E. Mandel and I. Wallerstein (eds), *New Findings in Long Wave Research*, New York, St. Martin's Press.

Tsoulfidis, L. (2003), *Economic History of Greece* (in Greek), Thessaloniki, University of Macedonia Press.

Villar, P. (1991), *A History of Gold and Money (1450-1920)*, London, Verso.

MONETARY THEORY OF PRODUCTION: A CLASSICAL-CIRCUITIST ALTERNATIVE INTERPRETATION

*Eladio Febrero**

Our aim in this paper is to offer an interpretation of what Keynes called a monetary economy of production, grounding our view on elements taken from the Theory of the Monetary Circuit and from the Classical Theory of production, as revived by Sraffa. The former provides a coherent explanation of the role of money and credit for the circulation of commodities, required for the expansion of the system. The second offers a sound view of the real *side of an economic system for output, prices and its relation to distribution and modes of production. Taking Edward Nell's lead, we assume a set of money channels through which money circulates in order to make possible the expansion of an economic system. This approach clarifies some of the interactions between the financial and real sides of an economic system.*

INTRODUCTION

In this paper we develop a wide-ranging viewpoint that takes under its belt the Classical theory of production as revived by Sraffa and the Theory of the Monetary Circuit (TMC from here onwards), associated with Parguez and Graziani, amongst others. Our aim is to provide a theoretical framework for what Keynes called a monetary economy of production. To do so, we follow Nell's lead (cf. Nell (1998, 2004)).

On the one hand, Sraffa (1960) provides us with a sound theory of value built in the Classical theory of production (cf. for instance, Kurz and Salvadori (1995)). Although, monetary and financial issues are almost totally absent in that theoretical strand. On the other hand, the TMC provides a coherent description for how money puts the wheels of production in motion. Yet, prices and distribution are explained in a Kaleckian fashion, without making explicit references to production.

We contend that Keynes himself might be a feasible link between both theoretical strands. He provides an explanation for output quantities in Sraffian systems and also (more in the *Treatise* and his post General Theory writings in the *Economic Journal* than in the *General Theory*) anticipates some aspects

* Department de Análisis Económico y Finanzas, Facultad de Ciencias Sociales, University of Castilla-La Mancha, Cuenca, Spain, e-mail: eladio.febrero@uclm.es

which are central to the TMC. Nonetheless, we are more than aware of the problems involved in this task. Particularly troublesome, we believe, is that the Sraffian approach assumes a long period standpoint whilst Keynes' analysis, and that of a TMC, adopt a short period view. For this reason, we shall adopt what Nell (1998), chapter 10, suggests as a *benchmark equilibrium methodology*. This involves assuming an economic system placed in *normal* or *natural* positions. Firms have to determine prices and adopt investment decisions in the light of the expected growth of output. The benchmark equilibrium serves as a guideline for current behaviour. Within this we are neither assuming that the economy fluctuates around a centre of gravity for output nor that firms always make the right predictions. It is simply an initial approximation to the real world taking this equilibrium position as a reference point. Thus short period analysis can be framed into a long period approach, with the former affecting the latter and *vice versa*.

THE THEORY OF THE MONETARY CIRCUIT

The central message of the TMC states that a bank (either private or the central one) creates money *ex nihilo* when it grants a credit to a creditworthy borrower (the government, a firm or an individual agent) to make a payment to a third agent. This is a balance sheet operation in which a bank simultaneously issues a liability (a bank deposit) and an asset (credit) on its own. Bank liability is an accepted means of payment by all members of the community. It commands purchasing power on the basis of existing and / or future wealth. Like the ebb and flow of the sea, it is created at the borrower's order and destroyed when the debt is paid back to the bank (cf. for instance, Graziani (2003) or Parguez and Seccareccia (2000) amongst others).

The TMC can be described as follows. For simplicity's sake, we start by assuming a closed capitalist economy in which three (groups of) agents exist: firms, workers (households) and a (private) bank. Production takes time and all economic activities are coordinated (i.e. all production processes start and finish on the same dates). Once all processes have finished, each firm has its output *at the plant's gate*. Commodities have to circulate before new processes can start.

- *Stage 1: Output decisions.* Once a production process has taken place, and before the next one can start, firms have to decide how much output should be produced, usually according to expected demand at *normal* prices. Such decisions also determine the amount of factors that should be hired (or purchased).
- *Stage 2: Monetary efflux.* A group of firms ask for a bank credit so a new production process can start. If banks consider that the collateral is adequate, credit claims will be accepted and borrowers will be provided with sufficient liquidity to make corresponding payments.
- *Stage 3: Monetary circulation.* Once some agents have access to liquidity, they can buy commodity inputs and hire labour to start new processes. So output starts to circulate and this spending provides other

producers with the liquidity needed to purchase further commodities and so on.[1]

- *Stage 4*: *Monetary refflux*. After circulation, the initial borrowers should recoup the liquidity required to reimburse their banks loans. When debts are cancelled money is destroyed as both sides of the bank's balance sheet cancel each other out.
- *Stage 5*: *The collection of savings*. We have implicitly assumed that no leakage exists in the monetary circuit (i.e. neither households nor firms hoard money). This being the case, the initial borrowers capture all the liquidity that they introduced into the circuit to pay back bank debt through the sale of their produce. However, usually households save and some firms spend less on capital goods than what they receive from the sale of their output. When this happens, initial borrowers will not be able to recoup the liquidity needed to cancel their pending debts with the sale of their output. Here, two solutions to this problem can be highlighted: (i) firms may issue assets in financial markets, or (ii) they may negotiate the conversion of short-term debt into long-term debt with the banks. Depending on savers' liquidity preference, savings will go to financial markets or to bank deposits.

The introduction of additional agents (e.g. the government, the central bank and international trade), alternative circuits (i.e. households may ask for credits for durable consumer goods or financial assets) or the possibility of banks creating money to fund not only circulating capital but also investment in fixed capacity or financial assets for speculative motives, does not radically alter the central message of the TMC. Furthermore, taking into consideration these factors enriches the analysis and may provide the answers to some pending questions (e.g. the fixing of the interest rate, the workings of fiscal policy, *et cetera*).

THE REAL SIDE OF THE ECONOMY

The real analysis can be broken down into three parts: (i) technology, (ii) the quantity system and (iii) the price system.

Technology

We shall assume a closed capitalist economic system with four sectors gathered into two groups: one, in Sraffian terminology, is basic and the other one is non-basic. Regarding the former, it includes three industries with four (groups of) firms. The first industry produces new machines (*NM*) by means of labour (*L*) and circulating capital (*Kc*), the second industry has two (groups of) firms: the first one produces circulating capital with new machines, circulating capital and labour, whilst the second one uses old machines (*OM*). The third industry produces consumer goods (*C*) by means of labour and circulating capital. The non-basic sector, which we shall call government, produces public services (*PS*) with labour alone.

The following table may be helpful:

Table 1

	d	Inputs Commodities NM	OM	Kc	L	PS	Outputs Commodities NM	OM	Kc	C	PS	
Industries	S.I.			Kc_1	L_1		$NM^{(1)}$					S.I.
	S.II.a	NM_{2a}		Kc_{2a}	L_{2a}			$OM^{(2a)}$	$Kc^{(2a)}$			S.II.a
	S.II.b		OM_{2b}	Kc_{2b}	L_{2b}				$Kc^{(2b)}$			S.II.b
	S.III			Kc_3	L_3					$C^{(3)}$		S.III
	Gov.				L_G						$PS^{(4)}$	Gov

We shall assume the usual axioms for the viability of this system (cf. Kurz and Salvadori (1995, chapter 7), Schefold (1989, Part II, Section B)) and to this we shall add the constancy of technical coefficients. All processes start and finish on the same dates and workers spend all their proceeds on consumer goods so that the labour vector can be replaced by a vector of consumer goods (Nell, 1998). The labour supply does not constrain output growth.

Next we define the following matrices:

$$\mathbf{A}^* = \begin{pmatrix} \mathbf{A}_{4x4} & \mathbf{a}_{4x1} \\ \mathbf{0}_{1x4} & \mathbf{0}_{1x1} \end{pmatrix} \tag{3.1}$$

$$\mathbf{A} = \begin{pmatrix} 0 & nm_{2a} & 0 & 0 \\ 0 & 0 & om_{2b} & 0 \\ kc_1 & kc_{2a} & kc_{2b} & kc_3 \\ c_1 & c_{2a} & c_{2b} & c_3 \end{pmatrix}; \mathbf{a} = \begin{pmatrix} 0 \\ 0 \\ 0 \\ c_G \end{pmatrix} \tag{3.2}$$

$$\mathbf{B}^* = \begin{pmatrix} \mathbf{B}_{4x4} & \mathbf{0}_{4x1} \\ \mathbf{0}_{1x4} & \mathbf{b}_{1x1} \end{pmatrix} \tag{3.3}$$

$$\mathbf{B} = \begin{pmatrix} nm^{(1)} & 0 & 0 & 0 \\ 0 & om^{(2a)} & 0 & 0 \\ 0 & kc^{(2a)} & kc^{(2b)} & 0 \\ 0 & 0 & 0 & c^{(3)} \end{pmatrix}; \mathbf{b} = \left(ps^{(4)}\right) \tag{3.4}$$

$$\mathbf{Q}^* = \begin{pmatrix} \mathbf{Q}_{4x1} \\ \mathbf{q}_{1x1} \end{pmatrix} \tag{3.5}$$

$$\mathbf{Q} = \begin{pmatrix} NM \\ OM \\ Kc \\ C \end{pmatrix}; \mathbf{q} = (PS) \tag{3.6}$$

Matrices **A** and **a** encapsulate the input coefficients of the basic and the non-basic systems, respectively. Matrix $\mathbf{A}^*$ accounts for the whole set of input coefficients. Similarly, **B** and **b** stand for basic and non-basic output coefficients, whilst $\mathbf{B}^*$ is the output matrix for all output coefficients. Finally, **Q** and **q** are (4 x 1) and (1 x 1)–dimension column vectors for basic and non-basic output levels. $\mathbf{Q}^*$ is a (4+1 x 1)–dimension column vector of output.

The Quantity System

The quantity system can be written as:

$$\begin{aligned} &\mathbf{A}^*\mathbf{Q}^*(1+g) + \begin{pmatrix} 0 \\ \mathbf{q} \end{pmatrix} = \mathbf{B}^*\mathbf{Q}^* \\ &NM = \overline{NM} \\ &g \le \frac{1}{\lambda_{\max(\mathrm{B}^{-1}\mathrm{A})}} - 1 \end{aligned} \tag{3.7}$$

Thus we fix, from the outside, the activity level for the industry producing new machinery and the rate of growth of the economic system, g. $\lambda_{\max(\mathbf{B}^{-1}\mathbf{A})}$ is the maximum eigenvalue of matrix $\mathbf{B}^{-1}\mathbf{A}$ (i.e. the rate of growth is lower than the maximum growth allowed by the basic system). Column vector $\mathbf{Q}^*$ has the attribute of making the ratio between each commodity output (given by $\mathbf{B}^*\mathbf{Q}^*$) and each commodity used as input (given by $\mathbf{A}^*\mathbf{Q}^*$) equal $(1+g)$, except obviously for the non-basic commodity. The size of such an industry (government) is a residual which shall be inversely related to the effective growth rate and directly related to the size of the rest of the industries. By no means does the economy have to be permanently in a full employment position: but labour should not constrain output.

The system will expand proportionally at a rate g. All of the surplus in the basic system is invested:

$$\mathbf{Q}_{t+1}^* = \mathbf{Q}_t^*(1+g) \tag{3.8}$$

The price system

We shall adopt the following assumptions:

- Wages are paid *ex ante*.
- Workers do not save and spend all proceeds on consumer goods.
- Consumer goods are properly normalized so one unit of labour equals one unit of consumer goods.
- Industries S.I, II and III are organized in a capitalist form: they earn a positive profit.
- The industry called 'government' is a non-profit making enterprise. It earns no profits since the product value of its product equals production costs.
- Competitive conditions prevail in the capitalist block: all industries earn the same profit rate.
- The government's budget is balanced.
- The tax burden is sustained by wages alone.
- All profits are saved and ploughed back into expanding capacity.

We define the input matrix **A'**:

$$\mathbf{A}'=\begin{pmatrix} 0 & nm_{2a} & 0 & 0 \\ 0 & 0 & om_{2b} & 0 \\ kc_1 & kc_{2a} & kc_{2b} & kc_3 \\ c_1(1+t) & c_{2a}(1+t) & c_{2b}(1+t) & c_3(1+t) \end{pmatrix} \tag{3.9}$$

Where t is the tax rate on nominal wages.

Hence the price system is as follows:

$$\begin{aligned} &\mathbf{pA}'(1+r)=\mathbf{pB} \\ &p_C c_G(1+t)=p_G ps^{(4)} \end{aligned} \tag{3.10}$$

With:

$$\mathbf{p}=\begin{pmatrix} p_{NM} & p_{OM} & p_{Kc} & p_C \end{pmatrix} \tag{3.11}$$

In (3.10) we have 5 equations and 5+3 unknown variables (the five prices, the profit rate, the nominal wage and the tax rate). To resolve this, we take p_C as a *numeraire*, the profit rate will equal the growth rate (see below) and then we can calculate the nominal wage and the tax rate according to the following equations.

$$\begin{aligned} &p_C=1 \\ &1L=1C \\ &w=p_C(1+t) \\ &t\sum wL_i=wL_G(1+t) \end{aligned} \tag{3.12}$$

One unit of labour consumes one unit of consumer goods, the nominal wage per unit of labour equals the price of the consumption basket times one plus the tax rate, t, and the tax rate is such that the sum of collected taxes (from labour alone, civil servants included) equals public spending, so that the government's budget is balanced.

One further condition is required to ensure the equilibrium of the system: the interest rate i should equal the profit rate r and the growth rate g.

MONETIZING GROWTH

We shall assume that a period of production has already finished. Before the next one can start, commodities have to circulate amongst industries. We are faced with a Marxian Commodity–Money–Commodity circuit where no value is created.

For simplicity's sake we adopt the Classical hypothesis on saving and spending: workers spend all their wages whilst capital owners save and plough back all their profits.

Now firms will expand their productive capacity according to their predictions of future demand. Uncertainty is at the very heart of the accumulation process and production is a lengthy process. Additionally, barter or commercial credits are the exceptions to the rule. To state the obvious, money has to be available before you can spend it.

Let us now see how the circulation of commodities between periods of production is monetized. What follows is a description of a monetary circuit understood as a set of money channels. This description does not preclude either the existence of alternative circuits or the co-existence of more than one.

(i) To start production processes wages have to be paid. Although, not all trades have to apply for credit to pay wages: those from the consumer goods sector should be paid with money that has already been created. Here we assume that the government asks for a credit from the central bank to pay civil servants' wages (cf. Bell 2000).[2] The central bank creates the money required. Additionally, S.I, S.II.a and S.II.b ask for credits from commercial banks. If borrowers are seen as creditworthy by banks, they will create deposits (i.e. bank money) when they grant them credits. S.II.a can start a new production process: it has labour, circulating capital (its output) and old machine (which was new in the previous period). This is the monetary efflux.

(ii) Workers in these sectors pay taxes and the rest will be spent on consumer goods.

(iii) Now the consumer goods sector S.III has liquidity. It pays wages to its workers. And again, the latter pays taxes and spends the rest on consumer goods.

(iv) The government, which had spent first, has now collected taxes from all workers and can cancel its debt with the central bank if the amount of taxes matches previous public spending. As Bell, *op.cit.*, states, taxes (and bonds) do not finance public spending. They are the mechanisms of the monetary refflux.

(v) S.III, the producer of consumer goods, has monetized its profits. With the liquidity from the sale of its output it will purchase circulating capital from S.II.a and S.II.b. Once it gets this input it can start a new production process.

(vi) S.II.b needs new machine. In the general case, its proceeds from the sale of circulating capital to S.III minus the short-term debt for wage payments will not be enough to pay for this so it will have to ask for a long-term bank credit (the maturity of the debt should match the life time of the machine; in our example two periods). With this additional borrowed money it purchases new machine from S.I. Now it can start its own process of production. And with the proceeds from the sale of new machine to S.II.b, S.I purchases circulating capital from S.II.a and S.II.b. What is leftover is used to reimburse the bank's initial debt (for the payment of wages). By and large, we can follow Davidson (1986) and assume that the producer of fixed capacity (S.I) will reach an agreement with its future purchaser (S.II.a) in order to deliver a particular type of output for a certain date, in exchange for a definite sum of money.

(vii) At the end of the circuit, S.I and the government have cancelled their debts. S.III did not ask for a bank credit. It got liquidity from third agent debtors. And S.II.a has a surplus equal in absolute terms to the deficit of S.II.b. The explanation for this finding is as follows: S.II.a, the producer of circulating capital with new machinery, obtained liquidity to pay for the second instalment of the long-term bank loan needed to purchase the fixed capital input one period earlier. This surplus equals the pending debt of S.II.b which has purchased new machinery during this period of time. In the next period, S.II.b will have to reimburse the bank with the second instalment plus interest. This is possible when the system expands at a rate g which equals the long term interest rate.

Now we shall consider the possibility of household savings. When firms expect a rate of growth of the economic system, say, g and the government expands its spending at the same rate, workers in sectors S.I, S.II.a, S.II.b and government will obtain proceeds according to what has been described above. However, if workers spend less than their incomes, the sales of S.III will be lower than its production. This will probably lead it to reduce its output growth and to hire less labour than in the situation described above. The first consequence is that the government will be unable to collect enough taxes to cancel its debt with the central bank. Secondly, S.III will purchase less circulating capital from S.II.a and S.II.b. Then S.II.a will not obtain sufficient proceeds to cancel its pending long-term bank debt (i.e. the liquidity for the second instalment). Thirdly, as S.II.b sales do not match production, it will probably shift its predictions for future demand of its output downwards and will try to purchase less fixed capacity than previously agreed with S.I. And fourthly, S.I will reduce its growth rate of output as demand for it falls. This process is fittingly described by means of multi-sectoral multipliers.

The Keynesian paradox of thrift can be clearly seen in this framework: workers' savings result in a fall in output that leads to a problem of effective demand. However, this model sheds light on some further problems: (i) Agents with long-term debt will not be able to accumulate the amortization funds required to make loan repayments on time. (ii) If liquidity preference is complete, all savings will be held in the form of bank deposits. Although, contrary to conventional economic theory (i.e. the loanable funds theory), this does not mean that banks are accumulating excess reserves which would lead them to bring down interest rates on loans. These deposits are the counterpart of pending debts (i.e. illiquid assets). We should expect an increasing liquidity preference from banks, resulting in fewer loans instead of a lower interest rate as a result of all of this. Alternatively, if liquidity preference is nill, all savings will go to financial markets. This makes it possible for firms to recoup all of the liquidity injected into the circuit so it can be destroyed at the end. Although, because of the lack of effective demand, the rate of growth of output for the next period is going to be lower. (iii) Current savings are the result of prior investment (from deficit-spending units). Thus, although savings and investment spending are made by different agents, the former depends on the latter[3] and such savings can take place later (in a logical temporal sense). This means that we cannot combine savings and investment in a market in order to determine the interest rate: it was already fixed when the demand for credit to finance investment took place. (iv) Lower interest rates reduce the requirements of liquidity to cancel the pending debts of long-term indebted agents. Thus, a reduction in interest rates may help to alleviate the debt burden, reducing the default rate. Nevertheless, when there is a problem of lack of effective demand low interest rates will not drive the economy towards a full employment position, as the capital controversies showed a long time ago (cf. for instance Cohen and Harcourt (2003)).

INTEREST RATES IN THE CLASSICAL-CIRCUITIST MONETARY ECONOMY OF PRODUCTION

In this Section we shall provide an explanation of how interest rates are determined and how the payment of interest is possible.

(i) Determination of the short-term interest rate

Let us assume that there are two commercial banks, A and B. Bank A grants credit to firm F for wage payments. Once these payments are made:

Commercial bank A			
M	Credit to Firm F	Deposit of L_F	M

Next workers of firm F, L_F wish to move their deposits to commercial bank

B.[4] Now bank B will have an excess reserve whilst bank A will owe that amount of money to bank B:

Commercial bank A			
M	Credit to Firm F	Loan from Bank B	M

Commercial bank B			
M	Reserve	Deposit of L_F	M

The net debt of the commercial banking system, taken as a whole, is zero.

At the end of the day no bank should have a negative balance. The central bank offers credit / deposit facilities to commercial banks at the end of the day. The following figure describes this (cf. Clinton 1997):

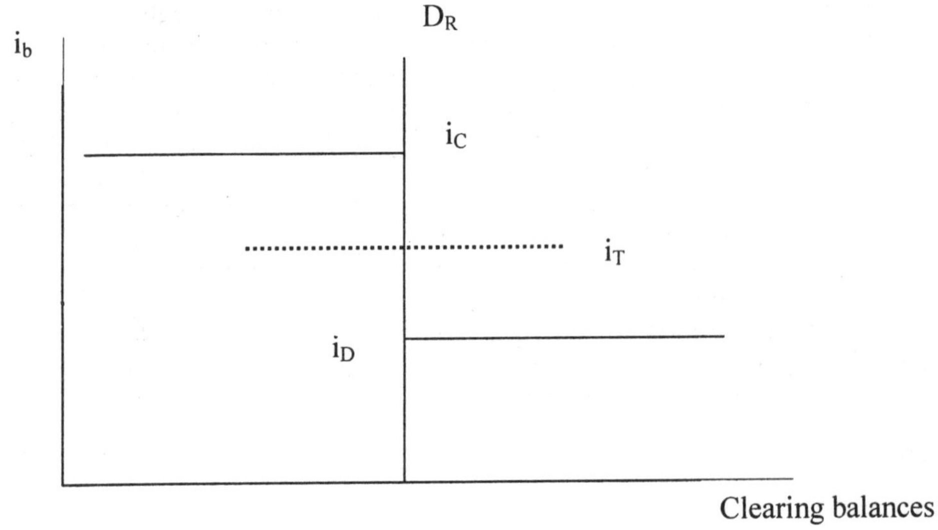

Figure 1

The commercial banking system taken as a whole shows a zero net debt: the deficit of bank A equals the surplus of bank B in absolute terms. Hence, the aggregate demand for reserves, D_R is a vertical line on the zero position. In order to control the interest rate, the central bank offers bank B the possibility of depositing its surplus in the central bank and remunerating this surplus at interest i_D. The horizontal line on i_D shows the supply of deposits at the central bank. Also, it offers bank A the possibility of borrowing the amount of liquidity needed to reach a balanced position from the central bank, at interest i_C. Now, the horizontal line at i_C shows the supply of reserves from the central bank. Hence bank B will prefer to lend its surplus to bank A, and the latter will prefer to borrow from bank B at a middle interest rate, i_T. The latter is the central bank's targeted short-term interest rate. Commercial banks will offer credits at a rate which is a mark up on i_T.

Next, as Wray (1998, chapter 5), has pointed out, when the government makes a payment to private agents (e.g. pensions) with newly created money from the central bank, and this payment does not match current tax collections, there will be an injection of liquidity into the commercial banking system leading to a shift leftwards of the aggregate demand for reserves. So i_T would shift downwards to i_D because (most) banks would not need to request reserves from other banks.

In order to prevent this shift from the target rate, the central bank has to wipe out commercial banks' excess reserves by either shifting deposits held by the government in commercial banks towards the central bank or through open market operations.

Additionally, when the central bank wishes to shift to another target rate, it formally announces its intention and the change takes place automatically.

(ii) Determination of the Long-term Interest Rate

The long-term interest rate can be viewed as the sum of two components: a weighted average of short-term interest rates plus a premium which depends on risk, liquidity and other factors regarding the desirability of the financial instrument in consideration (e.g. Bernanke (2005, p. 5)). In essence, it reflects all future short-term rates expected by market participants.[5] This is a market variable which the central bank can indirectly affect though it cannot fix it. When the central bank wants to influence the long-term rate it signals what it is going to do with the short-term rate in any particular context.

Circuitists provide an explanation about the mechanisms used to fix the long-term interest rate grounded on what Keynes termed the liquidity preference. This theory can be summarized as follows (cf. Graziani, *op.cit.* p. 123 and ff.). We are positioned in the last phase of the monetary circuit (stage 5 above): that is, agents have saved some of their proceeds and this amount equals outstanding firms' and government debt (excluding interest) to banks.

On the one hand, indebted agents with pending debt repayments may collect savings issuing debt assets in financial markets or, alternatively, renegotiate short-term bank loan conditions in order to postpone payments. On the other hand, savers can hold their monetary savings either in the form of bank deposits or in debt assets purchased in financial markets.

The supply of debt assets (D^S) will depend positively on the interest on bank credit (i_c) and negatively on the interest on securities (i_B), which is our long-term interest rate. The demand for debt assets (D^D) will be an increasing function of the interest on securities and a decreasing function of interest on bank deposits (i_D). This means that, in equilibrium, we have three unknown quantities (i_c, i_B and i_D) and one equation ($D^S = D^D$). We can assume that i_D equals zero and that i_c is determined as a mark up on the interest at which the central bank provides reserves (these assumptions are not far from the truth). Then, the equilibrium condition above determines i_B.[6]

This view adopts a purely subjective standpoint for the determination of the equilibrium long-term interest rate whose spread can *a priori* reach any level. Yet, we may wonder whether there exists any limit for the long-term interest rate in the long period.

For Circuitists, firms can always pay nominal interest rate (without any limit) on securities.[7] Though, as Sraffa (1960) clearly demonstrated, once the real wage is given there exists a ceiling for the real interest rate, given by the profit rate which, in turn and in our view, depends on the rate of growth of output and productive capacity.

Four points will be raised to ground our argument: (i) Money or credit is not a produced commodity so the interest rate cannot be subjected to any natural law as, for instance, the profit rate. (ii) When credit is used for productive ends, the interest on borrowed funds will be limited by the profit that the entrepreneur is going to obtain from these funds.[8] (iii) The (long-term, real) interest rate will be lower than the (real) profit rate during long periods of time. Yet, the opposite may hold for short periods.[9] (iv) Contrary to what some Sraffians have stated (e.g. Pivetti (1991)) and not unrelated to the points made above, the interest rate cannot be taken as the centre of gravity for the profit rate.[10]

(iii) Interest Payments

Briefly, how is it possible for firms to reimburse banks with $M' = M(1 + i) > M$, if banks create an amount of money M at the very beginning of the circuit?

Two explanations are offered here.

Our first explanation takes its lead from Robinson (1956) where we take into consideration the very fact that even banks need labour and capital to *produce* financial services. These factors are *paid* before banks make a profit (ruled by the interest rate). And it is this expenditure which makes the payment of (a part of) interest on debt possible. It could be argued that this assumption involves accepting that banks can create money for themselves (contrary to what, for instance, Graziani (2003, p. 60) states. But see Graziani, *op.cit.*, p. 117-8). However, we believe that this is not the case. What banks cannot do is to create more money for themselves than the profit they expect to earn. Otherwise the refflux mechanism would not work.[11]

As for our second explanation, we have already seen in our model that users of used fixed capital can pay interest on long-term debt when the economy expands at a rate *g* greater or equal to the interest rate. The mechanism which makes the payment of this interest possible resembles that of the former circuit: banks advance money so the economy can expand. And this money is channelled towards long-term indebted firms: thus, banks create the money for the payment of interest on debt. Yet, in this circuit this type of liquidity is not used by banks themselves, but by other borrowers.

In our model, we have implicitly assumed that the circulation of commodities only occurs between periods of production and at an infinite velocity. It is for this reason that short-term debt has not been explicitly dealt with. Of course, we realize that this is an oversimplification. Yet, this does not alter our main conclusion in this Section, which is that banks create the money required to pay interest on debt.

To sum up, the expansion of the banking industry (its real productive assets) together with the expansion of the productive capacity of the *real* economy makes the payment of interest on debt possible. There is a hierarchy of variables in this model, in the sense that the rate of growth of output is *the* exogenous variable. Then, this affects (positively) the profit rate and creates a ceiling for the interest rate. On the other hand, the central bank controls the short-term interest rate which is a floor for the interest rates at which commercial banks offer credits.

THE INTEREST RATE, THE PROFIT RATE AND THE PRICES OF PRODUCTION

In his Production of Commodities Sraffa (1960, p. 33), cryptically observes that interest rates may be taken as the centre of gravity for profit rates.[12] Ciccarone (1998, pp. 403-5) points out that this statement '*has been traditionally justified on the basis of the two-step view that: (1) the monetary authority can determine the money rates of interest* [...]; *(2) there exists a definite relationship between the rates of interest and profits*'. Following Kurz and Salvadori (1995, pp. 481-3), the second step can be divided into two approaches: (2a) the rate of profit results from adding up the rate of interest and the rate of profits of enterprise; (2b) the banking sector is considered a basic sector and it earns the average profit rate which is ruled by the interest rate. The following equations encapsulate the latter view:

$$\begin{aligned} \mathbf{pA'}(1+r)+i_C\mathbf{a}-i_D\mathbf{d}&=\mathbf{pB} \\ i_C&=\mathbf{pa_b}'(1+r)+i_TV+i_DD \end{aligned} \qquad (6.1)$$

Where $\mathbf{A'}$ is a socio-technical matrix (including both technical requirements and wage payments per unit of output: see expression 3.9 above) for the basic sector, excluding the banking system. i_C is the interest rate on credits requested by basic industries, $\mathbf{a}$ is a vector of bank credit advanced to basic industries per unit of output, i_D is the interest rate on deposits and $\mathbf{d}$ is a vector of industry's deposits. The price equation for the banking industry is in the second row. i_C is the price of one unit of credit, $\mathbf{a_b}'$ stands for the vector of socio-technical inputs of the banking industry, i_T is the interest rate on reserves V, and D are collected deposits.[13]

On the one hand, a rise in the interest rate i_C increases the price of basic commodities. On the other hand, this leads to an increase in the profit rate of the banking industry. Moreover, $\mathbf{p}$ will experience a further increase when firms discover that the profit rate they are obtaining is too low (compared to the current profit rate in the banking sector).

However, in our opinion this viewpoint is troublesome. There are some arguments that counter this (cf. Nell (1988, 1999)): (i) the central bank has the ability to control short-term nominal interest rates, not long-term real ones; the long-term interest rate is not subjected to any *natural* law unlike the profit rate, because money is not a produced commodity; (ii) in the real world, the rate of growth of demand is usually negatively correlated with the interest rate; when the rate of growth of output is high (low) the profit rate has to be high for firms to finance the requisite expansion of productive capacity; (iii) when the rate of growth of demand changes and this shift becomes longstanding firms will expand productive capacity *pari passu*. Only when the rate of growth of demand changes temporarily will the adjustment occur through changes in the degree of utilization of productive capacity.[14]

Additionally, we believe that there is a further drawback. Competition, in the Classical-Marxian sense, leads to the equalization of the profit rate in all trades, on the amount of value which is advanced to the process of production. In this sense, following Marx (1894, chapters XXII and XXIII), it makes no difference whether the amount of money advanced was first owned by the entrepreneur or the bank when we fix the prices of production. The interest rate is a mechanism for the re-distribution of surplus between industrial and financial capitalists. What this means is that if a production process needs an investment of, say, 100 monetary units to yield a 20% profit rate in *normal* conditions, the industrial capitalist will borrow some liquidity if the interest rate is no higher than 20%. Once profits have been realized, they will be distributed between the two types of capitalists according to the amount of money advanced and interest rates.

When this happens, the Sraffian approach for the calculation of production prices remains perfectly valid, as in expression (3.10), i.e. the interest rate should not enter the price system. And this raises, at the very least, a couple of questions: (i) What determines the profit rate? And (ii) what is the relation between the profit rate and the interest rate?

Regarding the first question, in the case of even conditions of accumulation, it is the rate of growth of output and capacity, through capitalists saving behaviour, which determines the profit rate, making the wage rate a residual (e.g. Kaldor (1956), Pasinetti (1974)). In our view, this is a fruitful standpoint for integrating the Classical and the Circuitist approaches (Cf. Nell (2004). Alternatively, see for instance Pivetti (1991)). As for our second question, we share Marx's view, *op.cit.*, that there is no natural law regulating interest rates.[15] The rate of growth of output (seen through the behaviour of savings) determines the *normal* profit rate and additionally sets a ceiling on the interest rate. Simultaneously, the central bank, under *normal* conditions, has the ability to influence the long-term interest rate (by manipulating the short-term one) and to set limits on it. The rate of interest affects the profit rate of the banking system (cf. Ciccarone, *op.cit.*) but does not affect the profit rate of the industrial system.[16] Unlike some Sraffians, we believe that causality runs the other way around: the profit rate in the industrial system affects the mark up on the base interest rate (determined by the central bank) on which commercial banks calculate the rate of interest at which they make loans, to enable the banking system to earn the *normal* profit rate.

When the interest rate matches the rate of growth of output and the profit rate, all the money introduced at the beginning of the circuit can be destroyed at the end. When interest rates are lower than the profit and output rates, some liquidity can remain at the end of the circuit without the system running down.

SUMMARY

This paper has presented an interpretation of what Keynes termed a monetary economy of production, taking elements from the Theory of the Monetary Circuit and from Sraffa. To do so, we have assumed that the economy is in a long period equilibrium. This is an instrumental assumption to facilitate an understanding of how an economy works.

The central variable is the growth rate of output, ruled by the Keynesian principle of effective demand. Under the Classical hypothesis of savings and spending, it determines the profit rate and then, together with technical conditions, the set of relative prices. Furthermore, it also determines the ceiling for the long-term interest rate. The central bank sets a floor on it. We have assumed that the degree of utilization of productive capacity remains at a *normal* position in a long period analysis.

Money is required for the growth of output. But what is crucial here is that we are talking about credit money not commodity money. Thus, banks have the ability to create money *ex nihilo* to finance the payments which are required to put the wheels of production in motion. In our idealized model, money begins with the circulation of commodities once a production period has finished and before the next one begins. It ends when this circuit is completed (i.e. all trades get rid of all of the requisite inputs).

Following Nell, we adopt a Monetary Circuit (understood as a set of channels through which money circulates). Here we visualise how interest payments can be made, how much money is needed to make the requisite commodities circulate, how profits are monetized and how this money is created and destroyed when credits are granted and debts are repaid. This Circuit also demonstrates how household savings or government surpluses are leakages which complicate the reimbursement of pending debts by indebted units to banks.

Obviously, our paper is not conclusive and many questions still have to be answered. For example:

- What happens when there is an uneven demand for growth and accumulation?
- What are the consequences of household borrowing?
- Under what circumstances does financial instability appear and what are its consequences?
- Open economy considerations.

Nevertheless, we hope that this Classical-Circuitist alternative provides a fruitful starting point for improving our understanding of how the real world works.

NOTES

1. Note that what circulates is output produced in t which is now input for a process in period t + 1.
2. When this is not possible, the government should apply for credit from commercial (i.e. private) banks. Our main conclusions remain unaltered within this assumption.
3. Actually, as Moore (2004) has put it, saving is the accounting record of investment.
4. Cf. Rochon and Rossi (2004).
5. Cf. for instance Moore (1988, p. 285-6).
6. It should be noted, as Graziani clearly states, that the equilibrium in the market for securities does not mean that all savings are held in securities.
7. Graziani (2005, p. 115-6) states that when the interest on securities paid by firms is spent either on consumer goods or securities, they can pay any amount, no matter how high, without any real cost.
8. For points (i) and (ii) see Marx (1894, chapters XXII and XXIII).
9. The reader should note that the demand for financial assets can be funded not only with savings but also with credit (e.g. speculative motive). In this case, the expectation of huge future yields may turn into current inflation of asset prices, leading to interest rates that are higher than the normal profit rate for certain periods of time (cf. Nell, 1999). Although this situation cannot be sustained for long since predictions of future profits need to be confirmed within the firms' accounts.
10. Cf. Nell, *supra*.
11. Actually, the interest on short-term debt, iwL_K (where L_K stands for labour in sectors S.I, II.a and II.b) should equal the outlay required for the banking sector to supply its credit services: cf. Nell (2004, p. 196), Ciccarone, *op.cit.* p. 407.
12. In a letter to Garegnani dated 13 March 1962, quoted in Bellofiore (2001, pp. 366-7), Sraffa writes: 'In conclusion, I'd say that the review [that Garegnani was intending to write of Production of Commodities for Moneta e credito] would do well not to insist too heavily on the passing remark about the monetary interest rate' (originally in Italian; translation by R. Bellofiore).
13. In the reference, i_T is replaced by r, the *normal* profit rate.
14. To these arguments we draw attention to the problematic meaning of vector **a** for the determination of production prices, a question posed by Mongiovi and Rühl (1993).
15. The same holds for Keynes when he writes: '... the rate of interest is a highly conventional [...] phenomenon' (1936, p. 203).
16. The disparity between the profit rate, the rate of growth and the interest rate can unleash as Nell, *supra*, has put it, a process of financial instability which we have not dealt with in this paper.

REFERENCES

Bell, S. (2000), Do taxes and bonds finance public spending? *Journal of Economic Issues*, 34, 603-20.

Bellofiore, R. (2001), Monetary analysis in Sraffa's writings: a comment on Panico, in T. Cozzi and R. Marchionatti (eds), *Piero Sraffa's Political Economy*, London, Routledge.

Bernanke, B. S. (2005), Implementing Monetary Policy, *The Federal Reserve Board,* Speech March 30.

Ciccarone, G. (1998), Prices and Distribution in a Sraffian Credit Economy, *Review of Political Economy*, 10, 399-413.

Clinton, K. (1997), Implementation of Monetary Policy in a Regime with Zero Reserve Requirements, *Bank of Canada: Working Paper 97–8*.

Cohen, A. and Harcourt, G. (2003), Whatever Happened to the Cambridge Capital Theory Controversies?, *Journal of Economic Perspectives*, 17, 199-214.

Davidson, P. (1986), Finance, Funding, Saving, and Investment, *Journal of Post Keynesian Economics*, 9, 101-10.

Graziani, A. (2003), *The Monetary Theory of Production*, Cambridge, Cambridge University Press.

Kaldor, N. (1956), Alternative Theories of Distribution, *Review of Economic Studies*, 23, 83-100.

Keynes, J. M. (1936), *The General Theory*, New York, Harcourt and Brace.

Kurz, H. D. and Salvadori, N. (1995), *Theory of Production*, Cambridge, Cambridge University Press.

Mongiovi, G. and Rühl, C. (1993), Monetary theory after Sraffa, in G. Mongiovi and C. Rühl (eds) *Macroeconomic Theory: Diversity and Convergence*, Aldershot, Edward Elgar.

Marx, K. (1894), *Capital. A Critique of Political Economy, Vol. III. The Process of Capitalist Production as a Whole*, Chicago, Charles Kerr and Co [1909].

Moore, B. (1988), *Horizontalists and Verticalists. The Macroeconomics of Credit Money*, Cambridge, Cambridge University Press.

Moore, B. (2004), Saving and Investment : Keynes Revisited, in R. Arena and N. Salvadori (eds), *Money, Credit and the Role of the State. Essays in Honour of Augusto Graziani* Aldershot, Ashgate.

Nell, E. J. (1988), Does the Rate of Interest Determine the Rate of Profit? Reprinted in E. J. Nell, *Transformational Growth and Effective Demand. Economics after the Capital Critique*, New York, New York University Press, 1992.

Nell, E. J. (1998), *The General Theory of Transformational Growth. Keynes after Sraffa*, Cambridge, Cambridge University Press.

Nell, E. J. (1999), Wicksell after Sraffa: 'Capital Arbitrage' and 'Normal' Rates of growth, Interest and Profits, in G. Mongiovi and F. Petri (eds), *Value, Distribution and Capital. Essays in honour of Pierangelo Garegnani*, London, Routledge.

Nell, E. J. (2004), Monetizing the Classical Equations: a theory of circulation, *Cambridge Journal of Economics*, 28, 173-203.

Parguez A. and Seccareccia, M. (2000), The Credit theory of Money: the Monetary Circuit Approach, in J. Smithin (ed.), *What is money?* London, Routledge.

Pasinetti, L.L. (1974), *Growth and Income Distribution*, Cambridge, Cambridge University Press.

Pivetti, M. (1991), *An Essay on Money and Distribution*, London, Macmillan.

Robinson, J. (1956), *The Accumulation of Capital*; Spanish version in México, *Fondo de Cultura Económica* [1960].

Rochon, L.P and Rossi, S. (2004), Central Banking in the Monetary Circuit, in M. Lavoie and M. Seccareccia (eds), *Central Banking in the Modern World. Alternative Perspectives*, Cheltenham, Edward Elgar.

Schefold, B. (1989), *Mr. Sraffa on Joint Production and Other Essays*, London, Unwin Hyman.

Sraffa, P. (1960), *Production of Commodities by Means of Commodities*, Cambridge, Cambridge University Press.

Wray, L. R. (1998), *Understanding Modern Money. The Key to Full Employment and Price Stability*, Cheltenham, Edward Elgar.

APPENDIX: A NUMERICAL ILLUSTRATION

Let us assume an economic system whose production techniques are described by the following matrices (see Section 3, expressions 3.1-4):

$$\mathbf{A} = \begin{pmatrix} 0 & 1 & 0 & 0 \\ 0 & 0 & 1 & 0 \\ 10 & 6 & 6 & 10 \\ 6 & 4 & 5 & 20 \end{pmatrix}; \mathbf{a} = \begin{pmatrix} 0 \\ 0 \\ 0 \\ 4 \end{pmatrix};$$

$$\mathbf{B} = \begin{pmatrix} 1 & 0 & 0 & 0 \\ 0 & 1 & 0 & 0 \\ 0 & 18 & 16 & 0 \\ 0 & 0 & 0 & 40 \end{pmatrix}; \mathbf{b} = (8)$$

(where the columns indicate production processes and the rows indicate commodities). We assume that in period t, S.I has produced 1 unit of new machinery and that the rate of growth of the system, g = 3% (=0.03) (which the reader can see is lower than the maximum one, is given by the maximum eigenvalue of matrix $\mathbf{B}^{-1}\mathbf{A}$).

For an output vector in period t:

$$\mathbf{Q}^* = \begin{pmatrix} 1 \\ 0.970874 \\ 0.942596 \\ 1.01282 \\ 1.11998 \end{pmatrix}$$

we have an output input ratio for each basic commodity equal $(1 + g)$.

The time sequence for this quantity system is:

Table 2
Quantity System Time sequence

	Period t										
	Inputs: A<Q(t)>						*Outputs: B<Q(t)>*				
	NM	OM	Kc	C	PS		NM	OM	Kc	C	PS
S.I.	0	0	10	6	0		1	0	0	0	0
S.II.a	0,970874	0	5,82524	3,88350	0		0	0,970874	17,47573	0	0
S.II.b	0	0,942596	5,65558	4,71298	0	⟶	0	0	15,08153	0	0
S.III	0	0	10,1282	20,2564	0		0	0	0	40,5128	0
Gov.	0	0	0	4,47992	0		0	0	0	0	8,9598
	Period t + 1										
	Inputs: A<Q(t+1)>						*Outputs: B<Q(t+1)>*				
S.I.	0	0	10,3	6,18	0		1,03	0	0	0	0
S.II.b	1	0	6	4	0		0	1	18	0	0
S.II.a	0	0,970874	5,82524	4,85437	0	⟶	0	0	15,5340	0	0
S.III	0	0	10,4320	20,8641	0		0	0	0	41,7282	0
Gov.	0	0	0	4,6143	0		0	0	0	0	9,2286

Our description of the monetary circuit is placed just after outputs have been obtained in period t, B <Q(t)> and before the next process in period t + 1 starts, A <Q (t+1)>. (The symbols <> denote diagonal matrices.)

As for the vector of prices, first we need to determine the tax rate, as in expression (3.12). It is $t = 0.12854$. Then for the price of the consumer good, taken as a *numeraire,* we have a set of prices, according to (3.10-12):

$$p_{NM} = 23.7265, p_{OM} = 9.8636, p_{Kc} = 1.6264, p_C = 1, w = p_C\,(1 + t) = 1.12854$$

Let us now describe the circuit.

(i) The government needs 5.2074 monetary units (m.u. from here onwards) to pay wages to civil servants (i.e. 4.6143 plus taxes, 0.5931: cf. the tables above and below). S.I, S.II.a and S.II.b need money for wage payments as well. This amounts to 16.9669 m.u.. Total: 22.1743 m.u..

(ii) These workers pay taxes (2.5256 m.u.) and spend the rest on consumer goods (19.6487 m.u.).

(iii) S.III has to pay wages to its workers. It has the liquidity from the sale of consumer goods to workers in other sectors (19.6487 m.u.). But it does not have enough money to meet wage payments. It needs a bank credit amounting to 3.8972 m.u. Workers in S.III pay taxes and spend the rest on consumer goods.

(iv) At this point the government has collected 5.2074 m.u. in taxes. It can repay bank debt.

(v) Workers in S.III spend their incomes on consumer goods. With this liquidity, S.III pays bank debt and with the remaining liquidity (16.9669 m.u.) it purchases circulating capital (kc) from S.II.a (9.5346 m.u.) and S.II.b (7.4322 m.u.), in proportion to their corresponding net outputs (i.e. output in period t minus the amount of output which will be used as an input in t + 1).

(vi) Now S.II.b needs new machine. With the proceeds from the sale of output to S.III it can pay back the short-term credit it held for wage payments, though it needs additional money to pay for new machine. It applies for a long-term bank credit (a two periods maturity, matching the life time of the machine) amounting to 20.8084 m.u. S.I sells its output to S.II.b and obtains 23.7265 m.u. It reimburses the bank with short-term debt (wage payments) and with the rest, 16.7521 m.u., purchases circulating capital from S.II.a (9.4138 m.u.) and S.II.b (7.3382 m.u.).

(vii) Finally, in this last stage, all commodities have circulated and all trades have the inputs required to start new production processes expanded at a rate $(1 + g)$. We also discover that S.II.a has a surplus amounting to 13.4702 m.u., whilst S.II.b has a pending debt with the bank for the same amount. Our interpretation of this is that S.II.a can now make a second payment on its long-term credit (for the purchase of new machine one period before) plus the interest on it. If we apply these assumptions to period t + 1, we will find that S.II.b's surplus matches its deficit in period t, plus g – times that amount. For this very reason we believe that the rate of growth sets a limit on the profit rate which in turn limits the interest rate.

Table 3 shows the production sequence in monetary terms.

Note that column C in Table 3 stands for consumer goods, not for wages. The latter should be greater than the former in a proportion given by the tax rate. If we replace

Table 3
Production Process in Monetary Terms
Period t

	Inputs (monetary units)						*Outputs (monetary units)*				
	NM	*OM*	*Kc*	*C*	*PS*		*NM*	*OM*	*Kc*	*C*	*PS*
S.I	0	0	16,2642	6	0		23,7265	0	0	0	0
S.II.a	23,0354	0	9,4743	3,8835	0		0	9,5763	28,4229	0	0
S.II.b	0	9,2974	9,1983	4,7130	0	⟶	0	0	24,5289	0	0
S.III	0	0	16,4727	20,2564	0		0	0	0	40,5128	0
Gov.	0	0	0	4,4799	0		0	0	0	0	4,4799

Period t + 1

	Inputs						*Outputs*				
	NM	OM	Kc	C	PS		NM	OM	Kc	C	PS
S.I	0	0	16,7521	6,18	0		24,4383	0	0	0	0
S.II.b	23,7265	0	9,7585	4	0		0	9,8636	29,2756	0	0
S.II.a	0	9,5763	9,4743	4,8544	0	⟶	0	0	25,2648	0	0
S.III	0	0	16,9669	20,8641	0		0	0	0	41,7282	0
Gov.	0	0	0	4,6143	0		0	0	0	0	4,6143

the (column) vector of wages for the corresponding vector of consumer goods (in the input side of the table above, for period t+1) we should have:

Table 4

	Period t+1 *wL*
S.I	6.9744
S.II.a	4.5142
S.II.b	5.4783
S.III	23.5459
Gov.	5.2074

ON THE (IN-)STABILITY AND THE ENDOGENEITY OF THE 'NORMAL' RATE OF CAPACITY UTILISATION IN A POST-KEYNESIAN/KALECKIAN 'MONETARY' DISTRIBUTION AND GROWTH MODEL

Eckhard Hein*

In Kaleckian models of distribution and growth the equilibrium rate of capacity utilisation may persistently diverge from the 'normal rate' of utilisation. We assess this problem following the approach by Dumenil / Levy (1999) who consider the 'normal rate' of utilisation in a monetary production economy as the rate which is associated with price stability. Since inflation in our model is driven by distribution conflict, the 'normal rate' of utilisation is associated with consistent claims of firms and labourers. Taking into account real debt effects of changes in inflation and distribution effects of monetary policy interventions we discuss the short-run stability of the 'normal rate' and address the issue of long-run endogeneity. Generally, we show that in a Kaleckian monetary distribution and growth model, which takes the major features of a credit economy seriously, the 'normal rate' of capacity utilisation is endogenous to distribution conflict and monetary policy intervention in the long run. And we also show that major Kaleckian results, in particular the paradox of costs, can be retained for the short and the long run.

INTRODUCTION

Within Post-Keynesian investment-driven growth theory we can broadly distinguish between the older Kaldorian/Robinsonian models and the more recent models based on the work of Kalecki and Steindl.[1] In the Kaldorian/Robinsonian model distribution is determined by capital accumulation when savings propensities out of profits and out of wages are given and the former exceeds the latter. In the long run, the utilisation of productive capacity determined by the capital stock is assumed to be at a 'normal' level, and there is an inverse relation between the real wage rate and the rate of profit, and also between the real wage rate and the rate of capital accumulation. In the Kaleckian/Steindlian model, however, distribution is determined by mark-up pricing in incompletely competitive goods markets, and utilisation of productive capacity determined by the capital stock is variable also in the long run. Therefore, there is not necessarily an inverse relation between the real wage rate and the rate of

* Macroeconomic Policy Institute (IMK) in the Hans Boeckler Foundation, Duesseldorf, Germany.

profit, nor between the real wage rate and the rate of capital accumulation in the long run. Whereas the extension of Keynes's 'paradox of thrift' to growth theory is common to both the Kaldorian/Robinsonian and the Kaleckian/ Steindlian models, only the latter also give rise to a 'paradox of costs'. A positive relation between the real wage rate and the rates of capacity utilisation, capital accumulation and profit can generally be found in the wage-led Kaleckian models pioneered by Rowthorn (1981), Dutt (1984, 1987) and Amadeo (1986, 1986a), which rely on a strong accelerator effect of rising demand on investment. Even if a negative cost-effect of rising real wages on investment is allowed for and profit-led expansion may occur, as in the model proposed by Bhaduri/Marglin (1990), wage-led expansion remains a possible regime also in this type of model.[2]

Kaleckian models, however, have been criticised by some neo-Marxian and neo-Ricardian authors (i.e. Auerbach/Skott 1988; Committeri 1986), because the equilibrium rate of capacity utilisation may permanently deviate from firms' target rate of utilisation, the long run 'normal rate', without any tendency of adjustment.[3] This seems to be inconsistent with the requirement that firms' investment decisions should be based on expectations of some 'normal rate' of utilisation of new productive equipment. Therefore, firms are supposed to adjust productive capacity to demand in the long run, and capacity utilisation should be equal to firms' target rate of utilisation in a 'fully adjusted long-run position'.

Dumenil/Levy (1999) have even argued that taking into account the adjustment of the goods market equilibrium rate of capacity utilisation to the long-run 'normal rate' yields a synthetic model which displays Keynesian/ Kaleckian properties in the short run, but regains classical properties in the long-run fully adjusted position. Therefore, in the long run both the paradox of thrift and the paradox of costs, although valid in the short run, disappear. The adjustment mechanisms Dumenil/Levy (1999) apply and the results they derive are similar to those proposed in the New Consensus macroeconomic model:[4] Deviations of the goods market equilibrium rate of capacity utilisation from the 'normal rate' trigger rising (or falling) prices which make monetary policies intervene bringing the economy back to the 'normal rate' of utilisation in the long run, which is then associated with stable prices.

Post-Keynesians/Kaleckians have reacted differently to the neo-Marxian/ neo-Ricardian critique. Whereas Chick/Caserta (1997) have argued that a 'provisional' goods market equilibrium may be more important than a fully adjusted long-run position when it comes to analysing a monetary production economy characterised by continuous change in historical time, others have proposed different adjustment mechanisms between the 'normal' and the goods market equilibrium rate of capacity utilisation. Lavoie (1996a), Dutt (1997), Park (1997) and Commendatore (2005) have argued that the firms' notion of the 'normal rate' of utilisation is slowly increased (decreased) when the actual rate is persistently higher (lower) than the 'normal rate'. In a model with full-cost-pricing Lavoie (2002) has made the target rate of return calculated on the basis of 'normal' utilisation adjust to the actual rate of return which depends on the goods market equilibrium rate of utilisation. And adding conflict inflation to this model, Lavoie (2002, 2003) has shown that firms' target rate of return becomes endogenous and equilibrium capacity utilisation is not necessarily the standard or 'normal' rate underlying target-rate-of-return pricing, i.e. capacity utilisation remains endogenous. These papers show that under certain conditions the main propositions of the Kaleckian model, the paradox of thrift and the paradox of costs, may still hold.

Although these Kaleckian models discuss important adjustment processes, they are far from complete. In particular, although they contain distribution struggle and inflation arising from unresolved conflict, they omit to discuss major effects of rising or falling inflation on demand and hence on capacity utilisation. In a credit economy these effects are associated with the influence of changing inflation on firms' real debt position, as has already been discussed by Fisher (1933) and Keynes (1936, p. 264). And these models also lack a discussion of monetary policy effects on distribution and demand in a credit economy. The present paper attempts to fill some of these gaps.

We start from the Dumenil/Levy (1999) notion that the long-run 'normal rate' of capacity utilisation in a monetary production economy should be associated with stable inflation. But unlike Dumenil/Levy (1999) we take a closer look at the causes of changing inflation in a monetary production economy, which remain unclear in their model and which we see originating from unresolved distribution conflict. And also unlike Dumenil/Levy (1999) and the Kaleckian models referred to above we integrate the feedbacks of changing inflation on demand into our model. And we fully take account of the short-run and long-run demand and distribution effects of monetary policies applying the interest rate tool in order to fight rising or falling inflation rates. Our discussion is based on a monetary extension of the Bhaduri/Marglin (1990) model, as developed in Hein (1999, 2006), in order to allow for potential profit-led growth, as in Dumenil/Levy's (1999) long run.[5]

The paper is organised as follows. Whereas the second section presents the basic model, the third section adds conflict inflation to the model and distinguishes the Stable Inflation Rate of Utilisation (SIRCU), as the long-run 'normal rate' of utilisation, from the Goods market Equilibrium Rate of Capacity Utilisation (GERCU). In the fourth section we discuss the short-run stability properties of the SIRCU, with and without monetary policy interventions. the fifth section addresses the endogeneity issue of the 'normal rate' and focuses on the long-run adjustments of GERCU and SIRCU. In the sixth section the validity of the paradox of thrift and the paradox of costs within our model is discussed, and the last section concludes.

THE BASIC MODEL

We assume a closed economy without economic activity of the state. Under given conditions of production, there is just one type of commodity produced that can be used for consumption and investment purposes. There is a constant relation between the employed volume of labour (L) and real output (Y), i.e. there is no overhead labour and no technical change, so that we get a constant labour-output-ratio and hence constant labour productivity (y). The capital-potential output-ratio (v), the relation between the real capital stock (K) and potential real output (Y^v), is also constant. The capital stock is assumed not to depreciate. The rate of capacity utilisation (u) is given by the relation between actual real output and potential real output. The basic model can be described by the following equations:

$$p = (1+m)\frac{w}{y}, \qquad m > 0, \tag{1}$$

$$h = \frac{\Pi}{pY} = 1 - \frac{1}{1+m}, \tag{2}$$

$$r = \frac{\Pi}{pK} = \frac{\Pi}{pY}\frac{Y}{Y^v}\frac{Y^v}{K} = hu\frac{1}{v}, \tag{3}$$

$$\Pi = \Pi^n + Z = \Pi^n + iB, \tag{4}$$

$$\lambda = \frac{B}{pK}, \tag{5}$$

$$h = h(i), \qquad \frac{\partial h}{\partial i} \geq 0, \tag{6}$$

$$\sigma = \frac{S}{pK} = \frac{\Pi - Z + S_Z}{pK} = h\frac{u}{v} - i\lambda(1 - s_Z), \qquad 0 < s_Z \leq 1, \tag{7}$$

$$g = \frac{\Delta K}{K} = \frac{I}{K} = \alpha + \beta u + \tau h - \theta\lambda i, \qquad \alpha, \beta, \tau, \theta > 0, \quad g > 0 \text{ for } r - i > 0, \tag{8}$$

$$g = \sigma, \tag{9}$$

$$\frac{\partial\sigma}{\partial u} - \frac{\partial g}{\partial u} > 0, \Rightarrow \quad \frac{h}{v} - \beta > 0. \tag{10}$$

Writing w for the nominal wage rate, we assume that firms set prices (p) according to a mark-up (m) on constant unit labour costs up to full capacity output with the mark-up being determined by the degree of price competition in the goods markets and by the relative powers of capital and labour in the labour market (equation 1). The profit share (h), i.e. the proportion of profits (Π) in nominal output (pY) is therefore determined by the mark-up (equation 2). The profit rate (r) relates the annual flow of profits to the nominal capital stock (equation 3).

Introducing monetary variables into the model, we follow the post-Keynesian 'horizontalist' monetary view developed by Kaldor (1970, 1982, 1985), Lavoie (1984, 1992, pp. 149-216, 1996) and Moore (1988, 1989) and assume that the interest rate is an exogenous variable for the accumulation process whereas the quantities of credit and money are determined endogenously by economic activity.[6] In this view, the central bank controls the base rate of interest. Commercial banks set the market rate of interest by marking up the base rate and then supply the credit demand of consumers and investors they consider creditworthy at this interest rate. The central bank accommodates the necessary amount of cash. For the sake of simplicity, in what follows we suppose that the central bank's interest rate policy controls the real long-term interest rate. The pace of capital accumulation, therefore, has no direct feedback on the interest rate and we follow Pasinetti's (1974, p. 47) recommendation to treat the rate of interest as an exogenous variable in the theory of effective demand.

The pace of accumulation is determined by the entrepreneurs' decisions to invest. We assume that long-term finance is supplied only by retained earnings or by long-term credit of rentiers' households (directly or through banks).[7] By means of this simplification we do not have to distinguish between creditor households receiving interest income, on the one hand, and shareholder households receiving dividend income, on the other hand, and their different saving propensities.[8] Introducing interest payments into the model, profit splits into profit of enterprise (Π^n) and rentiers' income (Z) (equation 4).[9] Rentiers' income is determined by the stock of long-term credit (B) granted to firms and the exogenously given rate of interest (i). Equation (5) defines the debt-capital-ratio (λ).

Considering the distribution effects of interest rate variations (equation 6) we assume that the mark-up is interest-inelastic in the short run but interest-elastic in the long run.[10] As the mark-up has to cover the firm's actual and imputed interest payments, the minimum mark-up is affected by the interest rate. For the same reason, the rate of interest determines the minimum rate of profit on real investment in the long run. In the short run, there need not be an immediate positive impact of interest rate variations on the mark-up, the profit share and the profit rate, but we rather suppose a direct effect on internal funds of the firm and hence on investment and employment, which will be discussed below. If changes in the interest rate are lasting, however, mark-up and profit share will have to change in the same direction, because in the long run firms can only sustain those production processes which yield the minimum rate of profit determined by the interest rate. This position which considers interest to be a part of firms' long-run costs of production can, in particular, be found in neo-Ricardian work (Ciccarone (1998); Panico (1985); Pivetti (1985, 1988, 1991)). There it is argued that the exogenously given monetary interest rate determines the rate of profit and closes the degree of freedom of the production price model by Sraffa (1960). When there is an effect on the mark-up and the profit share in our model, it will be a lasting change in the interest rate and not in the actual interest payments which is relevant, because we assume that firms are aware of imputed interest costs on own capital, i.e. accumulated retained earnings.

We assume a classical saving hypothesis, i.e. labourers do not save. The part of profits retained is completely saved by definition. The part of profits distributed to rentiers' households, i.e. the interest payment, is used by those households according to their propensity to save (s_z). Therefore, total saving (S) comprises retained profits (Π-Z) and saving out of interest income (S_z). Taking equations (3), (4) and (5) into account, we get the saving rate (σ) in equation (7) which relates total saving to the nominal capital stock.[11] Note λ that an increase in the rate of interest, *ceteris paribus*, decreases the saving rate because income is transferred from firms with a saving propensity of unity to rentiers' households with a saving propensity of less than unity. An increasing debt-capital-ratio of firms reduces the saving rate for the same reason.

The accumulation rate (g) relating net investment (I) to the capital stock (equation 8), is a monetary extension of the function proposed by Bhaduri/ Marglin (1990). In their non-monetary model based on the principle of effective demand, the decisions to invest are assumed to depend on the rate of profit. Assuming the technical conditions of production to be constant, the profit rate is decomposed into the profit share reflecting the development of unit costs and capacity utilisation indicating the development of demand. Firms have to finance -at least partially-their net investment spending by credit. Following Kalecki's (1937) 'principle of increasing risk' we assume that the firm's access to credit is positively correlated with its internal means of finance and hence negatively with the interest rate and with the debt-capital-ratio (see also Kalecki 1954, pp. 91-5). The higher the amount of the firms' own capital, the higher the amount of debt capital that can be obtained for investment will be. From these arguments it follows, that the rate of interest and the debt-capital-ratio have a negative impact on investment because of their adverse effects on internal means of finance.[12]

The goods market equilibrium is determined by the equality of saving and investment decisions in equation (9). The goods market stability condition in equation (10) requires that the saving rate responds more elastically to changes in capacity utilisation than capital accumulation does. The goods market equilibrium values (*) for capacity utilisation, capital accumulation and the rate of profit in the short run are as follows:

$$u^* = \frac{\lambda i(1 - s_Z - \theta) + \alpha + \tau h}{\frac{h}{v} - \beta}, \tag{11}$$

$$g^* = \frac{\lambda i\left[\beta(1 - s_Z) - \theta\frac{h}{v}\right] + \frac{h}{v}(\alpha + \tau h)}{\frac{h}{v} - \beta}, \tag{12}$$

$$r^* = \frac{\frac{h}{v}\left[\lambda i(1 - s_Z - \theta) + \alpha + \tau h\right]}{\frac{h}{v} - \beta}. \tag{13}$$

CAPACITY UTILISATION, WAGE BARGAINING, INFLATION AND MONETARY POLICY INTERVENTION: THE GERCU AND THE SIRCU

With constant productivity of labour and a given labour supply, the Goods Market Equilibrium rate of Capacity Utilisation (GERCU) determines a certain rate of employment and hence unemployment, and an increase in the GERCU is associated with a proportional increase in employment and the employment rate. Generally, in Kaleckian and post-Keynesian distribution and growth models full utilisation of productive capacity determined by the capital stock will not mean full employment of labour.

Inflation in Kaleckian and post-Keynesian models is determined by distribution conflict. Figure 1 displays a simple 'conflicting claims' model of employment and inflation ($\hat{p}$) assuming constant production coefficients and a constant mark-up, as mentioned above.[13]

Although wage bargaining is concerned with money wage rates, it is assumed that labour unions intend to achieve a certain real wage rate–and with labour productivity given or productivity growth correctly anticipated a certain wage share. The labour unions' target real wage rate (w^r_b) depends positively on the employment rate, because unemployment has a negative impact on union bargaining power. With our assumptions from above the labourers' target real wage rate is positively related to the rate of capacity utilisation:

$$w^r_b = \phi + \varepsilon u. \tag{14}$$

In this paper we assume that unions do not consider the macroeconomic effects of their nominal wage demands. There is neither co-ordination between unions in different firms or industries nor between wage bargaining parties and monetary policy.[14] For the sake of simplicity we assume that full utilisation of capacity is associated with a union target real wage rate equal to labour productivity (y). Therefore, unemployment has to be of a sufficient amount to curtail distribution claims of labourers and to allow for positive profits (Kalecki 1971, pp. 156-164).

The feasible real wage rate (w^r_p) is given by mark-up pricing of firms. From equation (1) we get for the target real wage rate of firms:

$$w^r_p = \frac{w}{p} = \frac{y}{1+m}. \tag{15}$$

With the simplifying assumptions of a constant coefficient technology and a constant mark-up up to full capacity output the feasible real wage rate curve in

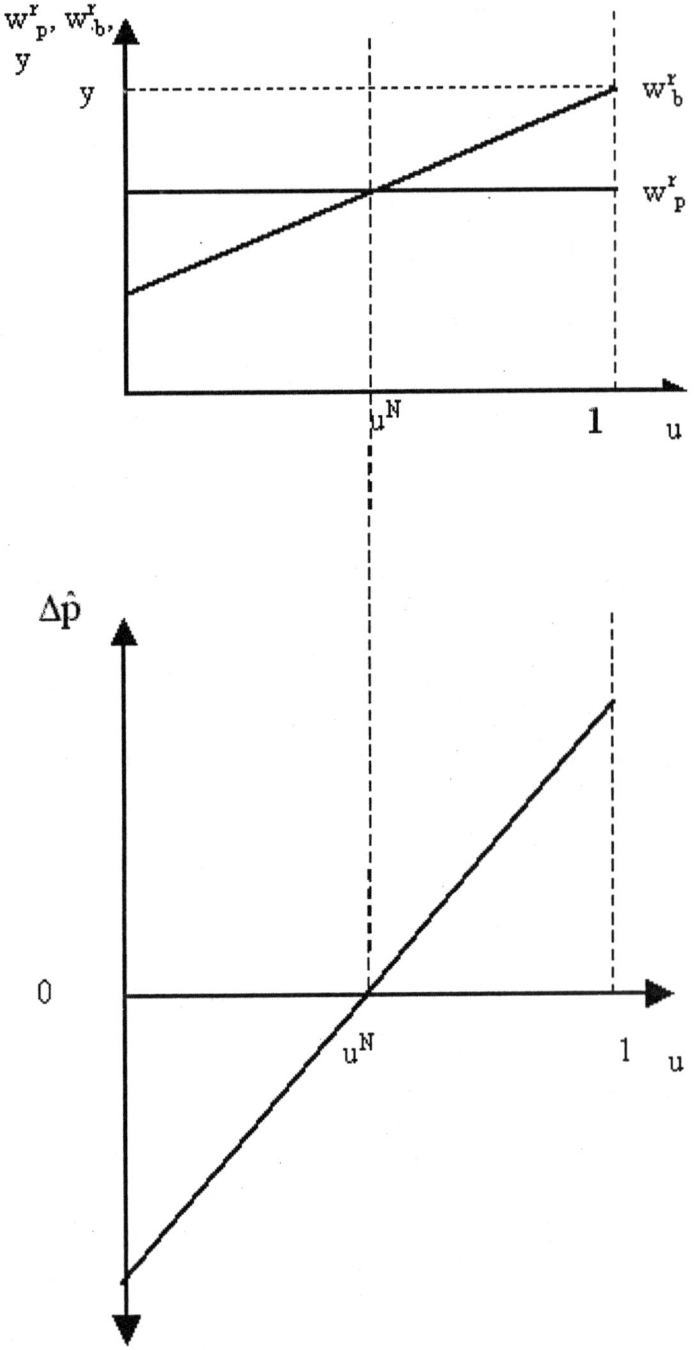

Figure 1: Capacity utilisation and distribution conflict

Figure 1 is just a horizontal line. The unions' target real wage and the feasible real wage only coincide by accident. From equations (14) and (15), and making use of equation (2), we get for the rate of capacity utilisation (u^N), which allows for the equality of the target real wage rate of labour unions and firms:

$$u^N = \frac{\frac{y}{1+m} - \phi}{\varepsilon} = \frac{y(1-h) - \phi}{\varepsilon}. \tag{16}$$

Only if the GERCU is equal to u^N, the distribution claims of labourers and firms will be compatible. Whenever the GERCU deviates from u^N we get rising or falling inflation rates (and finally deflation). Therefore equation (16) defines a Stable Inflation Rate of Capacity Utilisation (SIRCU) and hence a distribution equilibrium between the claims of labourers and those of firms. In a monetary production economy this rate of capacity utilisation can be considered to be the 'normal rate'.

SHORT-RUN STABILITY OF THE SIRCU AND MONETARY POLICY INTERVENTIONS

Discussing the short-run stability of the SIRCU we have to take a look at effects of rising or falling inflation on the GERCU. Let us assume in what follows, that firms set prices in the goods market after nominal wages in the labour market have been set, so that under the condition of a constant mark-up distribution between capital and labour does not change when the GERCU diverges from the SIRCU. And let us further assume that the stock of firms' debt is not indexed to changes in the inflation rate. Rising inflation rates will therefore decrease the debt-capital-ratio defined in equation (5), falling inflation rates will increase this ratio. These real debt effects associated with rising/falling inflation rates have already been highlighted by Fisher (1933) and by Keynes (1936, p. 264). If monetary policy does not respond to changes in the inflation rate and does not vary the nominal interest rate accordingly, real interest rates will fall in the face of accelerating inflation and will rise when inflation decelerates. Taken together, this implies that the interest-capital-ratio [$i\lambda = (iB)/(pK) = Z/(pK)$] will fall when inflation rises and will rise when inflation falls. Given that changes in the real interest rate do not affect the mark-up and hence the profit share in the short run, the effects of changes in the interest-capital-ratio on the GERCU are determined by equation (11) as follows:

$$\frac{\partial u}{\partial (i\lambda)} = \frac{1 - s_Z - \theta}{\frac{h}{v} - \beta} \tag{11a}$$

If only stable goods market equilibria are considered, equation (11a) shows that the effects of changes in the interest-capital-ratio on the GERCU depend on the parameters in the saving and investment function of the model. If the rentiers' propensity to consume ($1\text{-}s_z$) exceeds the firms' investment elasticity with respect to the interest-capital-ratio (θ), rising real debt-capital-ratios of firms and rising real interest rates will be associated with an increasing GERCU. This may be called the 'puzzling' case (Lavoie (1995)), usually not expected in post-Keynesian theory. If the conditions of the 'puzzling case' prevail, the SIRCU will be stable. Rising (falling) inflation rates will trigger falling (rising) debt-capital-ratios of firms and falling (rising) real interest rates which will then cause a falling (rising) GERCU. The GERCU will therefore adjust to the SIRCU.

If the rentiers' propensity to consume is smaller than firms' investment elasticity related to the interest-capital-ratio, rising indebtedness and rising real interest payments will have a negative effect on the GERCU. This can be called the 'normal case' (Lavoie (1995)), usually expected in post-Keynesian theory. If the conditions of the 'normal case' prevail, the SIRCU will be unstable. Rising (falling) inflation will cause falling (rising) real debt-capital-ratios of firms and falling (rising) real interest rates which will cause a rising (falling) GERCU, moving the economy farther away from the SIRCU.

In the 'normal case', stabilising the SIRCU requires monetary policy intervention, as suggested by Dumenil/Levy (1999) and also by modern New Consensus models. Different from New Consensus models, in our model central banks do not only have to change real interest rates by means of varying the nominal rate, but the change in the real rate has to be sufficient to overcompensate the counter-effects of the change in the debt-capital-ratio of firms on the GERCU. In general, this is not a problem in a situation of rising inflation, because there is no upper limit for the nominal interest rate set by the central bank. But in a situation of falling inflation or even deflation, central banks may not be able to reduce the nominal rate of interest by a sufficient amount to decrease real rates and to overcompensate the restrictive demand effects of rising debt-capital-ratios, because there is a zero lower bound for the nominal interest rate. Therefore, in this situation central banks may not be able to adjust the GERCU to the SIRCU and the economy may be trapped in a deflationary recession.

In the 'puzzling case', monetary policy interventions, which follow the Dumenil/Levy (1999)/New Consensus advice and increase the real rate of interest in the face of rising inflation and decrease it in the face of falling inflation or deflation, will have a destabilising effect. This may overcompensate the stabilising effect exerted by the change in the debt-capital-ratio and may cause a further deviation of the GERCU from the SIRCU. Table 1 summarises our results with respect to short-run stability of the SIRCU or the 'normal rate' of capacity utilisation.

THE LONG-RUN ENDOGENEITY OF THE SIRCU

In the 'normal case' we have monetary policies which can enforce short-run adjustment processes when the GERCU deviates from the SIRCU, provided that there is sufficient room of manoeuvre to vary real interest rates. In the long run, however, the distribution effect of persistent changes in the interest rate will make the SIRCU endogenous to short-run deviations of the GERCU.

Table 1
The short-run stability of the 'Stable Inflation Rate of Capacity Utilisation' (SIRCU)

	$1\text{-}s_z - \theta$	
	– ('normal case')	+ ('puzzling case')
No monetary policy intervention	unstable	*stable*
Monetary policy intervention	*stable*, if change in real interest rate overcompensates change in the debt-capital-ratio, otherwise *unstable*	*unstable*, if change in real interest rate overcompensates change in the debt-capital -ratio, otherwise *stable*

Assume for the reasons given above that persistent changes of the real interest rate are accompanied by changes of the mark-up in the same direction in the long run. In our model this has two effects:

First, changes in the mark-up affect the firms' target real wage rate: An increasing (a decreasing) mark-up shifts the firms' target real wage curve in Figure 1 downwards (upwards) and the SIRCU decreases (increases). From equation (16) we get:

$$\frac{\partial u^N}{\partial h} = -\frac{y}{\varepsilon} < 0. \tag{16.a}$$

Second, changes in the mark-up and hence in distribution between wages and profits have an additional long-run effect on the goods market equilibrium and hence on the GERCU, which adds to the short-run effect of monetary policy intervention. From equation (11) we get:

$$\frac{\partial u}{\partial h} = \frac{\tau - \frac{u}{v}}{\frac{h}{v} - \beta}. \tag{11.a}$$

The long-run effect of a change in the profit share on the GERCU is not unique in the present model. It rather depends on the elasticity of investment with respect to the profit share and on the initial GERCU, which has been established by the short-run effects of monetary policy interventions. A high profit share elasticity of investment and a low initial GERCU will be conducive to a positive relation between the profit share and the GERCU and we will see *profit-led expansion*:

$$\frac{\partial u}{\partial h} > 0, \text{ if} : \tau - \frac{u}{v} > 0 \tag{11.b}$$

A low profit share elasticity of investment and a high initial GERCU, however, will give rise to a negative relation between the profit share and the GERCU and we will see *wage-led expansion*:

$$\frac{\partial u}{\partial h} < 0, \text{ if} : \tau - \frac{u}{v} < 0 \tag{11.c}$$

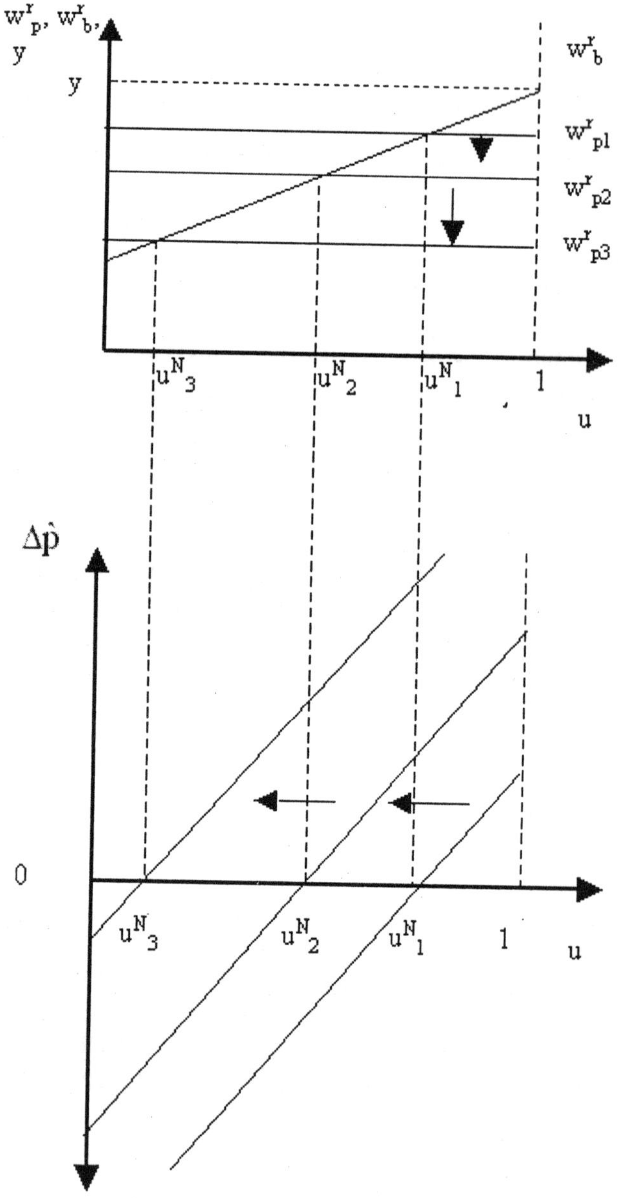

Figure 2: Long-run endogeneity of the Stable Inflation Rate of Capacity Utilisation (SIRCU) caused by monetary policy intervention

Let us now discuss the short- and long-run effects of monetary policy interventions in the 'normal case' (Table 1) of our model. Assume that by accident the GERCU exceeds the initial SIRCU at u^N_1 in Figure 2. Since rising inflation, a declining debt-capital-ratio and falling real interest rates are stimulating effective demand, the GERCU will further increase and inflation will speed up. In order to stabilise the inflation rate, central banks have to increase nominal interest rates in order to raise real interest rates by a sufficient amount to overcompensate the demand stimulating effects of falling debt-capital-ratios. Therefore, in the short run the central bank can bring back the GERCU to the SIRCU at u^N_1. In the long run, however, a higher real interest rate will induce firms to increase the mark-up. This will shift the firms' target real wage curve down from w^r_{p1} to w^r_{p2} and reduce the SIRCU to u^N_2. The redistribution at the expense of labour will also affect the GERCU. Here we have to distinguish between (A) wage-led and (B) profit-led regimes in order to discuss the further process:

(A) In the wage-led regime three scenarios (A.1-A.3) are possible depending on the relative (both negative) effects of changes in the mark-up on the GERCU and on the SIRCU in equations (11a) and (16a):

(A.1) If by accident $\frac{\partial u}{\partial h} = \frac{\partial u^N}{\partial h}$, the reduction of the GERCU caused by an increasing mark-up will make this new rate coincide with u^N_2 so that the economy gets to rest in a stable SIRCU at u^N_2.

(A.2) If $\left|\frac{\partial u}{\partial h}\right| > \left|\frac{\partial u^N}{\partial h}\right|$, the effective demand effect of redistribution at the expense of labour will make the GERCU fall below u^N_2 and we get falling inflation rates. This should make monetary policies reduce real interest rates, making the GERCU increase to u^N_2 in the short run. In the long run, firms then reduce mark-ups, which will increase the SIRCU as well as the GERCU, with the latter now overshooting the former, and monetary policy has to intervene again. This oscillation may converge to a stable SIRCU between u^N_2 and u^N_1, but it may also generate stable or exploding oscillation around that SIRCU, depending on the degree of over- and undershooting of the GERCU with respect to the SIRCU and the concomitant change in the real interest rate required for the short-run adjustment of the GERCU to the SIRCU.

(A.3) If $\left|\frac{\partial u}{\partial h}\right| < \left|\frac{\partial u^N}{\partial h}\right|$, the negative effective demand effect of redistribution at the expense of labour is weak, so that the GERCU remains above u^N_2. Again we get accelerating inflation inducing the central bank to increase real interest rates, forcing the GERCU down to u^N_2 in the short run. In the long run, firms again increase the mark-up which shifts their target real wage curve down to

w^r_{p3} and makes the SIRCU decline to u^N_3. The effective demand effect of redistribution also makes the GERCU fall, but it remains above u^N_3, inflation accelerates anew and central banks have to intervene again.

(B) If the economy is in a profit-led regime, the long-run distribution effect of rising interest rates, which have brought down the GERCU to the SIRCU in the short run, will again increase the GERCU to a level above the old SIRCU at u^N_1. The gap between the GERCU and the new SIRCU at u^N_2 will therefore be even wider than in the situation we have started from. Inflation will speed up again inducing monetary policies to increase real interest rates again, which will be able to bring down the GERCU to the lower SIRCU at u^N_2 in the short run. The long-run distribution effect will again reduce the SIRCU to u^N_3 but will increase the GERCU, and inflation will accelerate again.

From equation (11.a) we get that the lower the GERCU, the more likely the wage-led scenario (A.3) and finally the profit-led scenario (B) will become. This is what is shown in Figure 2: The rate of capacity utilisation which stabilises the inflation rate (at whatever level) becomes horizontal because of the nature of monetary policy interventions. In these scenarios, monetary policy is only able to stabilise the inflation rate in the long run at the expense of a continuously decreasing GERCU. Monetary policy interventions trigger a process in which stabilising inflation in the short run by means of increasing real interest rates and slowing down the economy re-establishes the inflation problem in the long run when the full distribution effects of real interest rate variations are felt. Therefore, if monetary policies combat inflation by means of raising real interest rates they will become a cause of the problem of stagflation.

Note that scenarios (A.3) and (B) also work in reverse: If the central bank intends to improve the GERCU, in the short run lowering real interest rates will be associated with rising inflation rates. In the long run, however, a falling mark-up increases the SIRCU. And since the long-run demand effect of redistribution in favour of labour is either not too strong (scenario A.3) or even negative (scenario B), so that the GERCU remains below the new SIRCU, there is again room for manoeuvre for the central bank to cut real interest rates. Since this process is associated with a gradually increasing rate of capacity utilisation, monetary policies lowering real interest rates and increasing the GERCU in the short run and the SIRCU in the long run can contribute to a transformation of a profit-led regime into a wage-led regime.

Summing up so far, in our model the 'normal rate' of capacity utilisation, the SIRCU, is endogenous to monetary policies determining the real interest rate. In the 'puzzling' case, the GERCU adjusts to the SIRCU because of the 'puzzling' real debt effects on demand and capacity utilisation. In the 'normal' case no such adjustment can be supposed and monetary policy interventions are required. In the short run, these will always be able to adjust the GERCU to SIRCU from above, but for an adjustment from below a sufficient room of manoeuvre for reducing real interest rates is required, and cannot be taken for granted. In the long run, distribution effects of changing interest rates will make the SIRCU endogenous to monetary policy, and demand effects triggered by redistribution will have a further influence on the GERCU. This will give rise to adjustment processes of the two rates which will not necessarily lead to a stable equilibrium but may rather generate a complex disequilibrium process of interacting GERCUs and SIRCUs, which is driven by monetary policy interventions in the face of deviation of these two rates and concomitant changes in inflation rates. This disequilibrium process may either lead to converging, constant or exploding oscillations of the GERCU around a SIRCU moving there and back, or to a disequilibrium process of continuously falling (or rising) GERCUs and SIRCUs.

THE PARADOX OF THRIFT AND THE PARADOX OF COSTS

Paradox of Thrift

Discussing the central features of Kaleckian models of distribution and growth we begin with the paradox of thrift. If we start from the coincidence of a goods market equilibrium with a distribution equilibrium ($u^* = u^N$), a change in the rentiers' propensity to save will only affect the GERCU negatively, but will have no effect on the SIRCU. From equation (11) we get for the change in the GERCU the well-known paradox of thrift outcome:

$$\frac{\partial u}{\partial s_Z} = -\frac{\lambda i}{\frac{h}{v} - \beta}\,. \tag{11d}$$

A falling (rising) rentiers' propensity to save will increase (decrease) the GERCU which will then exceed (fall short of) the SIRCU and will therefore trigger rising (falling) inflation rates. In the 'puzzling' case, the change in inflation rates will re-adjust the GERCU to the SIRCU and the economy will return to the former equilibrium. Therefore, in this case a change in the propensity to save will not have any effect on this joint equilibrium.

In the 'normal' case, the deviation of the GERCU from the SIRCU will not be self-correcting, but will trigger cumulative divergence and will hence require monetary policy intervention. Here the scenarios discussed in the fifth section apply. Therefore, monetary policy intervention will question the 'paradox of thrift' in the long run without being necessarily able to re-establish a new joint equilibrium of GERCU and SIRCU: Rising (falling) inflation caused by a decreasing (increasing) rentiers' saving propensity will trigger a rising (falling) real interest rate, and hence a rising (falling) mark-up and a falling (rising) SIRCU in the long run, to which monetary policy will then again try to adjust the GERCU. Also note, that a higher (lower) rentiers' propensity to save will make the 'normal' case more (less) likely (equation 11.a).

Paradox of Costs

To assess the relevance of the paradox of costs let us start again from a joint equilibrium of GERCU and SIRCU and assume that the mark-up and hence the profit share vary. This affects both the GERCU and the SIRCU as shown in equations (11.a) and (16.a). A falling (rising) mark-up will cause a rising (falling) SIRCU and in the wage-led regime a rising (falling) GERCU, whereas in the profit-led regime we get a falling (rising) GERCU. In the 'puzzling' case, however, the GERCU will adjust to the new SIRCU in both the wage-led and the profit-led regime due to the 'puzzling' real debt effects on demand and capacity utilisation. Therefore, in the 'puzzling' case the paradox of costs is generally valid, although we have in our model the Bhaduri/Marglin (1990) distinction between wage-led and profit-led expansion.

In the 'normal' case, the discussion of the fifth section applies. In the wage-led scenario (A.1) the paradox of costs is fully valid and a new joint equilibrium of GERCU and SIRCU is established. In the wage-led scenario (A.2) with a strong effect of redistribution on the GERCU, a falling (rising) mark-up will trigger increasing (decreasing) inflation and hence monetary policy intervention which in the long run will make the mark-up increase (decrease) again. Depending on the extent of the required interest rate variations, this effect may invalidate the paradox of costs without necessarily leading to a new joint goods market and distribution equilibrium. In the wage-led scenario (A.3) and in the profit-led scenario (B) with either a weak or even a negative (positive) demand effect of a falling (rising) mark-up, falling (rising) inflation rates will induce monetary policies to cut (raise) interest rates, which in the long run will reinforce the initial redistribution. Here the paradox of costs is fully valid and is even accelerated by real interest rate variations without leading to a new joint equilibrium of GERCU and SIRCU.

CONCLUSIONS

Starting from the problem that in Kaleckian models of distribution and growth the equilibrium rate of capacity utilisation may persistently diverge from the 'normal rate' of utilisation without endogenous adjustments, we have followed the approach proposed by Dumenil/Levy (1999) to consider the 'normal rate' of utilisation in a monetary production economy as the rate which is associated with stable inflation. But unlike Dumenil/Levy (1999) we have taken a closer look at the causes of changing inflation, which remain unclear in their model and which we have originating from unresolved distribution conflict. And also unlike Dumenil/Levy (1999) and their Kaleckian critics we have integrated the feedbacks of changing inflation on demand via real debt effects, and we have fully taken account of the short-run and long-run demand and distribution effects of monetary policies applying the interest rate tool in order to fight rising or falling inflation rates. Our discussion has been based on a monetary extension of the Bhaduri/Marglin (1990) model, in order to allow for profit-led growth, as in Dumenil/Levy's (1999) long run.

We have shown that in such a model the adjustment of capacity utilisation to the 'normal rate' may but need not necessarily require monetary policy interventions. And if monetary policy interventions applying the interest rate tool are necessary, this will affect the 'normal rate' of utilisation which will therefore become endogenous to the economic process. However, with monetary policy interventions, the establishment of a joint goods market and distribution equilibrium with stable inflation cannot be taken for granted. Generally, we will get complex disequilibrium processes of interacting 'normal' and goods market equilibrium rates of utilisation, which are driven by monetary policy interventions in the face of deviations of these two rates and concomitant changes in inflation rates.

With respect to the main results of Kaleckian models we have found that changes in the propensity to save either have no long-run effects on the joint distribution and goods market equilibrium, and hence on the 'normal rate' of utilisation, or that the paradox of thrift is invalidated by monetary policy interventions which are triggered by changes in the inflation rate following a change in demand. The paradox of costs, however, with only a minor exception, is valid also in the long run, when the adjustment of the 'normal rate' takes place, although we have allowed for the possibility of profit-led expansion already in the short run.

Generally, we have shown that in a model which takes the major features of a credit economy seriously, the 'normal rate' of capacity utilisation is endogenous to distribution conflict and monetary policy intervention in the long run. And we have also shown that some major Kaleckian results can be retained for the short and the long run. Therefore, we do not have to be 'Keynesian in the short term and classical in the long term', as suggested by Dumenil/Levy (1999).

NOTES

1. See Kaldor (1956, 1957, 1961), Robinson (1962), Kalecki (1954, 1971), Steindl (1952) and the overviews in Lavoie (1992, pp. 282-347) and Hein (2004, pp. 149-219).
2. See Blecker (2002) for a survey of the Kaleckian models.
3. See Lavoie (1995a, 1996a, 2003) for a review and discussion of the relevant literature.
4. See Lavoie/Kriesler (2005) on the similarity of the Dumenil/Levy (1999) model to the New Consensus model. For the New Consensus model see Clarida/Gali/Gertler (1999), McCallum (2001), Meyer (2001) and Walsh (2002). For post-Keynesian critique and amendment of the New Consensus models see Arestis/Sawyer (2004), Hein (2005), Lavoie (2004), Palacio-Vera (2005) and Setterfield (2004).
5. For a similar model based on the monetary extension of the traditional Kaleckian 'wage-led-only' approach see Hein (2005).
6. See for a similar procedure with respect to the introduction of monetary variables into post-Keynesian models of distribution and growth Lavoie (1992, pp. 347-71, 1993, 1995), Dutt/Amadeo (1993), Dutt (1989, 1992), Taylor (1985, 2004, pp. 272-78) and Hein (1999, 2006, 2006a).
7. The distinction between short-term finance for production purposes and long-term finance for investment purposes, not dealt with in the present paper, can be found in the monetary circuit approach (Graziani (1989, 1994); Lavoie (1992, pp. 151-69); Seccareccia (1996, 2003)).
8. Of course, our simplification implies that profits net of interest payments are all reinvested into the firm.
9. In what follows the terms 'profit', 'profit share' and 'profit rate' are related to gross profits as the sum of profit of enterprise and interest.

10. According to Kalecki (1954, p. 18), the degree of monopoly, and hence the mark-up, may but need not increase when overhead costs, including interest costs, increase.
11. This saving function is similar to the one used by Lavoie (1992, p. 365, 1995, p. 160), the only difference is that we explicitly consider the debt-capital-ratio.
12. On Kalecki's 'principle of increasing risk' see Arestis (1996) und Sawyer (1985, pp. 101-6, 2001a). A similar view was taken by Robinson (1962, p. 86) and Steindl (1952, pp.107-38). Recent empirical work has shown that the interest rate has important effects on investment through its impacts on internal funds and hence on the access to external borrowing in imperfect capital markets (Fazzari et al. (1988); Hubbard (1998); Schiantarelli (1996)).
13. See Arestis/Sawyer (2004, pp. 73-87), Cassetti (2002), Lavoie (1992, pp. 391-421, 2002), Rowthorn (1977) and Sawyer (2001, 2002) for post-Keynesian conflicting claims models of inflation.
14. See Hein (2002, 2005) for a discussion of the effects of effective wage bargaining coordination across the economy in which trade unions take into account the macroeconomic impacts of bargained nominal wages.

REFERENCES

Amadeo, E.J. (1986), Notes on Capacity Utilisation, Distribution and Accumulation, *Contributions to Political Economy*, 5, 83-94.

Amadeo, E.J. (1986a), The Role of Capacity Utilization in Long Period Analysis, *Political Economy*, 2, 147-60.

Arestis, P. (1996), Kalecki's Role in Post Keynesian Economics: An Overview', in J.E. King (ed.), *An Alternative Macroeconomic Theory: The Kaleckian Model and Post-Keynesian Economics*, Boston, Kluiwer.

Arestis, P. and Sawyer, M. (2004), *Re-examining Monetary and Fiscal Policy for the 21st Century*, Cheltenham, Edward Elgar.

Auerbach, P. and Skott, P. (1988), Concentration, Competition and Distribution–A Critique of Theories of Monopoly Capital, *International Review of Applied Economics*, 2, 42-61.

Bhaduri, A. and Marglin, S. (1990), Unemployment and the Real Wage: The Economic Basis for Contesting Political Ideologies, *Cambridge Journal of Economics*, 14, 375-93.

Blecker, R. (2002), Distribution, Demand and Growth in Neo-Kaleckian Macro-Models, in M. Setterfield (ed.), *The Economics of Demand-led Growth*, Cheltenham, Edward Elgar.

Cassetti, M. (2002), Conflict, Inflation, Distribution and Terms of Trade in the Kaleckian model, in M. Setterfield (ed.), *The Economics of Demand-led Growth*, Cheltenham, Edward Elgar.

Chick, V. and Caserta, M. (1997), Provisional Equilibrium and Macroeconomic Theory, in P. Arestis, G. Palma, and M. Sawyer (eds), *Markets, Unemployment and Economic Policy. Essays in Honour of Geoff Harcourt*, vol. 2, London/New York, Routledge.

Ciccarone, G. (1998), Prices and Distribution in a Sraffian Credit Economy, *Review of Political Economy*, 10, 399-413.

Clarida, R., Gali, J. and Gertler, M. (1999), The Science of Monetary Policy: A New Keynesian Perspective, *Journal of Economic Literature*, 37, 1661-707.

Commendatore, P. (2005), Are Kaleckian Models of Growth and Distribution Relevant in the Long Run?, in C. Panico and N. Salvadori (eds), *Classical, Neoclassical and Keynesian Views on Growth and Distribution*, Cheltenham, Edward Elgar.

Committeri, M. (1986), Some Comments on Recent Contributions on Capital Accumulation, Income Distribution and Capacity Utilisation, *Political Economy*, 2, 161-86.

Dumenil, G. and Levy, D. (1999), Being Keynesian in the Short Term and Classical in the Long Term: the Traverse to Classical Long-term Equilibrium, *The Manchester School*, 67, 684-716.

Dutt, A.K. (1984), Stagnation, Income Distribution and Monopoly Power, *Cambridge Journal of Economics*, 8, 25-40.

Dutt, A.K. (1987), Alternative Closures Again: A Comment on 'Growth, Distribution and Inflation', *Cambridge Journal of Economics*, 11, 75-82.

Dutt, A.K. (1989), Accumulation, Distribution and Inflation in a Marxian/Post-Keynesian Model with a Rentier Class, *Review of Radical Political Economics*, 21, 18-26.

Dutt, A.K. (1992), Rentiers in Post-Keynesian Models, in P. Arestis and V. Chick, (eds), *Recent Developments in Post-Keynesian Economics*, Aldershot, Edward Elgar.

Dutt, A.K. and Amadeo, E.J. (1993), A Post-Keynesian Theory of Growth, Interest and Money, in: M. Baranzini and G. Harcourt (eds), *The Dynamics of the Wealth of Nations*, London, Macmillan.

Dutt, A.K. (1997), Equilibrium, Path Dependence and Hysteresis in Post-Keynesian Models, in: P. Arestis, G. Palma and M. Sawyer (eds), *Markets, Unemployment and Economic Policy. Essays in Honour of Geoff Harcourt*, vol. 2, London/New York, Routledge.

Fazzari, S.M., Hubbard, R.G. and Petersen, B.C. (1988), Financing Constraints and Corporate Investment, *Brooking Papers on Economic Activity*, 1, 141-95.

Fisher, I. (1933), The Debt-Deflation Theory of Great Depressions, *Econometrica*, 1, 337-57.

Graziani, A. (1989), The Theory of the Monetary Circuit, *Thames Papers in Political Economy*, Spring.

Graziani, A. (1994), Monetary Circuits, in P. Arestis and M. Sawyer (eds), *The Elgar Companion to Radical Political Economy*, Aldershot Edward Elgar.

Hein, E. (1999), Interest Rates, Income Shares and Investment in a Kaleckian Model, *Political Economy. Review of Political Economy and Social Sciences*, 5, 5-22.

Hein, E. (2002), Monetary Policy and Wage Bargaining in the EMU: Restrictive ECB Policies, High Unemployment, Nominal Wage Restraint and Inflation above the Target, *Banca Nazionale del Lavoro Quarterly Review*, 55, 299-337.

Hein, E. (2004), *Verteilung und Wachstum. Eine paradigmenorientierte Einführung unter besonderer Berücksichtigung der post-keynesianischen Theorie*, Marburg: Metropolis.

Hein, E. (2005), Wage Bargaining and Monetary Policy in a Kaleckian Monetary Distribution and Growth Model: Trying to Make Sense of the NAIRU, *IMK Working Paper, 8/2005, Duesseldorf Macroeconomic Policy Institute (IMK) in the Hans Boeckler Foundation.*

Hein, E. (2006), Interest Rate, Debt, Distribution and Capital Accumulation in a Post-Kaleckian model, *Metroeconomica* (forthcoming).

Hein, E. (2006a), Interest Rate, Debt and Capital Accumulation-A Kaleckian Approach, *International Review of Applied Economics (forthcoming).*

Hubbard, R.G. (1998), Capital-Market-Imperfections and Investment, *Journal of Economic Literature*, 36, 193-225.

Kaldor, N. (1956), Alternative Theories of Distribution, *The Review of Economic Studies*, 23, 83-100.

Kaldor, N. (1957), A Model of Economic Growth, *The Economic Journal*, 67, 591-624.

Kaldor, N. (1961), Capital Accumulation and Economic Growth, in F.A. Lutz and D.C. Hague (eds), *The Theory of Capital*, London: Macmillan.

Kaldor, N. (1970), The New Monetarism, *Lloyds Bank Review*, 97, 1-17.

Kaldor, N. (1982), *The Scourge of Monetarism*, Oxford, Oxford University Press.

Kaldor, N. (1985), How Monetarism Failed, *Challenge*, May/June, 4-13.

Kalecki, M. (1937), The Principle of Increasing Risk, *Economica*, 4, 440-47.

Kalecki, M. (1954), *Theory of Economic Dynamics*, London, George Allen.

Kalecki, M. (1971), *Selected Essays on the Dynamics of the Capitalist Economy, 1933-70*, Cambridge, Cambridge University Press.

Keynes, J.M. (1936), *The General Theory of Employment, Interest, and Money*, in The Collected Writings of J.M. Keynes, vol. VII, 1973, London, Basingstoke, Macmillan.

Lavoie, M. (1984), The Endogenous Flow of Credit and the Post-Keynesian Theory of Money, *Journal of Economic Issues*, 18, 771-97.

Lavoie, M. (1992), *Foundations of Post Keynesian Economic Analysis*, Aldershot, Edward Elgar.

Lavoie, M. (1993), A Post-Classical View of Money, Interest, Growth and Distribution, in G. Mongiovi and C. Rühl (eds), *Macroeconomic Theory: Diversity and Convergence*, Cambridge, Cambridge University Press.

Lavoie, M. (1995), Interest Rates in Post-Keynesian Models of Growth and Distribution, *Metroeconomica*, 46, 146-77.

Lavoie, M. (1995a), The Kaleckian Model of Growth and Distribution and its Neo-Ricardian and Neo-Marxian Critiques, *Cambridge Journal of Economics*, 19, 789-818.

Lavoie, M. (1996), Horizontalism, Structuralism, Liquidity Preference and the Principle of Increasing Risk, *Scottish Journal of Political Economy*, 43, 275-300.

Lavoie, M. (1996a), Traverse, Hysteresis and Normal Rates of Capacity Utilization in Kaleckian Models of Growth and Distribution, *Review of Radical Political Economics*, 28, 113-47.

Lavoie, M. (2002), The Kaleckian Growth Model with Target Return Pricing and Conflict Inflation, in M. Setterfield (ed.), *The Economics of Demand-led Growth*, Cheltenham, Edward Elgar.

Lavoie, M. (2003), Kaleckian Effective Demand and Sraffian Normal Prices: Towards a Reconciliation, *Review of Political Economy*, 15, 53-74.

Lavoie, M. (2004), The New Consensus on Monetary Policy Seen from a Post-Keynesian Perspective, in M. Lavoie and M. Seccareccia (eds), *Central Banking in the Modern World. Alternative Perspectives*, Cheltenham, Edward Elgar.

Lavoie, M., Kriesler, P. (2005), Capacity Utilisation, Inflation and Monetary Policy: Marxian Models and the New Keynesian Consensus, *http://aix1.uottawa.ca/~robinson/Lavoie/Working/dal-RRPE-2.pdf.*

McCallum, B. (2001), Monetary Policy Analysis in Models without Money, *Federal Reserve Bank of St. Louis Review*, 83, 145-60.

Meyer, L.H. (2001), Does Money Matter?, *Federal Reserve Bank of St. Louis Review*, 83, 1-15.

Moore, B.J. (1988), *Horizontalists and Verticalists: The Macroeconomics of Credit Money*, Cambridge, Cambridge University Press.

Moore, B.J. (1989), The Endogeneity of Credit Money, *Review of Political Economy*, 1, 65-93.

Palacio-Vera, A. (2005), The 'Modern' View of Macroeconomics: Some Critical Reflections, *Cambridge Journal of Economics*, 29, 747-67.

Panico, C. (1985), Market Forces and the Relation between the Rate of Interest and Profit, *Contributions to Political Economy*, 4, 37-60.

Park, M.S. (1997), Accumulation, Capacity Utilisation and Distribution, *Contributions to Political Economy*, 16, 87-101.

Pasinetti, L.L. (1974), *Growth and Income Distribution*, Cambridge, Cambridge University Press.

Pivetti, M. (1985), On the Monetary Explanation of Distribution, *Political Economy*, 1, 73-103.

Pivetti, M. (1988), On the Monetary Explanation of Distribution: A Rejoinder to Nell and Wray, *Political Economy*, 4, 275-83.

Pivetti, M. (1991), *An Essay on Money and Distribution*, London, Macmillan.

Robinson, J. (1962), *Essays in the Theory of Economic Growth*, London, Macmillan.

Rowthorn, R.E. (1977), Conflict, Inflation and Money, *Cambridge Journal of Economics*, 1, 215-39.

Rowthorn, R.E. (1981), Demand, Real Wages and Economic Growth, *Thames Papers in Political Economy*, Autumn.

Sawyer, M. (1985), *The Economics of Michal Kalecki*, Armonk, New York, M.E. Sharpe.

Sawyer, M. (2001), The NAIRU: A Critical Appraisal, in P. Arestis and M. Sawyer (eds), *Money, Finance and Capitalist Development*, Cheltenham, Edward Elgar.

Sawyer, M. (2001a), Kalecki on Money and Finance, *European Journal of the History of Economic Thought*, 8, 487-508.

Sawyer, M. (2002), The NAIRU, Aggregate Demand and Investment, *Metroeconomica*, 53, 66-94.

Schiantarelli, F. (1996), Financial Constraints and Investment: Methodological Issues and International Evidence, *Oxford Review of Economic Policy*, 12, 70-89.

Seccareccia, M. (1996), Post Keynesian Fundism and Monetary Circulation, in G. Deleplace and E. Nell (eds), *Money in Motion*, London, Macmillan.

Seccareccia, M. (2003), Pricing, Investment and the Financing of Production within the Framework of the Monetary Circuit: Some Preliminary Evidence, in L.P. Rochon and S. Rossi (eds), *Modern Theories of Money*, Cheltenham, Edward Elgar.

Setterfield, M. (2004), Central Banking, Stability and Macroeconomic Outcomes: A Comparison of New Consensus and Post-Keynesian Monetary Macroeconomics, in: M. Lavoie and M. Seccareccia (eds), *Central Banking in the Modern World. Alternative Perspectives*, Cheltenham, Edward Elgar.

Sraffa, P. (1960), *Production of Commodities by Means of Commodities*, Cambridge, Cambridge University Press.

Steindl, J. (1952), *Maturity and Stagnation in American Capitalism*, 2nd. edition, 1976, London/New York, Monthly Review Press.

Taylor, L. (1985), A Stagnationist Model of Economic Growth, *Cambridge Journal of Economics*, 9, 383-403.

Taylor, L. (2004), *Reconstructing Macroeconomics. Structuralists Proposals and Critiques of the Mainstream*, Cambridge/Mass, London, Harvard University Press.

Walsh, C.E. (2002), Teaching Inflation Targeting: An Analysis for Intermediate Macro, *Journal of Economic Education*, 33, 333-46.

THE CONVENTIONAL VERSUS THE NATURAL RATE OF INTEREST

Oscar De-Juan*

The 'natural rate of interest' is one of the most important and controversial chapters in the history of economic thought. It continues to be a highly topical subject in modern macroeconomics and in the new consensus on monetary policy. On classical and post-Keynesian grounds, this paper considers that the interest rate is a (re)distributive variable with a monetary character. At any moment we can refer to the 'conventional' rate of interest, on which economic agents base their investments in real and financial assets. But this rate lacks the necessary conditions to be called 'natural'. Neither is it the gravity center *of market interest rates, nor does it gravitate around the natural (uniform) rate of profit or the natural (non-inflationary) rate of growth. A unique relationship between the rates of interest, profit, growth and inflation, as suggested by K. Wicksell, does not exist. Given this, the ability of monetary authorities to influence the market interest rate, both in the short run and in the long run, is enhanced.*

INTRODUCTION

Since 1995 OECD countries have had historically low interest rates and low inflation rates. One percent has been a normal real rate for ten-year bonds in most countries in a golden decade characterized by fast growth and high profitability. In contrast, the two decades that followed the 1973 crisis were familiar with stagnation, high inflation and high real interest rates (above 5%). Previously, the real rate averaged 3% in the long lasting boom (1950-1973) with high rates of growth and inflation.

After refreshing these data, the reader is asked to select one of the following options in a multiple choice test: (a) The rate of interest has been oscillating around the rate of profit (its 'natural' value which depends on stable forces such as productivity and thrift); (b) The rate of profit has adjusted to the rate of interest influenced by a changeable monetary policy; (c) There is only one rate of interest which warrants a non-inflationary growth; but this 'natural' rate lacks stable fundamentals and changes from time to time; (d) There is no such a thing as a 'natural rate of interest'; at most we can speak of a 'conventional rate', influenced by monetary policy and divorced from the rate of profit and the rate of growth.

---

* University of Castilla-La Mancha, Department of Economics and Finance, Albacete, Spain.

Our personal choice would be (d). This paper tries to justify such a choice. Our theoretical pillars are twofold. From the classical-Marxian theory of value distribution we learn that the interest rate is a re-distributive variable.[1] From post-Keynesian macroeconomics we borrow the hypothesis that the interest rate is a monetary phenomenon in a world of 'endogenous money'.[2] Our paper is structured in four Sections, apart from this *Introduction*. Section 2 explains why the rate of interest is a monetary and 'conventional' variable, but does not accomplish the requirements of 'natural' variables. Section 3 contends, contrary to neoclassical, Keynesian and Sraffian economists alike, that the interest rate and the profit rate may diverge for good. Section 4 rejects the Wicksellian idea, revived by the new monetary policy, that there is a unique relationship between the rate of interest, the rate of growth and the rate of inflation. In the final Section we highlight the implications of our thesis for monetary policy.

THE INTEREST RATE: A 'CONVENTIONAL' AND 'MONETARY' PHENOMENON

Money is endogenously created by the banking system. 'Money is credit-driven and demand-determined', to use the usual post-Keynesian definition (Moore (1988), p. 19). The temporal dimension of production forces firms to borrow from banks in order to advance wages and other expenditure before their products are sold. These loans are transformed into deposits and used as a means of payment, i.e. money. The central bank (CB) plays a crucial role in this scheme of things. By requiring commercial banks to keep a fraction of their deposits in liquid reserves, the CB becomes 'the lender of last resort' and is able to fix the official interest rate (i_o).[3] Market short-term interest rates are usually pegged to the official rate. Under normal circumstances, the market rate for medium and long-term credits can be computed as a multiple of the official rate, according to the following expression. It is a typical post-Keynesian expression, although nowadays it has a broader acceptance (Bernanke and Blinder (1992)).

$$i^* = i_o(1+\mu) \tag{1}$$

i^* is a representative interest rate that will be identified with 'one year preferential credits', i.e. credits granted by commercial banks to their best customers. Other interest rates are linked to i^* and can be determined by taking into account the specific risks associated to the lender, the borrower and the maturity period. i_o is the official interest rate set by the CB. μ is the normal 'mark-up' applied by commercial banks to the official rate. The 'mark-up' is supposed to be high enough to cover the usual banking costs and to warrant the general rate of profit on the capital invested. The interest rate determined in the financial markets may deviate from i^* when special risks show up: risk of default if the borrowers are too indebted, risk of inflation, risk of currency depreciation, and so on (Kalecki (1937), Minsky (1982)). In this paper we are interested in the analysis of 'normal' conditions, so equation (1) will suffice.

If the interest rate i^* lasts long enough, it may attain the status of 'conventional rate'. People will base their investments decisions in real and financial assets bearing in mind the conventional rate and market deviations from it. The 'conventional' rate, however, is not a 'natural' rate in the classical sense of the word, for two complementary reasons.

(1) A conventional variable lacks of the strong fundamentals that characterize natural variables; consequently, they are more volatile. Technology is the main determinant of natural prices and the associated rate of profit. We can expect that relative prices will evolve slowly along a one-way path, paralleling the increases in productivity. By contrast, if the conventional rate of interest can be influenced by monetary policy, one can expect sudden changes in both directions.

(2) Natural variables play the role of a *gravity center* determining the long period equilibrium for market prices and current rates of profit, influenced by demand shocks and capacity utilization. The conventional interest rate is not a magnetic pole of the market rate. Quite on the contrary, it is a *path-dependent* variable likely to adjust to new market circumstances. A shock on financial markets may displace the conventional rate if it lasts long enough. *Path-dependent* and *natural* variables cannot get along peacefully; they involve a *contraditio in terminis*.

The conventional rate of interest has practical relevance. Investment decisions take into consideration the 'conventional' or 'normal' rate in the recent past that is supposed to prevail in the foreseeable future. We should emphasize, however, that the interest rate is not the key determinant of investment. Post-Keynesian economists consider that investment decisions depend mostly on the expected growth of demand. The principle of acceleration allows us to write: $I_{d,t}=k \cdot g \cdot Y_t$. In the preceding expression, $I_{d,t}$, is the investment decided at the end of period t; k is the desired 'capital / output' ratio; g is the growth of autonomous demand to which aggregated demand adjusts via the multiplier; Y_t is the current level of production. The implementation of this decision may take several years if the desired investment is too high in relation to the firms' annual sales or to any sensible referent. This idea is accounted for by the *flexible accelerator* contained in equation (2). φ indicates the temporal distribution of investment decisions. Deviations from the conventional interest rate ($Di = (i-i^*)/i^*$), may slow down or speed up the execution of investment decisions.

$$I_t = kgY_t(\varphi - bDi) \tag{2}$$

For the purposes of this paper the most relevant conclusions from (2) are: (1) The interest rate does not affect the decisions of investment but the implementations of such decisions; (2) What matters is not the actual level of interest rates, but the deviations of the interest rate from the conventional rate (Di); (3) The conventional rate is *path-dependent*. A fall in market rates speeds up investment. But if the new rate remains constant for a long time, it may gain the status of 'conventional' and cease to stimulate the execution of investment.

The conclusion that the conventional rate of interest is not a natural rate, in any meaningful sense, has to overcome two additional hurdles. First we need to prove that the interest rate does not gravitate around a 'natural rate of profit', as neoclassical theory asserts. Nor does the rate of profit adjust to a monetary rate of interest as most Keynesian and Sraffian economists claim. In our opinion both variables have different determinants and may be separated for good. Second, we need to prove that the interest rate does not gravitate around a 'natural rate of growth' defined as the one which ensures price stability or keeps inflation on target. Countering modern macroeconomics (both neoclassical and Keynesian), we shall contend that there is no a unique relationship between interest rates, investment, the rate of growth and the rate of inflation.

THE RATE OF INTEREST AND THE RATE OF PROFIT: SEPARATION OR DIVORCE?

Classical and Marxian political economy views the rate of interest as a (re)distributive variable. Given technology and the real wage, competition enforces a system of prices, which grants the 'normal' rate of profit for the representative or regulating firms in each industry. The 'operating surplus' of the firm appears as a 'residual' that is further redistributed among interest payments to moneylenders and profits of enterprise to shareholders. The level of the interest rate determines the terms of the redistribution of surplus between 'rentiers' and 'capitalists' (to use the classical-Marxian terminology). The profit of enterprise is supposed to remunerate the 'risk and trouble of productively employing capital' (Ricardo, 1821, pp. 90 and 120). This remuneration, however, is a simple residual. There is no a precise 'profit of enterprise' determined by competition or other economic mechanisms.

Smith's and Ricardo's are sometimes ambiguous. Marx (1894, chs 22 and 23) is crystal-clear about. The interest rate is a monetary category that is exogenously determined by institutional factors reflecting the relative powers of money capitalists and industrial capitalists. Distribution occurs in two stages. The rate of profit is determined together with the real wage by capital-labour conflict. The conflict between the two capitalists groups determines the rate of interest, while the profit of enterprise appears as the residual variable (Hein, (2006)). In Marx's own words:

'The average rate of interest prevailing in a certain country –as distinct from the continually fluctuating market rates–cannot be determined by any law. In this sphere there is no such thing as a natural rate of interest in the sense in which economists speak of a natural rate of profit and a natural rate of wages' (Marx (1894), p. 362).

'For the productive capitalist who works on borrowed capital, the gross profit falls into two parts –the interest, which he is to pay the lender, and the surplus over and above the interest, which makes up his own share of the profit. If the general rate of profit is given, this latter portion is determined by the rate of interest' (Marx, (1894), 364 and 373).

Neoclassical economics revolutionized the theory of distribution, in general, and the theory of the interest rates, in particular (Walras (1889), Section V; Fisher (1930)). The interest rate now appears as a real and natural phenomenon. In equilibrium it coincides with the rate of profit, which is determined by the forces of productivity and thrift. *Thrift* refers to the *intertemporal preferences of individuals* that show up in the upward-sloping supply of capital. *Productivity* lies behind the downward-sloping demand for capital explained by the decreasing *marginal productivity of capital* (MPC): the more capital you invest the lower will its marginal productivity be. The downward demand for capital is the mechanism that brings about the equalization between the interest rate and the rate of profit to the point where productive investment coincides with savings corresponding to full employment income. Unfortunately for neoclassical economics, the capital controversies of the sixties (after Robinson (1956) and Sraffa (1960)) made it clear that if capital is a collection of heterogeneous goods, it is impossible to derive a well-behaved (downward-sloping) demand for capital. And without it the whole neoclassical analysis collapses (Eatwell and Milgate (1983), *Introduction* and *Conclusions*).

Keynes (Keynes (1936), ch. 15) found an additional pitfall in the neoclassical theory of the interest rate. The capital market (and the loanable funds market), which relates productive investment to full employment savings, does not exist at all. The interest rate was determined in the *money market*, by the interplay of an *exogenous supply of money* and *liquidity preference.* Interest rates appear, therefore, as a monetary phenomenon, which can be manipulated by central banks. In equilibrium –he admitted–the rates of profit and interest coincide, but it is the rate of interest which determines the rate of profit, not the other way around. Given the downward-sloping investment function (now called, *marginal efficiency of capital*), firms are supposed to invest until their returns equal the interests determined in the money market. But is Keynes' marginal efficiency of capital justified? Garegnani (1978) warns that this function suffers from the same basic weakness as the neoclassical marginal productivity of capital. Despite that, Keynes makes an important and reliable contribution we can rely on: the interest rate is a monetary phenomenon with a 'conventional' basis, in the terms we defined in the previous Section.

'It might be more accurate, perhaps, to say that the rate of interest is a highly conventional, rather than a highly psychological, phenomenon. For its actual value is largely governed by the prevailing view as to what its value is expected to be. *Any* level of interest which is accepted with sufficient conviction as *likely* to be durable *will* be durable; subject, of course, in a changing society to fluctuations for all kinds of reasons round the expected normal' (Keynes (1936), p. 202; his emphasis).

Freed from neoclassical remnants, one might expect that Sraffians would admit to the divorce between interest and profit rates. But this hasn't been the case. As it is well known, the Sraffian system of relative prices of production has one degree of freedom. One can take as given, either the real wage or the rate of profit. Sraffa, following Ricardo, initially opted for the real wage but shortly afterwards shifted to the rate of profit.

'The rate of profits, as a ratio, has a significance which is independent of any prices, and can well be 'given' before the prices are fixed. It is accordingly susceptible of being determined from outside the system of production, in particular by the level of the money rates of interest' (Sraffa (1960), p. 33).

Sraffians have taken seriously this suggestion[4] in order to stress the importance of monetary policy. But their thesis is so extreme and weak that it causes a natural rejection. We have assumed that monetary policy may affect the redistribution of income between rentiers and capitalists. They go further and conclude that monetary policy affects the primary distribution of income between factors of production. The money rate of interest would determine the general rate of profit and, therefore, the real wage. In our opinion it is saver to take the real wage as the independent variable. We should simply accept that trade unions have the desire and the power to keep the real wage 'conquered' in the past.[5]

Let us comment briefly on the three explanations provided by distinguished Sraffian economists. **Panico (1988)** considers that the banking industry provides basic services required for other industries. An increase in the rate of interest on bank loans will raise the financial costs of industrial firms. The general increase in prices will increase the profit rate and decrease the real wage. Mongiovi and Rühl (1993) have rightly rejected the idea of 'debt coefficients' since debt structure differs among firms and changes through time. If highly indebted firms raised prices after an increase in interest rates, they would be swept away by lowly indebted firms. **Ciccarone (1998)** argues that profits in the banking sector result form the difference between the interest on loans and the interest on deposits. In a competitive equilibrium, he concludes, the rate of profit of the banking sector coincides with the general rate of profits. Our equation (1) says something similar except for one thing: he considers the 'mark-up' μ as a constant parameter, while we relate it to the general profit rate (r). We do not know the value of μ until we know r. The third explanation, proposed by **Pivetti (1991)**, is based on a more direct but imprecise idea: 'arbitrage'. Arbitrage between real and financial assets and arbitrage among different financial assets, is supposed to bring about the equality between the interest rate (the independent variable), the profit of enterprise and the general rate of profits on the capital invested. Arbitrage is also the driving force for post-Keynesian economists such as Nell (1998) and Seccareccia and Lavoie (2004).[6]

In our analysis of the classical economists and Marx, we have argued that arbitrage does not accomplish this function. Modern textbooks on finance do also provide a support to our thesis (Brealey and Myers (1996), ch. 17). When discussing the implications of the Modigliani–Miller propositions, they take the separation of both rates as the norm and conclude that if the profitability of the firm remains constant, changes in interest rates and leverage coefficients will not affect the fundamental value of the firm.

In our opinion, arbitrage does not work in the desired direction once the endogeneity of money and the central role played by banking is taken seriously. Consider the following expression.

$$r^* = i^* \lambda + \alpha(1 - \lambda) \qquad (3)$$

- λ stands for the *leverage coefficient*, i.e. the ratio of borrowed funds to total funds. It depends mainly on historical and institutional factors.

- r^* stands for the 'normal' rate of profit of a representative firm that we take as given and constant for our period of analysis (a decade or so). Cyclical fluctuations associated to the degree of capacity utilization are irrelevant.

- i^* is the conventional rate of interest, as defined earlier. The asterisk indicates that we abstract from market fluctuations. This seems reasonable, since we are interested in analyzing the effects of permanent changes in i^* associated to a persistent monetary policy.

- α stands for the 'profit of enterprise', i.e. the yield from 'own – capital'. It results from dividing dividends by the current value of shares.[7] Despite the formal presentation, α is the true dependent variable. It is a residual that indicates what the yield from own-capital should be in order to ensure the correspondence between the market value of the firm and its economic value (related to r^*).

Let us suppose that initially $\lambda = 0.5$ and $i^* = r^* = 0.10$. Then α equals 0.10. Imagine, now, that a consistent monetary policy succeeds in halving market interest rates. Given r^* and λ, the profit of enterprise corresponding to $i^* = 0.05$ turns out to be $\alpha = 0.15$. What will the consequences of a permanent fall in interest rates be?

A redistribution of wealth in favor of the former owners of bonds and equities. These windfall profits will be cashed in when old assets are sold. After a time, old bonds will disappear and new ones will be sold at their face value, despite lower interest on them. This is because firms can get bank loans at 5%. Banks will be eager to lend at this rate since they can also borrow cheaper from CB. Households will be forced to accept these new financial conditions. The wealth that they whish to retain in low-risk assets (either long-term deposits or bonds) will yield lower returns. It is a consequence of the hypothesis of the endogeneity of money and the recognition that the credit market rules the roost.

Equity prices will eventually converge to their fundamental value, which we have supposed to be constant since r^* does not change. The profitability obtained from shares is higher, but the equities' discount rate has increased *pari passu*. This is so because the discount rate is supposed to be the yield from assets with a similar risk (i.e. the 15% offered by the equities of other firms).

A permanent fall in the interest rate might also have an impact on the leverage coefficient. This change usually takes a long time and does not contradict our main thesis: the permanent separation between the rates of interest and profit. A higher λ would simply broaden the difference between the interest rate and the profit of enterprise.

One could explain the previous example as an increase in the 'risk premium' of capitalists. It would be more appropriate to say that the economy has experienced a change in the terms income is (re)distributed between rentiers and capitalists and between financial capital and industrial capital. Industrial firms are the real winners in this process. They will find it easier to finance their own expansion using retained profits, once the profit of enterprise has increased from 10 to 15%. They can borrow cheaper from banks and from households at 5% (instead of 10%). And, of course, they can continue issuing equities. Immediately after the fall in interest rates, it was the best option because new equities could be sold above their face value. After a time, new equities will be sold in the stock market at par value.

THE INTEREST RATE AND INFLATION: HOW 'NATURAL' IS THE NON-INFLATIONARY RATE OF INTEREST?

Knut Wicksell (1898) was one of the first economists to recognize the endogeneity of money and the monetary nature of the rate of interest.[8] He admitted that the money rate of interest (i) could temporarily depart from its fundamental value, the real rate of profit (r). But the separation–he concluded–could not mean a divorce because it would result in 'price instability' and a resetting crisis. There are three possible scenarios. (a) $i < r$ would spur investment and growth over and above the potential level, triggering a process of 'cumulative inflation'. (b) $i > r$ would put a break on investment, and trigger a process of recession and cumulative deflation. (c) The third position follows suit: 'There is a certain rate of interest on loans which is neutral in respect to commodity prices, and tends neither to raise nor to lower them' (Wicksell (1898), p. 102).

Nowadays macroeconomists (both neoclassical and Keynesian) are busy in the search for the 'non-inflationary rate of interest' (NIRI, for short). They are urged on by the governors of central banks, who ask for rules clarifying when and how much should they raise the official rate to prevent inflation. The 'Taylor rule' is the most popular of them. (Taylor (1993, 1998)). The natural rate of interest would be the one which ensured a zero output gap and a constant rate of inflation. A more detailed definition would take demand and supply shocks away.

'The natural rate is defined to be the real fed funds rate consistent with real GDP equalling its potential level (potential GDP) in the absence of transitory shocks of demand. Potential GDP, in turn, is defined to be the level of output consistent with stable price inflation, absent transitory shocks to supply. Thus, the natural rate of interest is the real fed funds rate consistent with stable inflation absent shocks to demand and supply' (Williams (2003), p.1; see also Laubach and Williams (2003)).

In this standard definition of NIRI, the first thing to notice is the omission of the fundamentals. The NIRI is defined with regard to results (absence of inflation), not to causes (permanent deviation from the profit rate). The profit rate is not an observable variable but we know, at least, its determinants (productivity, in particular). Wicksell devoted considerable time and effort to examining the effects of an increase in productivity, which raises the profit rate but not the money interest rate. Nowadays the NIRI is computed by analyzing econometrically past data on market interest rates, output, unemployment and inflation. The models yield a 'natural rate', but it changes continuously, because it is a mere average of market results. Since the determinants of the natural interest rate are not identified, the whole idea becomes a non-scientific (i.e. non refutable) hypothesis. If their forecasts are not confirmed by the facts, they can always lay the blame to the change in the natural rate of interest. A similar problem occurs with the natural rate of unemployment (NAIRU), whose relationship with the NIRI and the Phillips curve is evident. A fall in the interest rate below its natural level is bound to accelerate the rate of growth and to reduce the unemployment rate below its natural level, accelerating inflation. When this does not occur, they tend to suspect that the NAIRU has fallen.

The NIRI and the NAIRU contains both theoretical and empirical flaws (Arestis and Sawyer (2005), chs 2 and 4). It takes for granted that aggregate demand and particularly investment are highly sensitive to interest rates. And it focuses exclusively on demand-pull inflation. None of these hypotheses have been confirmed by empirical evidence.[9] They are certainly not required in our post-Keynesian model where investment depends mostly on the expected growth of demand, while inflation is mostly a cost-push phenomenon.

Keynes learned from Wicksell that the interest rate is a monetary variable. Had Wicksell known about the Keynesian principle of effective demand, his investment function would have given more importance to demand expectations than to interest rates. In periods of recession, when entrepreneurs expect a weak growth in demand, investment will be nil despite real interest rates approach zero. In boom periods, when entrepreneurial expectations are buoyant, investment and interest rates usually grow *pari passu*. Had Wicksell lived half a century longer, he would have realized hat high inflation, high interest rates and massive unemployment may exist together. He would have concluded that the 'natural rate of interest' and the 'natural rate of unemployment' are 'conventional' variables. That both of them are path-dependent in the sense that once people become accustomed to the new rates, they loose their destabilizing properties.

Our point in this Section is that there is no a unique relationship between the interest rate, the rate of growth and the rate of inflation. Two economies, identical in every way, except for the rate of interest, may be in dynamic equilibrium. After a time, differences in the distribution of income and wealth will emerge. The rate of growth might also differ. Yet, both economies could grow steadily and efficiently, and both could keep inflation on target. If the conventional rate of interest is path-dependent and accommodates to a persistent monetary policy, there is no point to search for the natural, non-inflationary rate of interest. As we said in Section 2, *path-dependent* variables and *natural* variables are a *contraditio in terminis*.

CONCLUSIONS

In a world of 'credit money', endogenously created and destroyed, the interest rate is a monetary phenomenon in the sense that it is related to the official interest rate set by the CB. A persistent monetary policy may help to determine the conventional rate on which investment decisions are based. This would not be possible if the interest rate gravitated around a rate of profit determined by forces as stable as productivity, thrift and the like. The effectiveness of an autonomous monetary policy would also be questionable if there was a unique non-inflationary rate of interest (NIRI). A rate lower than the NIRI would cause, according to Wicksell, an inflationary spiral that would bring the economy to a standstill and force a realignment of the official rate to the natural one. Our paper has tried to prove that both conceptions of 'natural rates' are theoretical flawed and empirically void. There is no a unique relationship among the rates of interest, the natural (uniform) rate of profit and the natural (non inflationary) rate of growth. We have also rejected the hypothesis, so cherished by many Sraffian and Keynesian economists, that the money rate of interest regulates the rate of profit (and, indirectly, the real wage). It would be too pretentious and the justification is not clear.

In agreement with Keynes (1936, ch. 24), we suggest to central banks that instead of looking for a 'mysterious' natural rate of interest and binding themselves to it, they should try to keep the official rate as low and stable *as possible*. The official rate should be treated as an 'anchor', instead of a 'battle-axe'. It might be impossible and imprudent to maintain a low rate, if the economy faces pure credit-demand inflation or if the exchange rate is depreciating steadily. Apart from these rather special cases, a low interest rate may be possible and efficient. It would also be convenient to avoid the capricious redistribution of wealth associated with sudden movements of the conventional interest rate (which enters into the discount rate).

NOTES

1. Smith (1776, book I, ch. IX), Ricardo (1817, chs I, XXI and XVII), Tooke (1826), Marx (1894, chs XXI-XXVIII), Kalecki (1937, 1943), Sraffa (1960), Kurz and Salvadori (1995).
2. Moore (1988), Wray (1990), Lavoie (1992), Rochon (1999), Arestis and Sawyer (2004).
3. Even in the countries without compulsory reserve requirements, banks are obliged to balance assets and liabilities every day. To ensure the daily balance they borrow in the money market.
4. Probably, Sraffians have taken their master's suggestion too far. In a letter to Garegnani dated 13 March 1962, Sraffa writes: 'In conclusion, I'd say that the review [of my book] would do well not to insist too heavily on the passing remark about the monetary interest rate' (quoted in Bellofiore (2001), p. 366-7).
5. Real wages may fluctuate during the cycle, but in the determination of prices of production (and the natural rate of profit associated to them), short-term fluctuations are irrelevant.
6. In our opinion, Pivetti is trapped in the assumption of the '*necessary long-run connection between the normal profit and money interest*' (Pivetti (2001), p. 113). Nell could be saved if one interprets the proposed equality between the rates of growth, profits and interest as a 'golden rule' for secure accumulation of real and financial capital. But Nell sometimes suggests that g determines r and arbitrage forces the equality between r and i.
7. We are supposing that all the profits of enterprise are distributed entirely as dividends. If a part of them is saved (firms' reserves), there will be an automatic rate of appreciation that we should add to dividends.
8. The origins of this idea can be traced back to Tooke (1826).

9. After revising a vast array of empirical papers, Arestis and Sawyer conclude that a percentage point increase in interest rates leads to a 0, 21 decline in the rate of inflation after five years.

REFERENCES

Arestis, P. and Sawyer, M. (2004), *Re-examining Monetary and Fiscal Policies in the 21st Century*, Aldershot, Edward Elgar.

Bellofiore, R. (2001), Monetary Analysis in Sraffa's Writings: A Comment on Panico, in T. Cozi and R. Marchionatti (eds), *Piero Sraffa's Political Economy*, London, Routledge.

Bernanke, B.S. and Blinder, A.S. (1992), The Federal Funds Rate and the Channels of Monetary Transmission, *Amercian Economic Review,* 82, 901-21.

Brealey, R. and Myers, S. (1996), *Principles of Corporate Finance*, New York, McGraw-Hill.

Ciccarone, G. (1998), Prices and Distribution in a Sraffian Credit Economy, *Review of Political Economy*, 10, 399-413.

Fisher, I. (1930), *The Theory of Interest*, New York, Macmillan.

Eatwell, J. and Milgate, M. (eds) (1983), *Keynes's Economics and the Theory of Value and Distribution*, London, Duckworth.

Garegnani, P. (1978), Notes on Consumption, Investment and Effective Demand, *Cambridge Journal of Economics*, 2, 335-533, and 3, 63-82.

Hein, E. (2006), Money, Interest and Capital Accumulation in Karl Marx's Economics: A Monetary Interpretation and Some Similarities to post-Keynesian Approaches, *The European Journal of the History of Economic Thought*, 13,113-40.

Kalecki, M. (1937), The Principle of Increasing Risk, *Economica*, 3, 440-7. A revised version appears in M. Kalecki (1971), *Selected Essays on the Dynamics of the Capitalist Economy, 1933-1970,* Cambridge, Cambridge University Press, Chapter IX: 'Entrepreneurial Capital and Investment'.

Kalecki, M. (1943), *Studies in Economic Dynamics,* London, Allen and Unwin.

Keynes, J.M. (1936), *The General Theory of Employment, Interest and Money,* London, Macmillan.

Kurz, H. and Salvadori, N. (1995), *Theory of production*, Cambridge, Cambridge University Press.

Laubach, T. and Williams, J.C. (2003), Measuring the Natural Rate of Interest, *Review of Economics and Statistics*, 85, 1063-70.

Lavoie, M. (1992), *Foundations of Post-Keynesian Economics*, Aldershot, Edward Elgar.

Marx, K. (1894), *Das Kapital*, vol. III. English translation: *Capital,* Moscow, Progress Publishers (1972).

Minsky, H. (1982), *Can 'It' Happen Again?,* Armonk, New York, Sharpe.

Mongiovi, G. and Rühl, C (1993), Monetary theory after Sraffa, in G. Mongiovi and C. Rülh (eds), *Macroeconomic Theory: Diversity and Convergence,* Aldershot, Edward Elgar.

Moore, B.J. (1988), *Horizontalist and Verticalist: The Macroeconomics of Credit Money*, Cambridge, Cambridge University Press.

Nell, E. (1998), *The General Theory of Transformational Growth. Keynes after Sraffa*, Cambridge, Cambridge University Press.

Panico, C. (1988), *Interest and Profit in the Theories of Value and Distribution*, London, Macmillan.

Pivetti, M. (1991), *An essay on money and distribution*, London, Macmillan.

Pivetti, M. (2001), Money Endogeneity and Monetary Non-Neutrality: a Sraffian Perspective, in L. P. Rochon and M. Vernengo (eds), *Credit, Interest Rates and the Open Economy*, Cheltenham, Edward Elgar.

Ricardo, D. ([1817] 1950), *The Principles of Political Economy and Taxation*, Cambridge, Cambridge University Press.

Robinson, J. (1956), *The Accumulation of Capital*, London, Macmillan.

Rochon, L.P. (1999), *Credit, Money and Production: an Alternative Post Keynesian Approach,* Cheltenham, Edward Elgar.

Seccareccia, M. and Lavoie, M. (2004), Long-Term Interest Rates, Liquidity Preference and the Limits of Central Banking, in *Central Banking in the Modern World. Alternative Perspectives*, Cheltenham, Edward Elgar.

Smith, A. ([1776] 1976), An Inquiry into the Nature and Causes of the Wealth of Nations, (2 vols), Oxford, Oxford University Press.

Sraffa, P. (1960), *Production of Commodities by Means of Commodities. Prelude to a Critique of Economic Theory*, Cambridge, Cambridge University Press.

Taylor, J. B. (1993), Discretion versus policy-rules in practice, *Carnegie Rochester Conference Series on Public Policy*, 39, 195-214.

Taylor, J. B. (1998), Monetary Policy Guidelines for Employment and Inflation Stability, in R. Solow and J. B. Taylor, *Inflation, Unemployment and Monetary policy*, Cambridge (MA), The MIT Press.

Tooke, T. (1826), *Considerations on the State of the Currency*, London, John Murray.

Walras, L. (1889), *Eléments d'économie politique pure*, Lausanne, F. Rouge.

Williams, J.C. (2005), The natural rate of interest, *Federal Reserve Bank of San Francisco, Economic Letter*, n. 32, 1-4.

Wicksell, K. (1898), *Geldzins und Guterpreise*. English translation: *Interest and prices*, New York, Macmillan (1936).

Wray, L. R. (1990), *Money and Credit in Capitalist Economies,* Cheltenham,Edward Elgar.

MINSKY ON INCOME DISTRIBUTION, EFFECTIVE DEMAND AND CAPITALIST PERFORMANCE

George Argitis[*]

In the macroeconomic debates over income distribution and economic performance, different models of capitalism with diverse institutional structures have been main points of reference. In most of them, the role of monetary and financial forces is largely absent especially in equilibrium models. This paper introduces a Post Keynesian framework, which develops from Hyman Minsky's financial approach to economic instability, and considers the distributional and demand effects of non-financial corporate sector's debt and of monetary policy on investment and capital accumulation. The econometric evidence supports paper's fundamental hypotheses for the USA and the UK.

INTRODUCTION

Hyman Minsky's *Financial Instability Hypothesis* would seem to have obvious application to the recent experience of poor industrial and macro-economic performance of many developed and developing countries, especially in the current era of financial liberalisation. It is surprising that only few studies have attempted to use Minsky's ideas and concepts to analyse the role of monetary and financial forces in capital accumulation. One factor which might have contributed to the neglect of Minsky's work is that the two conventional macro-processes, the neo-classical and the new-Keynesian, focused on specific aspects of the functioning of the financial markets, ignoring the role of corporate debt in income distribution and in aggregate demand.

The neo-classical macro-process presumes that financial markets function smoothly and firms' investment decisions are isolated from financial influences. Modigliani and Miller (1958), who worked within the Arrow-Debreu economic environment, developed a theorem with which they assume that firms' investment decisions are independent from their financial structure under the assumption of perfect capital markets. Neo-classical theoretical and empirical models of investment are heavily based on the assumption of a 'representative firm' that responds to prices set in self-equilibrated and perfectly competitive capital markets. If all firms have equal access to capital markets, then their financial structure is irrelevant to their productive investment, because external funds appear to be a perfect substitute for internal capital. With perfect capital

* Department of Economics, University of Crete, Rethimno, Greece.

markets, firms' investment decisions and their profit optimisation problem could be solved without considering effects of financial factors. In the neo-classical macro-process financial and monetary factors do not play an important role. The neo-classical macro-process is marked by a strong causation running from labour markets to good markets and in turn to financial markets.

New-Keynesian credit rationing (e.g. Stiglitz and Weiss (1981); Greenwald and Stiglitz (1984, 1989); Blinder (1987); Stiglitz (1988)) and equity rationing models (e.g. Stiglitz (1992)) construct the micro foundations of the effects of external finance failures in investment decisions. Credit and equity rationing exists due to uncertainty and to informational asymmetries among the participants in the markets, conditional to human inability to eliminate them in the context of probability. In credit rationing models, banks face moral hazard and adverse selection problems, while they select the rate of interest that maximises their profits, regardless of whether at this rate of interest the demand for credit is greater than the supply of credit. In the new-Keynesian macro-process, credit and equity rationing cause a failure of investment and the aggregate supply. The new Keynesian theoretical and empirical research has made important advances in the way external financial constraints may influence investment, capital accumulation and market disequilibrium positions.

The contention of this paper is that the neo-classical and the new-Keynesian macro-processes are based on a failure to consider the macro-implications of the endemic instability of financial markets as well as the importance of the non-financial corporate sector's (henceforth industrial sector) financial structure. Debt and interest payments may influence income distribution and may play an important role in industry's investment decision-making. To conceptualise the importance of industry's debt in macroeconomic performance we develop (Section 2) a Post Keynesian framework, which is based on Minsky's financial theory of investment that highlights the distributional and demand effects of debt and of interest payments on capital accumulation. In Section 3 we use econometric techniques to test our basic hypothesis, using annual data of the USA and the UK for the period 1974-2002. Finally, Section 4 summarises and concludes the paper.

INTEREST PAYMENTS, FINANCIAL INSTABILITY AND CAPITAL ACCUMULATION

Opposite to the standard economic theory that adopts barter, pure exchange economy paradigm, Minsky has developed a Wall Street paradigm that begins with the picture of a money economy with sophisticated financial institutions. Minsky's institutional analysis of capitalism develops from the dynamics of cash flows (wages and salaries to consumers, sale proceeds to firms, interest payments to banks) and the interdependence among firm's balance sheets. Variato (2001) observes that Minsky shifts the research interest from the analysis of the relationships driven by relative prices and decisions taken by consumers and producers to the analysis of the relationships driven by changes in cash flows between firms and their suppliers (savers or banks).

In a closed, small government economy, which is Minsky's basic model, the connection between finance and investment commits firms to past decisions and makes present behaviour dependent on monetary dynamics. Bellofiore and Ferri (2001) note that Minsky's perspective is a full-blown theoretical alternative to standard economic theory in the way it incorporates the categories of money, finance, profits and income distribution. Minsky's *Financial Instability Hypothesis* illustrates the importance of the financial practices of the industrial sector in the functioning of a market economy. More specifically, Minsky conceptualises the 'world we live in' as to be a capitalist economy with long-lived capital assets and complex financial processes. Capital accumulation involves financing arrangements between the industrial and the banking sector. In Minsky's conceptualisation, finance has its own place and movements in capitalist reproduction and that industry and finance must be considered as mutually interactive.[1] Their exact relation follows a historical path and is shaped by institutions, policies, uncertainty, societal actions and class conflicts, entrepreneur and state strategies resulting overtime in a historically-specific, but changeable economic structure, which considerably marks out the active role of finance in the process of capitalist evolution. The essential problem of the non-financial corporate sector centres on the way investment and positions in capital assets are financed. The funds that industrial firms needs in order to acquire control over capital assets are obtained by a variety of financial instruments, such as bank loans, bonds, mortgages, equity shares etc. Each financial instrument creates commitments to pay money in the future; one example is the payment of interest and repayment of the principal on debts. These cash payment commitments are money flows set up by the financial structure of a firm.

Arestis and Glickman (2002) note that the essence of Minsky's originality is his thesis that forces capable of producing financial fragility and instability are built into the system itself. In Minsky's words 'in a world of uncertainty, given capital assets with a long gestation period, ...the successful functioning of an economy within an initially robust financial structure will lead to a structure that becomes more fragile as tile elapses. Endogenous forces make a situation dominated by hedge finance unstable (1986, p. 213). Minsky follows Keynes's (1936) *General Theory* and considers investment decisions to be taken under uncertainty and in calendar time, with no scientific basis to calculate probabilities of future events. His major concept is that industrial and macroeconomic performance hangs on the fulfilment of industry's financial commitments to banks and other financial institutions.

More specifically, Minsky (1977; 1982a; 1982b; 1986; 1992) argues that financial instability and crisis occurs whenever the financial practices of the business sector deteriorate. In his framework, the robustness or fragility of a financial system depends on two relations: financial system's cash flow patterns and the way the functioning of a financial system affects lending, which enable business, households and financial institutions to fulfil their financial commitments. Debt creates a complex set of relations between the industrial sector and the banking sector. Increasing indebtedness is likely to cause industrial sector's inability to fulfil its debt commitments, triggering an endogenous disequilibrating process.

Minsky defines corporate profits to be the cash flow that do or do not validate any particular structure of business debt. A debt structure is validated when maturing commitments to pay are fulfilled and expectations are sustained that future remaining commitments will be fulfilled. The validation of industrial debt depends upon expected profits being large enough so that payment commitments to banking sector can be fulfilled either out of current profits or by refinancing. The expected level and stability of industry's profit determines the debt structure that industrialists, their bankers, and the ultimate holders of the economy's assets will accept. In particular, in an economy where there are serious consequences to default on financial obligations, the potential negative deviation of realized profits from expected levels is an important determinant of acceptable debt structures. When some industrial units can not refinance their position through the normal channels (credit markets) are forced to raise cash by unconventional instruments or by trying to sell out their position to increase their liquidity (Minsky (1982b)).

There are three fundamental determinants of this happening; when the corporate sector increases its reliance on debt to finance new investment; when economy's liquidity falls and when finance becomes more speculative and *ponzi*. According to Minsky (1977), in a modern capitalist economy economic units control a structure of capital assets that yield cash flows over time, which depends on the demand for output produced by these capital assets and the output price. Combinations of debt and equity constructing a structure of firm's liabilities and firm's gross profits finance such capital assets. At any point in time, the liability structure determines a time series of payments. The cash flow problem for a unit concerns the balancing between the cash receipts from operations and the cash payments due to debts. If the expected cash receipts exceed the cash payment commitments during a period of time, then, a unit is a hedge unit. If the unit can meet the payment commitments on liabilities, which represent only interest, but not all its payment commitments over the same period, is a speculative financing unit. A *ponzi* financing unit is a speculative unit for which the interest of its payment commitments exceeds the net income receipts. The continuation of the functioning of a *ponzi* financing unit depends on its ability to borrow money. Both *ponzi* and speculative units are vulnerable to changes in the financial markets and changes in the rate of interest. Financial constraints and higher interest rates raise the fragility of the financial system and lead *ponzi* and speculative units to bankruptcy.[2]

Minsky's argument that every economic unit –firm, household, government, nation- face, like a bank, the problem of daily balancing cash inflow against cash outflow is the essence of his concept that capitalism is essentially a financial system. For him and in contradistinction with the conventional economic theory, the major problem faced by economic units is not the problem of maximizing profit or utility subject to a budget constraint, but the problem posed by what Mehrling (2001) has called the survival constraint, which requires that cash outflow not exceed cash inflow. To meet this constraint economic units must balance their cash commitments and their cash flows. And because it is likely that cash flows falls short from time to time, economic units must have access to reliable sources of refinance, which makes them possible to meet current cash flow needs by pledging expected future cash flows. However, borrowing does not relax the survival constraint. Financial assets represent future cash outflows to the debtor and future cash inflows to the creditor and hence transfer the constraint from one economic unit to another.

The only way for the industrial sector to relax the survival constraint is to create new non-financial capital assets, which are expected to be profitable, that is future cash inflows are expected to exceed by some margin the cash payment commitments required to finance the initial investment. Minsky adopts Kalecki's (1971) profit equation according to which a shortfall of realised profits below anticipated profits requires a prior shortfall of investment. It is the decline in investment that has therefore to be explained. Minsky's financial theory of investment arises from a cumulative rise in interest payments that cannot be paid within an institutional structure that squeezes liquidity for the industrial sector. The root of macro-economic instability is hence to be found in industry's financial structure.

Kalecki's (1971) paper on entrepreneurial capital and industry's investment decisions adds dynamics on the importance of the financial structure of capital accumulation. It will be argued that in Kalecki's context, Minsky's *Financial Instability Hypothesis* is getting endogenous dynamics that arise from a cumulative increase in interest payments. Kalecki has pointed out that entrepreneurial capital, which is the amount of capital owned by a firm, is of decisive importance in limiting investment and the size of a firm. Kalecki (1971) distinguished between two types of capital, entrepreneurial capital and rentier capital. The former is capital owned by the firm while the latter is the capital it tries to borrow. What is crucial in Kalecki's argument is the idea that a firm's access to the capital market is determined, among other factors, by the amount of its entrepreneurial capital. In other words, the available finance to industry in the form of lending is determined by the amount of profits remain to industry (internal funds) after paying interest payments to banks for its outstanding debt.

To better understand the importance of Kalecki's argument in the context of Minsky's *Financial Instability Hypothesis*, we shall first consider Minsky's analysis of the cyclical behaviour of an economy. Minsky's starting point is an economy that is currently doing well. An increase in investment is most likely to be initiated in a financially robust environment in which industrial firms are in liquid positions with not much accumulated debt, while interest rates as well as interest payments are low. In Minsky's model, an increase in investment always leads to larger current profits, and larger current profits stimulate expectations of higher future profits; these, in turn, will trigger more investment. Growing investment and profits will increase confidence on the part of the banking system. Industrialists will make greater use of debt; banks will make more loans and possibly riskier loans. The upshot of Minsky's argument is that in such a scenario the expected gross cash flows of all economic units become increasingly committed contractually to other units. The possibility of default increases and the ability of most units to fulfill their payment commitments in the face of an unexpected economic downturn declines. Economic expansion unavoidably creates financial fragility. As financial fragility grows, the interest rates increase and financial institutions curb finance, making a fall in investment spending more likely. An economy with private debts is especially vulnerable to changes in the pace of investment, for investment determines both effective demand and the viability of debt structures. Lower investment means lower demand and profits than expected. Financial instability follows from the subjective nature of expectations about the future course of investment and the subjective determination by bankers of the appropriate liability structure for investment financing. In an economy with capitalist financial usages, uncertainty is a major determinant of the path of financing, investment, income and employment. Minsky (1996) concludes that in a new financially fragile and unstable environment industrialists are forced to sell illiquid assets to meet interest and principal payments. In a dynamic manner, a recession and a debt-deflation crisis may occur unless institutional developments (a lender of last resort, big government) stabilize the economic system (Papadimitriou and Wray, 2001).

After Kalecki's distinction between internal and external finance, the way investment is financed is fundamental for investment to be self-reinforcing. As investment grows, industrial firms make greater use of debt. The necessity of external finance increases the interest rates. The combination of higher interest rates and debt increases interest payments and negatively affects industry's realized and expected internal funds. The inverse relation between internal funds and interest payments can be shown by making use of some 'income accounting', regarding the distribution of income between industry, finance and labour. The following identities relate to the income produced by the production system.

$$IP = (Y - W) - FP \qquad (1)$$

where: IP = industry's internal funds Y = total income, W = wages, Y-W = total capitalist profit, FP = interest payments paid to banks by industry.

Expressing this in the form of shares dividing by total capitalist profit:

$$IP/(Y - W) = 1 - FP/(Y - W) \qquad (2)$$

The inverse relation between IP/(Y-W) and FP/(Y-W) gives rise to a mechanism through which interest payments might set limits on industry's investment decision-making.

$$CA = \varphi(FP/(Y-W)) \qquad (3)$$

Where: CA = Capital Accumulation in the industrial sector.

An increase in corporate debt and a tight monetary policy might have a negative effect on capital accumulation via three channels. *Firstly*, it increases the interest payments paid and hence causes a distributional effect worsening industry's internal funds, while it increases industry's reliance on debt. *Secondly*, in a Kaleckian manner, the availability of external finance to industrial sector falls because of the decrease in internal funds. A permanent redistribution of income towards the banking system makes these effects stronger, exacerbating this inherent antithesis in the process of investment-financing. In addition, a fall in industry's investment reduces industry's total profit and makes firms unable to meet their interest payments for their debt, generating possibilities of financial instability and crisis. In this context, financial fragility and macroeconomic instability is an unavoidable outcome of the distributional effects stemming from a rise in industry's debt and in interest payments paid to banks. The stance of the monetary policy appears, therefore, to be a crucial determinant of the finance-investment relation and the macro-behaviour of an economy. *Thirdly*, changes in income distribution at the expense of industry and labour are likely to cause an aggregate demand failure with negative feedback effects on industry's investment. In addition, from (2) we observe that a rise in labour's income share will reduce, *ceteris paribus*, industry's internal funds exacerbating the aforementioned effects.

ECONOMETRIC ANALYSIS

Equation 4[3] formalizes our major hypotheses developed in the previous Section in order to empirically assess new channels of finance's influence on business investment decisions.

$$GCS = f(FINPS, CU, WSS) \qquad (4)^{4}$$

The growth rate of business capital stock, GCS, is our dependent variable. The expansion of the capital stock captures both the materialization of new investment and the dynamics of the investment decision-making. The variable FINPS, is the interest payments as a percentage of total capitalist profit. We select this variable because it reflects the distributional impact of debt and of monetary policy on business internal funds. A rise in the financial profit share normally reflects higher interest payments and less available internal funds[5] for firms to finance new investment as well as pessimistic expectations about future profits and banks' lending. In our specification, industry's investment decisions are also allowed to be affected by changes in aggregate demand, a very well know hypothesis in the Post Keynesian empirical literature (Fazzari and Mott (1986-87); Fazzari (1993)). The standard accelerator hypothesis underpins this relation. The best way of incorporating this effect into an empirical investment equation would be to include a capacity utilisation variable, as a proxy of the aggregate demand. Our last explanatory variable is the labour income share, WSS. An increase in labour's income share is a source of industry's profit fall and hence causes negative effect of industry's internal finance. Furthermore, the use of the WSS variable allows us to capture the impact that workers' power might have on wage-setting and on income distribution.

Assuming a linear function and a stochastic relationship, equation (4) including the error term results in the following specification of our estimating equation.

$$GCS_t = a + bFINPS_t + cCU_t + dWSS_t + u_t \quad (5)$$

The expected signs being: $f_{FINPS}<0$; $f_{CU}>0$; $f_{WSS}<0$

Note that in our specification the variables are in real terms and because they are defined in growth rates (GCS) or ratios (FINPS, WSS) are non-trended. An investigation of the data pattern shows that CU is also a non-trended variable. An autoregressive distributed lag (ARDL) structure of equations is tested using 29 observations.[6] The Akaike Information and the Schwarz Bayesian criteria suggest that a lag structure of the model up to the second order is preferred by the Data.

REGRESSION RESULTS

We regard the ARDL (2,2,2,2) model as a starting point and attempt to optimise the fit for each country by narrowing down the number of parameters, taking the t-value as an indicator. The information we wish to extract from the ARDL model is whether the variables should be included in levels, in differences and in lags. Table 1 (in Appendix) presents the estimated regressions preferred by the data.

After the application of a full range of misspecification tests in the estimated regression, which are reported in Table 2 (in Appendix), we fail to reject the null hypothesis. Therefore, there is no evidence of serial correlation, or of a rejection of the linearity, normality, homoskedasticity assumptions at the 5% and 10% level of significance by the standard Langrage Multiplier test. Moreover, the CUSUM and CUSUMSQ tests provide no evidence of structural instability in any of the reported regressions. The coefficient of determination, R^2, which is .89 for the USA indicates a good fitness of our estimated regressions. The insignificance of CU in the UK reduces the value of R^2 to .59.

The estimates reveal that the first lagged value of the dependent variable has a positive and significant influence on the current value of the growth rate of capital stock. The statistical significance of the lagged dependent variable shows the autoregressive nature of investment. The financial profit share appeared to be an important determinant of the growth of capital stock. The results show that in both countries it is statistically significant at the 5% level and has the expected negative sign. An increase in the interest payments reduces the internal funds for the business sector and discourages investment. The share of financial profits to total profits emerges therefore, as a channel through which finance and monetary policy affects investment and industrial accumulation. Durable changes in the interest rate and the implementation of a restrictive monetary policy act as a potent source of internal financial constraints on investment. The opposite distributional and financial effects will occur if monetary policy is expansionary.

Turning to the other explanatory variables, we see that the coefficients have the expected signs and are statistically significant, but the CU in the UK. The change of capacity utilization appears to exert a significant positive impact on the growth rate of capital stock. Macro-policies that stimulate demand will have a strong, positive impact on investment. Yet, income redistribution towards workers exerts a negative impact on investment as it is expected.

CONCLUSIONS

The Minsky's type macro-process developed in this paper attempts to show the way a rise in rentiers' income might destabilize the macroeconomic and financial system of a capitalist economy. This process builds upon Minsky's and Kalecki's ideas and allows for the multiplicity of institutions, structures and practices in today's capitalism.

We have argued that an increase in financial profits is likely to cause distributional and demand effects, which could have a negative influence on income, profits, industry's investment decisions and financial stability. The results presented here demonstrate that finance, demand and income distribution influences investment. Lower business profits and higher interest payments reduce internal cash flows and thus weaken investment. In addition, lower sales reduce the need to expand industry's capacity. The indebted firms and industries are likely that first meet investment problems, when monetary policy becomes more restrictive. The distributional consequences of monetary policy and external financial bottlenecks stimulate changes in the production process and in firms' ability to fulfil their repayment commitments and thus increase the possibility of a Minskian type financial instability and crisis.

Seen in this context, a challenge is to think about institutional changes and a new policy structure that is able to transcend the constraints imposed by financial markets and financial elites on income distribution, on effective demand, on capital accumulation and employment. In this Keynes's intellectual support is again of crucial importance. Among the few explicit policy statements that Keynes offers in Chapter 24 of his *General Theory* are a call for the 'euthanasia of the rentier' and for a 'comprehensive socialization of investment'. Yet, for Keynes strong market intervention policies were necessary to channel financial resources away from speculative markets and towards productive activity. These Keynesian policy themes are relevant today if we wish to create favorable conditions for a rentier-targeting policy structure, alternatively to neo-liberalism, and industrial favor financial markets, which will be a great advantage of the order of events that might reinforce industry's accumulation and macro-economic stability.

NOTES

1. In this respect, Minsky's perception of capitalism is close to Marx's ([1894] 1991) analysis developed in Part Five of *Capital III*, where the method of structure of *Capital* is applied to deploy the monetary and financial facets of capitalist instability (see Harris (1976); Panico (1988); Argitis (2001)). Marx has developed a monetary framework of distribution in which he paid attention to the distribution of surplus value between industrial and money capitalists. In this part of Marx writings, the type of the relation between the industrial and the financial section of capital, whether conflicting or cooperative (see Epstein and Schor (1986); Epstein (1992, 2002)) has a major role to play in financial arrangements between the two sectors and in the determination of industrial and financial interests in distribution. Marx's analysis assumes an antagonistic relation between the two capitalist groups (Minsky implicitly makes the same hypothesis), which is a significant institutional determinant of the interaction between 'real' and monetary forces in capitalism.

2. In the General Theory Keynes ([1936] 1991) offered a painstaking critique of speculative nature of financial market practices and their negative impact on channelling resources towards the expansion of productive capacity. It is worthy also to recall the 'euthanasia of the rentier' which bodes ill for the banks also, but it is quiet sufficient to state that Keynes' macro-process necessitate the incorporation of rentiers' effects on economic activity. Post-Keynesian economists (e.g. Weintraub (1958); Davidson and Smolensky (1964); Davidson (1978, 2002)) have emphasize the rentier aspects of capitalism and the macro-instability caused by the malfunctions arise in financial markets.
3. The investment function has been the subject of a large number of econometric studies, which have provided very important evidence with significant implications for theory and policy (Jorgenson (1971), Gertler (1988), Fazzari and Mott (1986-87); Fazzari *et al.* (1988); Fazzari (1993), Chirinko (1993)).
4. Data: Definitions and Sources: FINPS = FINP/Y-W, Y-W = non wage income = GTP = Gross Trading Profits of the non-financial corporate sector before providing for depreciation and stock appreciation, and before taxes, FINP = Interest Payments, Survey of Current Business, US Department of Commerce (USA), Blue Book, National Accounts (UK). WS = Wages and salaries paid by the non-financial corporate sector. Source the same as above. WSS = W/Y, Y = W + GTP. CU = Capacity Utilization, Main Economic Indicators, OECD. GCS = Business Capital Stock, OECD, National Accounts.
5. The issue of the causation between internal funds and investment has been addressed by other empirical works (e.g. Fazzari and Mott (1986-87); Fazzari (1993); van Ees *et al.* (1997)).
6. ARDL models have been shown to have desirable properties even in the face of unit roots (Pesaran and Shin (1995)).

REFERENCES

Arestis, P. and Glickman, M. (2002), Fianncial Crisis in Southeast Asia: Dispelling Illusion the Minskyan way, *Cambridge Journal of Economics,* 26, 237-60.

Argitis, G. (2001), Intra-Capitalist Conflicts, Monetary Policy and Income Distribution, *Review of Political Economy*, 14, 453-70.

Bellofiore, R. and Ferri, P. (2001), Introduction: Things fall Apart, the Centre cannot Hold, in R. Bellofiore and P. Ferri (eds), *Financial Keynesianism and Market Instability: The Economic Legacy of Hyman Minsky*, vol. I, Cheltenham, Edward Elgar.

Blinder, A. (1987), Credit Rationing and Effective Supply Failures, *The Economic Journal*, 97, 327-52.

Chirinko, R. (1993), Business Fixed Investment Spending: Modelling Strategies, Empirical Results, and Policy Implications, *Journal of Economic Literature*, 31, 1875-911.

Davidson, P. (1978), *Money and the Real World*, 2nd edn, London, Macmillan.

Davidson, P. (2002), *Financial Markets, Money and the Real World,* Cheltenham, Edward Elgar.

Davidson, P. and Smolensky, E. (1964), *Aggregate Supply and Demand Analysis,* New York, Harper and Row.

Epstein, G. (1992), Political Economy and comparative central banking, *Review of Radical Political Economics*, 24, 1-30.

Epstein, G. (2002), Financialization, Rentier Interests, and Central Bank Policy, Discussion paper, Political Economy Research Institute.

Epstein, G. and Schor, J. (1986), The Political Economy of Central Banking, *Discussion Paper*, 1281, Harvard University.

Fazzari, S. and Mott, T. (1986-87), The investment theories of Kalecki and Keynes: an empirical study of firm data, 1970-1982, *Journal of Post Keynesian Economics*, 9, 171-87.

Fazzari, S., Hubbard, G. and Petersen, P. (1988), Financing Constraints and Corporate Investment, *Brookings Papers on Economic Activity*, 1, 141-95.

Fazzari, S. (1993), Monetary Policy, Financial Structure and Investment, in G. Dymski, G. Esptein and R. Pollin (eds), *Transforming the US Financial System*, New York, M.E. Sharpe.

Gertler, M. (1988), Financial Structure and Aggregate Economic Activity: An Overview, *Journal of Money, Credit and Banking*, 20, 559-88.

Greenwald, B. and Stiglitz, J. (1984), Informational Imperfections in the Capital Market and Macroeconomic Fluctuations, *American Economic Review*, Papers and Proceedings, 74, 194-99.

Greenwald, B. and Stiglitz, J. (1989), Financial Market Imperfections and Business Cycles, *The Quarterly Journal of Economics*, 103, 77-98.

Harris, L. (1976), On interest, credit and capital, *Economy and Society*, 5, 145-77.

Jorgenson, D. (1971), Econometric Studies of Investment Behaviour: A Survey, *Journal of Economic Literature*, 9, 1111-147.

Kalecki, M. (1971), *Selected Essays on the Dynamics of the Capitalist Economy, 1933-1970*, Cambridge, Cambridge University Press.

Keynes, J.M. ([1936] [1991]), *The General Theory of Employment, Interest and Money*, Macmillan, Cambridge University Press.

Marx, K. ([1894] 1991), *Capital: A Critique of Political Economy*, vol. III, intr. E. Mandel, trans. D. Fernbach, London, Penguin Books- New Left Review.

Mehrling, P. (2001), Minsky, Modern Finance and the Case of Long Term Capital Management, in R. Bellofiore and P. Ferri (eds). *Financial Keynesianism and Market Instability, The Economic Legacy of Hyman Minsky*, vol. I, Cheltenham, Edward Elgar.

Minsky, H. (1977), A Theory of Systemic Fragility, in E. I. Altman and A. W. Sametz (eds), *Financial Crises: Institutions and Markets in a Fragile Environment*, A Wiley-Interscience Publication.

Minsky, H. (1982a), The Financial-Instability Hypothesis: Capitalist Processes and the behaviour of the economy, in Ch. Kindleberger and J. P. Laffargue (eds), *Financial Crises. Theory, History, and Policy,* Cambridge, Cambridge University Press.

Minsky, H. (1982b), *Inflation, Recession and Economic Policy*, New York, Whetsheaf Books.

Minsky, H. (1986), *Stabilising an Unstable Economy*, New Haven, Yale University Press.

Minsky, H. (1992), The Financial Instability Hypothesis, The Jerome Levy Economics Institute of Bard College, Working Paper, No. 74.

Minsky, H. (1996), Uncertainty and the structure of the capitalist economies, *Journal of Economic Issues*, 30, 357-68.

Modigliani, F. and Miller, M. (1958), The Cost of Capital, Corporation Finance and the Theory of Investment, *American Economic Review*, 48, 261-297.

Panico, C. (1988), *Interest and Profit in the Theories of Value and Distribution*, London, Macmillan.

Papadimitriou, D. and Wray, L. R. (2001), Minsky's Analysis of Financial Capitalism, in R. Bellofiore and P. Ferri (eds), *Financial Keynesianism and Market Instability, The Economic Legacy of Hyman Minsky*, vol. I, Cheltenham, Edward Elgar.

Pesaran, H. and Shin, Y. (1995), An Autoregressive Distributed Lag Modelling Approach to Cointegration Analysis, Working Paper No. 9514, Department of Applied Economics, University of Cambridge.

Stiglitz, J. (1988), Money, Credit and Business Fluctuations, *Economic Record*, 64, 307-22.

Stiglitz, J. (1992), Capital Markets and Economic Fluctuations in Capitalist Economies, *European Economic Review*, 36, 269-306.

Stiglitz, J. and Weiss, A. (1981), Credit Rationing in Markets with Imperfect Information, *American Economic Review*, 71, 392-410.

van Ees, H., Kuper, G. and Sterken, E. (1997), Investment, Finance and the Business Cycle: Evidence from the Dutch Manufacturing Sector, *Cambridge Journal of Economics*, 21, 395-407.

Variato, A.M. (2001), Hyman Minsky: what kind of (post-) Keynesian?, in R. Bellofiore and P. Ferri (eds), *Financial Keynesianism and Market Instability, The Economic Legacy of Hyman Minsky*, vol. I, Cheltenham, Edward Elgar

Weintraub, S. (1958), *An Approach to the Theory of Income Distribution*, Philadelphia, Chilton.

APPENDIX

Table 1
Regression Results

Period	*Country*					
1974-02	USA	GCS=-.033 +.66GCS(-1)-.0006FINPS+.0028DCU-.004WSS				
	R^2=.87	*-3.4*	*6.9*	*-2.58*	*4.78*	*-3.38*
1974-02	UK	GCS=.43+.40GCS(-1)-.29FINPS-.37WSS				
	R^2=.59	*2.15*	*2.08*	*- 2.34*	*-2.12*	

Note: Italic numbers are t-values.

Table 2
Diagnostic Tests

Test Statistics	*LM Version* *USA*	*UK*
Serial Correlation	CHI-SQ(1)=.39	CHI-SQ(1)=1.36
Functional Form	CHI-SQ(1)=.062	CHI-SQ(1)=3.89
Normality	CHI-SQ(2)=.21	CHI-SQ(2)=2.13
Heteroscedasticity	CHI-SQ(1)=.34	CHI-SQ(1)=2.69

Note: Critical values for CHI-SQ (1) and CHI-SQ (2) at 5% and CHI-SQ (1) at 1% level of significance are 3.84, 5.99 and 6.63, respectively.

THE POLITICAL ECONOMY OF SUSTAINABLE DEVELOPMENT

Persefoni V. Tsaliki*

In this paper we present and evaluate the premises of sustainable development literature. We show that mainstream as well as most radical views, more often than not, do not explicitly incorporate in their analysis the way in which the dominance of capitalist mode of production shapes the phenomena that relate to issue of sustainable development. We suggest an alternative perspective that allows for the political element to play more active role through the creation of the necessary institutions that may regulate economic life to desired directions, where the profit motive continues to dominate in the reproduction of capital but also takes into account the environmental dimension.

INTRODUCTION

Discussions and actions on preventing environmental degradation and favouring sustainable development are relatively recent phenomenon. This is not an issue of neglect but rather reflection of the lack of awareness on the issues at hand. As a matter of fact, the roots of the current concern for the importance of environment policy and of sustainable development can be found in the report of the World Commission on Environment and Development (1987), in which it was established that the traditional economic principles of rational utilization and efficiency were not enough to achieve sustainability.

The constituent components of sustainable development (hereafter SD) refer to the needs of the poor nations and the limits of the environment, and it is conceptualised as a process that meets the needs of the present without compromising the ability of future generations to meet their own needs (Charter (1992)). In a more formal manner, SD is defined as a process that secures continuous and indefinite provision of welfare for society through the implementation of policies which satisfy human needs and, at the same time, take into account ethical and environmental issues which are left aside in the normal functioning of the economy.

The claim of this paper is that the quest for SD should not limited on how the environmental, ethical, moral and other related issues may influence the economy, but rather its focus must be on how exactly the political and economic variables may influence all the above issues and practices. We argue that the

* Department of Economics, Aristotle University of Thessaloniki, Thessaloniki, Greece.

economic dimension and the specific social relations originated in a capitalist mode of production are the source of the problems that emerge within SD; hence, the suggested analyses and policy proposals towards SD must take into consideration the dimension of the character of capitalist production. The remainder of the paper is structured as follows: Section 2 deals with the literature on SD and summarizes its main arguments. Section 3 highlights some of the limitations and inconsistencies which arise from the way SD is presented and dealt within the relevant literature. Section 4 places the emphasis on the necessary steps that should be taken toward economic growth associated with cleaner environment. The final section presents our conclusions, and makes some remarks about future research efforts.

SUSTAINABLE DEVELOPMENT IN THE LITERATURE

There is no consensus in the literature on the exact meaning of SD.[1] Within the mainstream economics, several perspectives on SD have been developed; one of them claims that because of concrete limits to ecological capacity, there is a need to preserve and respect the environment without explicitly introducing social and economic dimensions of sustainability; in another perspective, social, economic and ecological issues are combined and the emphasis is placed on the human dimensions of sustainability; a third perspective assigns crucial importance to economic and technological advances in achieving sustainability (Carvalho (2001); Farrell and Hart (1998)). If there is a general conclusion shared by these mainstream studies is that ecological problems arise due to poverty, population growth and underdevelopment. However, mainstream studies usually do not examine the roots of these problems and, as a result, their policy suggestions attempt to reconcile economic growth and environmental protection through technological advances and appropriate developmental strategies.[2]

Radical views, on the other hand, argue that SD becomes possible only if there is a complete transformation of the way humans deal with the natural environment. This transformation can take place through the ethical and spiritual transformation of individuals, the control of natural resources by small communities, the wealth redistribution aligned to poverty alleviation, the recognition that development involves broader human development goals, the strong social policies, the strong civil societies, *etc.* In short, these authors favour alternative models of development in which capital accumulation should not necessarily be the primary purpose of society, but instead, the local participation and inclusion of different social groups in the process of economic development (Ocampo (2002); Chatterjee and Finger (1995)).

In the core of SD discussion is the dispute over the extent to which economic growth is required. The argument is that economic growth is not only a prerequisite but a necessity for any proposed policy prescription towards sustainability and there have been attempts to quantify the exact amount of growth required in both developed and underdeveloped economies to make sustainability gradually feasible.[3] On the other hand, many have attacked the idea that 'the more growth the better for all members of society and in all respects' on the grounds that it neglects to introduce the need for a changed pattern of economic development (Panayotou (1994); Broad (1994)). From these studies a consensus is formed according to which in a society there is a need for the integration of four types of sustainability, namely environmental, social, institutional and economic sustainability (Rowledge *et al.* (1999); La Grega *et al.* (1994)). Hence, the assumed theoretical and empirical research attempts to show how these four interrelated dimensions may form a new model of SD and also to point out the practices that should be followed for its implementation.

In the relevant literature, social sustainability refers to the capacity of a society to offer to its members the characteristics of social cohesion, whose core elements include education, income distribution, social contracts, communication and participation, social security, *etc.* (Hediger (2000)). In contemporary societies, employment[4] is linked to most of the above mentioned conditions for social cohesion and thus policy proposals for job creation are encouraged in order to achieve the goals of SD. One way of achieving higher records in employment and SD is through economic growth, but a counter argument related to the 'jobless' growth hypothesis raises the issue whether more growth is the cause for rising levels of unemployment in both developed and underdeveloped economies. Another argument is associated with the hypothesis that economic growth leads to higher income levels and thus to an increase of individuals' welfare.[5] There is no doubt that economic growth increases the average income but it does not necessarily reduce the distributional inequalities. Hence, within this framework of analysis the quest remains as to what extent economic growth consists a necessary and a sufficient precondition to guarantee social sustainability.

The social network needed to enhance social cohesion and SD refers to institutional sustainability.[6] Social cohesion is achieved and enhanced considerably in a society by the core institutional objectives which are accountability, civil society, empowerment, gender's equity and knowledge formation. These objectives are linked to economic growth and they describe essential characteristics of how wealth is produced, distributed and used in a society. Further, objectives referring to inter-linkages of the institutional and social dimensions of sustainability such as health, employment, fair income distribution and workers' rights facilitate the SD's targets. It is generally acknowledged that there is a need for broad reforms and the commitment of all nations to cooperate through efficient multinational institutions that would make and observe rules in areas such as trade, investment, environment, *etc.* (Ocampo (2002); Carvalho (2001)). It is argued that SD requires the emergence of world level organization, rested on democratic principles that will control and govern the various levels of world development (Griethuysen (2002)).

Environmental sustainability refers either to the solution of current environmental problems such as pollution or to the reduction of resource depletion. Some studies argue that economic growth lessens the environmental problems suggesting that economic growth is not an obstacle to, but the main way to achieve environmental sustainability (Grossman and Krueger (1992)).

Other studies have shown that some environmental problems such as land use, waste generation, loss of biodiversity, and green house gas emissions will get worse with economic growth (Daly (1991)). As a result of this direct relation between economic growth and resource consumption, the idea of zero-growth policies has become particularly popular as a way to prevent the increase in resource consumption and thus of environmental degradation.

Finally, within sustainable development literature, the evolution of economic activities (trade, production, distribution, *etc.*) has been the focus of analysis and they have been viewed from many different perspectives. At the centre of this analysis lies the idea that the dominant forms of economic growth, since the industrial revolution, have accelerated the transformation of nature, have generated ecological imbalances and degradation of the environment, and have created unsustainable conditions on a global scale. This concern with environmental and social degradation has prompted many motives to propose new ideas, policies and alternative approaches to economic growth.

The main idea behind all these proposals is that the economic system has either entered or is entering a new stage. In this new era, a new form of capitalism is required in order to facilitate an easier transition to sustainable industrial development. Consequently, various proposals and steps have been suggested to accommodate the need for a change in that direction. Among these proposals are:

- *'natural capitalism'* hence the idea is that environmental issues should penetrate and influence all economic activity, from the accounting system reports to managerial decisions. Moreover, 'natural capitalism' proposes specific steps to achieve 'that kind of change of heart' that will make sustainable development a core business target (Birkin (2001); Hawken *et al* (1999)).
- *'fair trade'* in the sense that current trade behavior should change and new principles should be implemented that will establish an equal basis of exchange between the developed and the less developed countries and thus contribute to the development of long-term SD (Strong (1997); Brown (1993)).
- *'new consumer'* whose environmentally friendly consumption behavior can contribute to SD (Birkin (2001)).
- *'new management'* which may organize a new economic system that will not violate the basic laws of the natural system. Thus, new management should implement the necessary rules and practices which will account for the limited capacity of the environment, such as renewable resources, minimization of waste discharges, *etc.* (Lamberton (1998)).

The list can be extended to include several other proposals, such as green accounting, ethical concerns, *etc.* Finally, it would be an omission not to mention the views expressed by those (neo liberals) supporting that only the principles of the free market have the capacity to provide SD in the world. The supporters of this view argue that only the unhampered competitive market economy through the price mechanism can reveal the most efficient allocation of resources, eliminate the economic degradation and meet, in general, the goals of SD.[7]

SUSTAINABLE DEVELOPMENT AND CAPITALISM

Capitalism is a system in which there is a complex interdependent social network whose reproduction requires precise complementarities among different activities undertaken by individuals (Shaikh (2004)). What drives the system and allows it to reproduce itself should occupy centre stage in our understanding of the functioning of real economy. For Smith, the self-interest is the principle that keeps capitalist society together, whereas for mainstream economists is the satisfaction of the unlimited needs and desires of humans with the limited available natural resources. On the other hand, for Marx profit motive is the driving force of capitalism.

In classical economics in general and Marx in particular, profit is the life blood of capitalism and the profit motive, which is socially constructed and maintained, subordinates everything to its own particular goals giving rise to recurrent economic patterns (Marx (1894)). The profit motive regulates the competition of capitals and makes individual capitals to rush and take advantage of areas of higher profitability, to seek the cheapest labour possible and even be in command of macroeconomic processes (*i.e.*, employment level, investment, *etc.*). Technical change is self-initiated and an ongoing process in capitalism, manifested through the mechanization of the production process. Both, profit motive and competition should be viewed as a process that paradoxically produces balance through constantly offsetting imbalances, growth through perpetual fluctuation, order through disorder (Shaikh (2004)). This view of capitalism in action is quite opposite to the usual neoclassical analysis according to which consumers and producers, in harmony, maximize their utility and profit, respectively. In this harmonic classless analysis of capitalism, all transactions take place in an equilibrium framework and nothing changes except for forces outside the economic system.

All matters associated with SD are shaped by the capitalist mode of production and, as such, they cannot escape from their subordination to profit motive. The usual treatment of SD issues in the literature, however, lacks to acknowledge this fact and as a result several analytical shortcomings arise.

Fetishism of Hidden Social Relations

The classical analysis of capitalism is in sharp contrast to that of mainstream economics which concentrates on the system's order. The notion of perfect competition deprives from real actors of production process, capital and labour, any function and everything is left to powerful market mechanism. The action from the production process and the concomitant social relations generated within capitalist mode of production is shifted to market place, where prices automatically move to bring balance in demand and supply. This logic of harmony goes through all analytical arguments of mainstream economics and it is applied in all markets including that of labour. In so doing, the social relations formed in the production process are hidden and fetishism of these relations is cultivated, such as between consumer and commodity, employer and employee, state and citizens, *etc.*

The perception of capitalism as a harmonious system gives rise to the idea that the ultimate goal of capitalism is the satisfaction of the needs and desires of human beings and consumers. Within this analysis, commodities are deprived from their social substance and consumers are viewed as powerful agents to determine exchange and production. Additionally, within mainstream analysis, labour and entrepreneurship are considered separate and independent factors of production whose remuneration is determined in the market and, as a result, the derived distribution of output is the outcome of an objective market mechanism. In this analysis of commodities, wages, profits, *etc.* there is no reference to social relations of production. No reference is made to the exploitation of labour from capital, and instead, wages and profits are defined in the market, like any product, through the supply and demand mechanism.

Similar fetishisms arise in all types of relations developed in a capitalist society and they penetrate into various proposals and practices developed within SD literature. The suggestions for a new approach to management, consumer behaviour, *etc.* fall short in understanding these underlying and hidden social relations. The arguments supporting collective consciousness and actions by consumers and capitalist underline this type of vision of capitalism. Capitalism promotes individualistic behaviours from the side of capital and consumer. Cut-throat competition among capitals allows no room for alliances to prevent environmental degradation and proposals based on collective actions fall short in applicability.

Private firms make investment and production decisions that are best for their own profits; often private interests push government policies that promote their own growth, frequently at the expense of natural resources (air, land or water). Hence, the fight against pollution and for SD, in general, is ultimately a fight to restrict and change the private enterprise system. The understanding of the often hidden social and economic relations maintained in capitalism becomes imperative and only the abolition of fetishisms might help and show how government may intervene more actively in an economy and how public may exert pressure on private firms.

The Role of Institutions-State

The institutional dimension of sustainability argues for the development of a social network of institutions and organizations which will guarantee the social cohesion of a society. However, the quest here is to what extent this network of institutions developed within capitalist mode of production can provide the ground to meet the goals of SD.

Neoclassical and Keynesian economists share, to a great extent, a common vision about how capitalism works. On the surface, neoclassicals seem to argue for the opposite of Keynesians, that is perfect competition versus imperfect competition, price taking versus price setting, full employment versus persistent unemployment, market driven laws of motion versus state regulated paths, *etc.* However, both approaches regard the market system fundamentally as efficient, equitable, stable and socially desirable in which the equilibrium is a natural state. The difference is that neoclassical economics view the market system itself alone capable to give optimal results, while Keynesians view many imperfections in the operation of the market system which might be corrected through government intervention. Almost all modern debates in economics, ranging from the effects of rising budget deficits and debt to the consequences of globalization, can be seen within these two alternative perceptions of the way with which the economy works, perfectly or imperfectly.

In contrast, for classical economists and Marx, in particular, capitalism is a turbulent system which, in its quest for equilibrium, never rests and always exists at disequilibrium. Competition among capitals (active business) and between capital and labourers define the accumulation process which is driven from profitability. As a matter of fact, anything in the capitalist mode of production is subsumed under the quest for more profits, and so are the various institutions, profit or non-profit.

For example, the state is a characteristic example of an institution that exists and operates with the purpose of providing the necessary guaranties so that the system based on profit motive can operate normally. Capital requires the state, while the state requires economic continuity and this in turn rests on the proper functioning of capital. While the state can regulate the outcomes produced by profit motive, it cannot eliminate the motive itself. Indeed, it cannot even significantly undermine the continuity of the circuit of capital, for when the latter falters, the whole system shakes. This is not to undermine the role of the state which can intervene in the operation of an economy and may alter (within strictly defined limits) the outcomes produced by the profit motive. Although the limits of state intervention may be wider during periods of prosperity and narrower during downturns, nevertheless state's intervention is confined within strict limits specified by the profit motive (Shaikh (2004)).

This vision of a hierarchically structured capitalist society stands in sharp contrast to the way modern economics represent capitalism as an idyllic society in which a set of equal partners, *i.e.*, households, business and state, operate on a distinct principle, utility, profits and economic management, respectively. Modern economics extend this notion of capitalist society to international institutions, which, as argued, may play an especially important role in implementing strategies to promote SD globally. The truth is that these organizations and institutions have enjoyed enormous power in shaping the development agenda and even policy process within developing countries. But these 'agents' also obey the law of profitability which governs capitalism and this is the reason why there are so many cases that reflect their failure to promote and implement appropriate strategies for SD (Ocampo (2002)). In fact, these cases reflect the worst aspects of current model of development and point to its lack of regard for natural environment and social equity.

Employment

Both, neoclassical and Keynesian economic approaches see the business sector as a passive player in economic life, whereas as an active player the first views the market and the second the public sector. This theoretical framework penetrates throughout their analysis. For instance let us consider the question of unemployment; neoclassical theory tells us that unfettered capitalism will automatically generate the full employment of labour, whereas Keynesians insist that only state intervention can guarantee full employment. Both sides, however, agree on the feasibility of the outcome and both implicitly characterize firms as passive players in this process. Their only difference lies in the way that the equilibrium, which is certain, can be attained.

But the decisive question here is to what extent does the proper function of capitalism requires the full employment of labour? The operation of capitalism needs, at least, the full capacity utilization of capital, regardless the level of labour employment. As a matter of fact, classical economists and Marx in their analysis of capitalism never implied that the proper functioning of capitalism requires the full employment of labour. This proposition is derived from the argument of subsistence wage by Smith and Ricardo and reserve army of labour by Marx. Within the Marxian analysis, the successful capitalist is the one who has replaced the last worker by a machine, because for him 'the machine is a perfect worker and the worker is an imperfect machine' (Marx (1865)). This view is supported by the functioning of capitalism itself, whereby the competition among capitals forces for higher mechanization of the production process and the concomitant replacement of labour by machines. Additionally, wages are suppressed in the presence of unemployment and so poverty and inequalities of any sort are permanent features of modern societies.

Consequently, full employment and equitable distribution of income, which constitute essential requirement for SD can not be achieved within capitalism, since they are not required for its proper functioning. Meanwhile, the state and the institutions developed within a capitalist society cannot escape from the limits set by capital accumulation. The state cannot set aside the profit motive itself, because it will weaken the continuity of the circuit of capital, and, by extension, jeopardize its own existence. In good times, the limits to the state interventions may be less restrictive and thus we may witness policies promoting 'full employment' and also a 'fair' distribution of income, but in the long run these cannot escape the limits set by the profit motive. Studies show that there is no basis to support the existence of a 'social wage' and thus there is no redistribution of income in favour to low income groups through the existed tax mechanism or public spending.[8]

Economic Analysis of Environment and SD

A common argument in SD literature is that the process of production, based on profit orientated private ownership and the tendency to maximize short-term gains has transferred social costs, such as environmental pollution, ecological destruction and deterioration in the quality of life onto nature and society. Hence, assuming a perfectly competitive economic environment, the concurrent analyses show how these externalities should be coped to produce maximum social welfare (Gillis *et al* (1996); Panagyotou (1993); Pearce and Turner (1990); Tietenberg (1988)).

A response to these 'bad' externalities was a set of proposed practices and proposals, which heavily rely on the idea that monetary measures of institutional performance do not capture enough relevant information to render institutions not only economically but also ecologically and socially sustainable. Thus, 'green' instead of traditional accounting measures were presented. Other proposals suggest a more active role either from the state or from the consumers' side towards meeting the goals of SD, whereas others indicate the need for a new prototype of management.

Within the neoclassical framework of perfect competition, businesses are passive entities and the market is an active and a powerful mechanism in determining all relations. The market itself determines the technology used in the production process and all firms adopt it immediately. Thus, the supply curve of the industry is defined by the same marginal cost curves of each individual firm. Consumers' behavior, on the other hand, shapes the demand curve for the product in the market. According to the neoclassical theory, a rational consumer with perfect information maximizes his/her total utility, which might include along other things, such as habits, perceptions of different sorts image *etc.*, also environmental concerns. There is no reason why a rational consumer should not incorporate in his/her utility function the element of environmental concerns?

Thus, within mainstream analysis, there is no room for any problem related to environment and market should function in way to solve this problem automatically. Since there is a uniform technology and all firms face the same average cost, the protection of environment should not be treated differently from all other costs faced by firms. If a problem arises, this can only be in a short-run, since the powerful market mechanism and consumers' demand function[9] impose on firms the same production technique. A rational consumer, in his utility function, should include environmental issues and thus the demand which is an essential part of the analysis, should shape the functioning of the market which in turn affects the supply. Thus, within the neoclassical framework there is no room for externalities related to environmental issues.

Similarly, within the Keynesian framework if market equilibrium is not in place because of improper functioning of market mechanisms, externalities, *etc.*, the state can intervene to reach the desired equilibrium point that encompasses the necessary environmental concerns. But here again the question arises as to what extent the capitalist state can escape from its own limits set by capital accumulation as this will jeopardize the continuity of capital circuit for environmental issues.

Another common economic goal for SD is to provide future generations with more assets per capita than current generation, since, as it is argued, capital produces well-being. In mainstream analysis, the dilemma of growth and environmental degradation ceases to exist if we consider that capital-assets may take different forms such as: man-made capital (machinery, factories, equipment); human capital (stock of knowledge, skills, health); natural capital (environment, nature); and social capital (sets of relations between people and institutions). Thus, it follows that the sum total of these assets must rise through time, in per capita terms, for there to be potentially SD. Hence, the increase of any of the above forms of capital will generate growth and, as a result, it turns to be only an issue of priorities how the goal of SD will be met within mainstream analysis.

TOWARD A SUSTAINABLE DEVELOPMENT

International experience has shown that capitalism generates a polarized system of great wealth together with extreme poverty, as well as, waste of natural and human resources. This mode of development imposes a huge burden on modern societies not only in terms of opportunities forgone, but also for the costs of managing social control and welfare tasks. Can a market-driven strategy bridge the chasm that is self- generated? The answer is clearly *no*, because a market-driven strategy has repeatedly proved that it cannot bridge the chasm that itself generates. The reason is that market signals, by and large, benefit profit motive and the identification of opportunities and possibilities of implementing approaches that provide SD requires more than well-intentioned policies. SD requires a restructuring of social forces and a move towards broad-based democratic participation in all aspects of life, within each country.

A pragmatic analysis and feasible proposals for SD should rely on the principles upon which capitalism operates. The driving motive of capitalism is self-expansion as a purpose in itself. We have to acknowledge the fact that societies normally are hostages to its growth since capitalism is by its very nature an expanding system. The expansion of economic activity creates new markets, products and technologies that make it possible for business to make profits. This overall expansion creates more opportunities and gives what the system needs, growth. But capitalist growth, as it turns out, involves environmental and social destruction and any proposed law to restrict pollution and enhance social cohesion decreases profits and results in stagnation and recession. Hence, a dilemma is put forward to modern societies.

A small step towards a sustainable growth is to establish a better way of assessing economic progress. GNP measures instead of placing high value to private benefits should count for social costs. In that way, measures on economic development and long-term growth will be lower or even negative and a major argument for profit motivated growth will vanish.[10] Of course, an alternative measure of economic activity by itself will not ensure a better natural and social environment. The fight against pollution and the achievement of sustainability goals is ultimately related to restriction and change of the private–enterprise system. Changing corporate behaviour requires organized pressure by a citizen movement which will force businesses to fully absorb the cost of their 'evils'. Reducing pollution is one part of a solution, but it does not eliminate capitalism's growth imperative, nor does eliminate the conflict between jobs and environment.

Another necessary step is assigning the public sector a more active role in determining industry policy. National and regional planning is necessary to direct investment toward development that preserves, rather than destroys the environment and only through public action an adequate number of jobs can be provided. The capitalist state has functional limits which are predetermined by the profit motive. Thus, if planning is left to the state, a democratic popular movement should be built to counterbalance the power of private businesses and the state itself. The experience of centrally planned economies showed that if state is driven solely by a growth imperative and not controlled by a people, its policies can abuse the matters of SD as badly as can private firms. Hence, a strong democratic well-informed and active population might be the answer to these issues.

In recent years, the environment crisis has worsened to the point where no one can ignore. Thus, minimal government involvement is present in many countries which, however, do not escape from mainstream economic analysis. The emphasis of these environmental policies is placed on controlling pollution and they have been unsuccessful. In fact, the goal of eliminating environmental degradation will be elusive as long as we rely on practices and technologies that generate pollution. Few real improvements will be achieved by adding control devices or concealing pollutants.

The answer to policy failures about SD is to direct public and private investments to research and developments programs that aim to develop new technologies and products which are environmentally friendly. Without denouncing the profit motive which is the driving force of a private capital, production with less polluted emissions because of new technologies or use of renewable resources might be steps forward to sustainability. Moreover, these efforts can take the form of a crusade by an international organization which will guide funds to appropriate programs. After all, globalization is here and it is time to turn it to a positive.

Sustainability is not 'simply' a matter of the environment, economic justice, and development. It is increasingly clear in our societies that pursuing development strategies must change and different approaches must be followed which will require more than the defence of our natural environment. We share the belief that something new is needed. But our argument leads us that an alternative strategy needs to be guided by vision supported by solid pragmatic analysis of capitalism and its laws of motion. In fact, vision and analysis are intertwined and as a result it is not enough just to describe the desirability of SD, but also to provide the detailed methods to implement it.

To our view, an alternative policy towards sustainability must take into account market signals and the way the economy operates. However, market signals and profit motive must be guided in a very precise way so as to lead to SD. This guidance cannot take the form of a command type of economy, simply because it will deprive people of incentives to actively participate in the decision making process. In addition, a command economy comes in direct conflict with the profit motive and the end result might be much worse from the current situation. We favour the idea of creating new democratically run national and international institutions which on the one hand will put new rules in the operations of markets so as to adjust cost and redirect supply decisions of firms; on the other hand, the same institutions will provide the necessary information to general public and make it increasingly more aware and sensitive to environmental issues. Consequently, if profit motive can be redirected to production of goods and services that account for the protection of the environment, the idea of SD might be possible.

CONCLUDING REMARKS

In conclusion, we can see the political element to play an increasingly important role by creating institutions that can regulate economic life to directions that on the one hand allow the reproduction of the society and on the other hand put more attention to sustainability issues. Of course, we must recognize the limitations that exist to political element which however can be strengthen by the support of segments of the society. In fact, our vision for SD cannot be parted from that capitalism is a society dominated by the profit motive, and all social relations (state, business sector, *etc.*) are constrained by the particular limits set by the pursuit of profits. The analysis of capitalism should not start from, or remain within the domain of markets, commerce and business, since these aspects represent only the outward face of the reality that we have to deal with.

NOTES

1. References have been kept to a minimum, although the literature on the topic is extensive.
2. These policies have been criticized on the grounds that they reflect a degree of 'northern' bias, since they consider that environmental problems are mainly a problem of the 'south' and that, although the 'north' has made some mistakes along the way, now it is on the right track. Hence, now, the 'north', in an arrogant way, attempts to prevent the 'south' from committing the same mistakes on the path to SD (Lohmann (1990)).
3. The Brundtland Commission in late 1980's has called for sustained growth rates of 5-6% in the developing countries and for 3-4% in the developed countries for the next 30 years in order to achieve a green-growth globally.
4. Education and life training is part of the working life, income distribution and social security are based on current or past participation in the labour force, whereas, social contracts, communication and participation are important elements of the working place and essential aspects to individual's well being. Hence, employment rate is suggested as a good indicator for social sustainability taking, however, into consideration the differences that individual societies might bear. The reason is that, in less developed countries where the informal sector dominates the economy or where social security is based not on public programs but rather on strong family ties, other indicators than paid work would be more relevant to use in exploring the social aspect of sustainability (Spangenberg (2004)).
5. Empirically, the Kuznets hypothesis suggests that economic growth at first leads to increased income disparities but the same growth, in a later phase, contributes to a more egalitarian pattern of income distribution. Studies have shown that the

Kuznets hypothesis is applicable only if public income is raised due to economic growth and it is used to establish a welfare state through its redistribution mechanisms (Spangenberg (2000, p. 77)).

6. 'The Social network refers to institutions, relationships and norms that shape the quality and quantity of a society's social interactions and it is not just the sum of the institutions within a society but the way which holds it together' (World Bank (1999)).
7. For Latin America countries studies have indicated that economic liberalization in the developing world has failed to generate dynamic economic growth, whereas its distributive effects have generally been adverse (Ocampo (2002)).
8. There are several studies showing that the 'social wage' does not exist, since what a labourer is called to pay (taxes, social security contribution, *etc.*) negates what he/she receives as public goods in developed countries (Maniatis, Tsaliki and Tsoulfidis (1999); Shaikh and Tonak (1987)).
9. In fact, firms' supply is derived from demand function.
10. Many industrialized countries, among them Japan, France, Germany and Norway, have similar measures that account for environmental destruction.

REFERENCES

Birkin, F. (2001), Steps to Natural Capitalism, *Sustainable Development,* 9, 47-57.

Broad, R. (1994), The Poor and the Environment: Friends and or Foes?, *World Development*, 22, 811-22.

Brown, B. (1993), *Fair Trade*, London, Zed Books.

Carvalho, O. G. (2001), Sustainable Development: Is It Achievable Within the Existing International Political Economy Context, *Sustainable Development*, 9, 61-73.

Charter, M. (1992), *Green Marketing*, Sheffield, Greenleaf Publication.

Chatterjee, P. and Finger, M. (1995), *The Earth Brokers: Power, Politics and World Development*, New York, Routledge.

Daly, H.E. (1991), *Steady State Economics*, Washington DC, Covelo.

Farrell, A. and Hart, M. (1998), What Does Sustainability Really Mean? The Search for Useful Indicators, *Environment*, 40, 26-31.

Gillis, M., Perkins, D.H., Roemer, M. and Snodgrass, D.R. (1996), *Economics of Development*, Norton, New York.

Griethuysen, P. (2002), Sustainable Development: An Evolutionary Economic Approach, *Sustainable Development*, 10, 1-11.

Hawken, P., Lovins, A. and Lovins, L. H. (1999), *Natural Capitalism: Creating the Next Industrial Revolution*, Boston, Little Brown.

Hediger, W. (2000), Sustainable Development and Social Welfare, *Ecological Economics*, 32, 481-92.

La Grega, M.D., Buckingham P.L. and Evans, J.C. (1994), *Hazardous Waste Management*, New York, McGraw-Hill.

Lamberton, G. (1998), Exploring the Accounting needs of an Ecologically Sustainable Development, *Accounting Forum*, 22, 186-209.

Lohmann, L. (1990), Whose Common Future?, *The Ecologist*, 20, 82-4.

Maniatis, Th., Tsaliki, P. and Tsoulfidis, L. (1999), *Issues in Political Economy: The Case of Greece* (in Greek), Athens, Sakis Karagiorga's Foundation.

Marx, K. (1865), *Capital I,* New York, International Publishers (1967).

Marx, K. (1894), *Capital III,* New York, International Publishers (1967).

Ocampo, J. A. (2002), Rethinking the Development Agenda, *Cambridge Journal of Economics,* 26, 393-407.

Panayotou, T. (1993), *Green Markets: The Economics of Sustainable Development*, San Francisco, ICS Press.

Panayotou, T. (1994), *Financing Mechanisms for Agenda 21*, Boston, Harvard Institute for International Development.

Pearce, D.W. and Turner, R.K. (1990), *Economics of Natural Resources and the Environment*, Baltimore, John Hopkins Press.

Rowledge, L.R., Barton, R.S. and Brady, K.S. (1999), *Mapping the Journey: Case Studies in Strategy and Actions Towards Sustainable Development*, Sheffield, Greenleaf.

Shaikh, A. (2004), The Power of Profit, *Social Research*, 71, 1-12.

Shaikh, A. and Tonak, A. (1987), The Welfare State and the Myth of the Social Wage, in R. Cherry *et al.* (eds), *The Imperiled Economy*, New York, Monthly Review Press.

Spangenberg, H. J. (2004), Reconciling Sustainability and Growth: Criteria, Indicators, Policies, *Sustainable Development*, 12, 74-86.

Strong, C. (1997), The role of Fair Trade Principles Within Sustainable Development, *Sustainable Development,* 5, 1-10.

Tietenberg, T. (1988), *Environmental and Natural Resource Economics*, Glenview, ÉÉÉ, Scott, Foresman.

World Bank (1999), What is Social Capital, www.world-bank.org

MID-RANGE THEORY AND THE DEVELOPMENTAL STATE DEBATE: THE CASES OF JAPAN AND SOUTH KOREA

Richard Westra*

This article develops the contribution of the Uno School's mid-range theorizing of capitalism for the study of economic development and advances its insights as key to sorting out issues in the state / market debate over the newly industrialized country (NIC) phenomenon in East Asia. It demonstrates how the production of knowledge of the East Asian NIC phenomenon and explanation of the role of market and state in development of Japan and South Korea proceeds through the periodizing of capitalism in the Uno approach and establishing by it of the core architecture of capital accumulation and state support in the post-war stage of consumerism. *The article concludes with comments on the potential held out by the capitalist market and capitalist state for development in Japan and Korea in the era of neo-liberal globalization.*

INTRODUCTION

Current market vs. state debate on economic development is rooted conceptually in an earlier face-off between modernization theory and dependency theory and empirically in competing views of the East Asian newly industrialized country (NIC) phenomenon (Westra (2006)). For modernization theory the market, meaning *capitalism*, is the telos of human history and the end-point at which economic development culminates. In dependency theory, the market, meaning capitalism as a 'world-system', is the source of asymmetric world-economic outcomes bringing capitalist development a-la-modernization theory to some and 'underdevelopment' and social impoverishment to others. What dependency theory proposes as the remedy to this predicament is for the state to act as a bulwark against global market forces, to promote indigenous national development, and as an apparatus for redistributing the fruits of this, possibly even fostering socialism. Leading up to the East Asian NIC posting of remarkable growth rates in the late 1970's and through the 1980's dependency theory had the upper hand as countries acceding to its policy implications to 'de-link' from global capitalism and advance national development and social redistribution made comparatively significant gains as measured by vital health and welfare indicators. The ascendancy of city-states Singapore and Hong Kong up the income ladder and South Korea and Taiwan into the forefront of world market

* Division of International and Area Studies, Pukyong National University, Pusan, South Korea.

competition in heavy industry and consumer durable production, purportedly through their free market links to global capitalism, served to vindicate modernization theory and neo-classical economics' neo-liberal policy prescriptions. So enamored over evidence of decades of NIC growth the neo-liberal global policy community codified its understanding of the NIC phenomenon and began peddling it as the panacea for the travails of the developing world as a whole (World Bank (1993)).

However, while the NIC phenomenon called into question the starker versions of dependency theory which maintained de-linking from global capitalism as the only development option, it never exorcized claims for the important role of the state in capitalist development. Focusing in on Japan and its ties to the NIC phenomenon, in particular to capitalist development in South Korea, a burgeoning literature challenged the redressed modernization theory of neo-liberalism with evidence that East Asian states were in fact 'developmental' (Johnson (1996)), and 'governed' the market (Wade (1990)) with market interfering policies to pick and support 'winning' companies (Amsden (1989)) while maintaining an 'embedded autonomy' (Evans (1995)) from market-generated social class outcomes. That this literature 'brings history back in' to the development discussion, integrating work on so-called 'catch-up development' which probes historical situations where late development is 'rationally' undertaken under state auspices (Hoogvelt (1997)), is important for enhancing understanding of some development processes and possibly making socially beneficial policy choices. But, it leaves a set of crucial questions unanswered. For example, what is it about the ontology of capitalism that allows for the analytical separation of market and state in the first place? Does exposing the deep structure of capital carry important ramifications for assessing potential limits of capitalist development? Is there in fact a unit of analysis problem or are national and global markets interchangeable concepts? And, are there varying historical forms and patterns of capitalist development that impact upon the realm of possibilities for the development of any developer?

A promising approach to the market/state debate in the critical neo-Marxist tradition, which attempts to overcome the deficiencies of dependency theory while accounting for the East Asian NIC phenomenon, is work of the Marxist *regulation school* (Lipietz (1987); Hurtienne (1989)). Regulation theory argues that analysis of capitalist development requires a 'mid-range' theory which studies capitalism at an 'institutional' level to capture the interfacing of markets and states in ways that ensure successful long-run accumulation across historical periods or *stages* of capitalism. According to regulation theory it is not a question of market *vs.* state but what sort of key labor processes the capitalist market operates with and what configuring of institutional structures are markets best embedded within to optimally 'regulate' their inherent contradictions. In the period following World War 2, it was the capitalist stage or 'regime of accumulation' of *fordism*, emanating from the United States (US), characterized by an institutional ensemble of assembly-line mass production, monopoly forms of competition, high wage and benefit bargains with labor, Keynesian state demand management, that regulated markets in core capitalist countries.

Regulation theory claims that profits were compromised when rising investment costs to meet economy of scale requirements could no longer be offset as technical limitations were reached in intensifying assembly-line work. Thus the task fragmentation and functional specialization characterizing key fordist industries became the foundation for spatially separating parts of the production process in order to recoup profits. The disciplined labor force, and legacies of the colonial past such as the absence of a landed class and presence of an industrial infrastructure, made Korea and Taiwan optimal locales for the spatial relocation of industrial branches historically coveted by core countries.

The contribution of this approach to the state/market debate over development is that it combines historical study of concrete development situations with analysis of predominant global patterns of capital accumulation in a fashion that captures systemic aspects of development elided in neo-liberal accounts while highlighting the geo-specific potential for capitalist development in East Asia under the auspices of developmental states that dependency theory missed. Its weaknesses are both conceptual and empirical. On the one side, regulation theory never expounds upon its notion of mid-range theory with respect to other ranges of theory–the abstract economic theory and economic history–that would presumably work together to study capitalist development (Westra (1998, 2003a)). As such its analysis never comes to grips with the historical specificity of the capitalist market and *capitalist* state in a way that captures the limits to capitalist development in the world as a whole. Further, the epistemology of concepts such as fordism is never clarified. Does fordism, for example, simply systematize empirical history of US capitalism? If this is the case, does development of Japan and South Korea require theorizing a 'new model' that accounts for their empirical nuances (Amsden (1990))? On the other side, Regulation theory was subjected to similar critiques as dependency theory that it simply 'read off' world economic outcomes such as NIC development in East Asia as a 'function' of core accumulation needs (Kiely (1995)).

This said I believe it is important not to throw out the baby with the bathwater. The purpose of this article is to develop the contribution of mid-range periodizing of capitalism for the study of economic development and advance its insights as key to sorting out issues in the state/market debate over the NIC phenomenon in East Asia. The position taken here, however, is that regulation theory is not the optimal vehicle with which to further that project. Rather it is maintained that critique of neo-liberalism, with its a-historical rendering of the market/state debate, and the salvaging of important elements of dependency and regulation theory, is best undertaken by the Japanese Uno approach[1] to political economy and mid-range theory. In the next section this article will summarize the provocative approach of the Uno School to the study of the deep inner structure of capital and outline its core conceptual architecture marshaled to treat problems of capitalist development. In the succeeding third section the Uno approach will be applied to post-World War 2 development of Japan and South Korea. This article demonstrates how the production of knowledge of the East Asian NIC phenomenon and understanding of the role of market and state in development proceeds through the periodizing of capitalism in the Japanese approach and establishing by it of the core structures of capital accumulation in the post-war stage. The article will conclude with a few words on the potential held out by the capitalist market and capitalist state for development in Japan and Korea in the era of neo-liberal globalization.

THE HISTORICAL SPECIFICITY OF CAPITALISM AND 'LEVELS OF ANALYSIS' IN DEVELOPMENT THEORY

From the perspective of the Uno approach, to effectively grapple with the array of complex questions marking the development field requires an understanding of the ontological peculiarity of capitalism as a social subject matter. In the economic historian Karl Polanyi's oft-cited observation, differing from pre-capitalist societies, the capitalist economy tends to 'dis-embed' itself from the politics, religion, etc, within which economic life had been historically enmeshed. Marx referred to this as capitalist 'fetishism' or 'reification' whereby the capitalist market converted social relations of production into impersonal, objective 'relations among things'. It is no accident therefore that economic theory emerges in the age of capitalism as its very condition of possibility is this rendering transparent by objective market operation of human economic relations. Yet this reifying of social relations also saddles the study of capitalist development with a problematic set of issues: First, capitalism manifests a certain *constant* or inner logic linked to its managing of economic life through objective society-wide, integrated systems of self-regulating markets; a logic that to a greater or lesser extent operates within each and every capitalist society irrespective of historical differences between them. Second, the history of capitalism has been marked by the existence of world-historic *stages* or phases of capitalist development with diverging geo-spatial dimensions and structures of accumulation; and the emergence of which, were *not* a teleological outcome of capital's logic. Third, capitalism has assumed multifarious forms throughout its historical existence, has been supported historically to greater or lesser extents by non-capitalist and non-economic social practices, and has always been subject to resistance and challenge by human agency, as well as the very exigencies of diverse use-value production.

It is to meet the conceptual demands of adequately capturing the homogenizing commodity-economic logic of capital in theory while treating diversity and compromising of that logic in history that Unoists prescribe a research strategy entailing three *levels of analysis*, each marshaling epistemologies appropriate to the specific aspect of their subject-matter, and operating in a division of labor, to produce the most complete and robust knowledge of capitalism. In the Unoist configuration, Marx's project embarked upon in his unparalleled *Capital*–the three volumes of which Unoists have recast and completed as *the theory of a purely capitalist society* (TPCS)[2]–constitutes the most abstract level of theory, given its task of exploring the logical inner principles of operation of the capitalist commodity economy. The abstract tenure of the theory of a purely capitalist society derives from the rigorous demands of its subject terrain, where to fully apprehend the commodity-economic logic of *capital*–that constant of all historical capitalism's–it must study it unencumbered by any non-economic, non-capitalist interference. To robustly defend the methodological procedure required for the theorizing of capital in the theory of a purely capitalist society would outstrip the bounds of this article. It may, however, be caricatured as follows: The working proposition is that the role of economic theory is to investigate the *modus operandi* of a reified 'economic' society where all use-values including human labor power itself are comodified and human economic life itself reproduced for the abstract purpose of value augmentation. The process of theory construction is guided by the very abstract and objective structure of its subject-matter, such that the TPCS logically unfolds all the categories of capital in a *dialectical* thought experiment.[3] Beginning with the 'contradiction' between value and use value in the commodity, as in Marx's *Capital*, the TPCS traces out the circulation, production and distribution forms of capital and achieves closure with the generation of the category of *interest* when capital, which germinates in the commodity, ultimately returns to it.

While the theory of a purely capitalist society studies capital with the highest degree of precision and objectivity possible in a social research endeavor, this is accomplished at the cost of creating a gulf between the theorizing of capital and the study of actual capitalist history. It is to mediate that movement in thought that necessitates the mid-range level of analysis or what Unoists dub *stage theory*.[4] Now the TPCS was predicated upon the necessary assumption that the march of value in history faces no resistance and capital can simply realize a global commodity economy where all use-values are converted into value objects and material life regulated by integrated systems of self-regulating markets. Only in this way, by permitting capital to have its way with the world, is it possible to expose capital for what it truly *is*. The TPCS also establishes the ontological foundation of the analytical separation of market and state in the study of capitalism. That is, at its level of abstraction, the TPCS demonstrates the possibility of economic life of an entire human society being reproduced solely through the commodity-economic operation of the self-regulating market with no extra-economic, extra-capitalist support. Across its history however, actually existing capital has never materialized such a stark society. The recalcitrance of use-values, non-capitalist ways of being, class struggle, etc. have in so many unique ways cropped up as obstacles to capital and refract capital's logic and its logical contradictions. Stage theory, therefore, concretizes the contradiction between value and use-value in the TPCS through its *structural* epistemology analyzing world-historic stages of capitalist development characterized by distinct structures of capital accumulation reflecting the *interplay* of the logical constant of capital (its self-regulating market) and capitalist augmenting of value with production of stage specific use-values.

These use-values–*wool*, *cotton*, *steel*, and the *automobile*–underpin leading sectors of capitalism and shape the structure of accumulation in its world-historic stages. They also require capital to assume concrete stage specific forms, respectively *merchant capital*, *industrial capital*, *finance capital*, and *corporate capital*, to manage their production. It is at the mid-range stage level of analysis that theory must confront the fact that though held implicit in the TPCS, capital itself necessarily 'brings the state back in' to support accumulation and manage the externalities that plague it across its history. The Uno approach names stages according to the characteristic stage specific *state* policies which support capital and manage the key externalities facing it. Respectively, these are *mercantilism, liberalism, imperialism*, and *consumerism*. While the TPCS theorizes value augmentation as it proceeds with geo-spatial homogeneity to materialize a global commodity-economy the world economic spread of capitalism historically has been extremely uneven. Stage theory treats this by theorizing accumulation at representative stage specific geographic sites and with the identification of predominant *national* accumulator(s) of each stage. For mercantilism and liberalism this was Britain. Germany and the United States (US) were the dominant imperialist capital accumulators. And for the stage of consumerism, the US was the representative stage specific site (See Figure 1).

It is precisely the problematic of actually existing capitalism's geo-spatial development–that, on the one hand, capital historically germinates within the geo-spatial contours of the nation state, yet maintains global pretensions, while on the other hand, its uneven development leads to the rise of a particular state in which accumulation initially advances – that requires mid-range analysis to theorize a stage specific international dimension of capital; though in the same epistemological terms as stage theoretic analysis as whole, where international accumulation is theorized as a dominant type or pattern.

Finally, *historical analysis* – the third level of analysis in the Uno approach – is epistemologically distinct from stage theory as it is concerned with *process* and *agency*, regarding the becoming, actual geo-spatial spread, transformation and passing of capital. And historical analysis focuses upon the panoply of historical-empirical variety in human material life.

To sum up, in operationalizing of levels of analysis several points must be kept in mind. First, if by so-called market development is meant an *economic* process, purged of all extra-capitalist, extra-economic interferences, such is possible solely under the highly restrictive conditions of value augmentation elaborated in the TPCS. In capitalist history, if there ever exists a stage of capitalist development where the modalities of accumulation approximate the 'purity' of capital captured in theory, it is the stage of *liberalism* theorized through the prism of Britain's domestic 'golden age' of laissez faire with its small business, entrepreneurial, price-competitive economy. Though even here, the involvement of the state looms large in managing the international dimension of liberalist capital. Other stages of capitalist development, as illustrated in Figure 1, necessitate even greater quotients of state support for accumulation.

Second, while there constitutes a family resemblance with regulation theory in theorizing post-war capital in terms of the structure of US accumulation it is superficial (Westra (1998, 2003a)). With its structural epistemology stage theory is synchronic and theorizes the characteristic forms and patterns of accumulation based on the advanced type of capital and state support system abstracted from capital's most advanced geographical site for the stage. Though structures of US capital constitute the basis for theorizing the stage of *consumerism*, to actually study really existing US capitalism would require historical analysis. In other words, no historical outcomes can be read-off stage theory. Whether stage

Figure 1
Stages of Capitalism

Stage	*Golden Age*	*Representative Use-value*	*Form of Capital*	*Structure of Accumulation*	*State Form + Management of Key Externalities*
Mercantilism (British Hegemony)	1700-50	Wool	Merchant Capital	- 'putting out system' - primitive accumulation - commodification of labor-power+ land	-emerging legal form of *rechtsstaat* -consolidation of national market
Liberalism (British Hegemony)	1850-73	Cotton	Industrial Capital	-entrepreneurial/owner operated business - external transactions/ market price signals - internationalization of commodity circuits	- *laissez faire* 'night-watchman' state domestically -colonialism+ coveting of raw materials - control over colonial markets
Imperialism (Germany/USA Hegemony)	1890-1914	Steel/ Chemicals	Finance Capital	- monopoly/oligopoly - bank/industry union - joint stock company - internationalization of portfolio finance circuits	- *Sozialpolitic* welfare state - *Weltpolitik* expansionism -international competition for resources and markets - militarization+division of globe into spheres
Consumerism (USA Hegemony)	1950-73	Automobile (consumer durable complex)	Corporate Capital	-oligopoly/MNC's -economic programming/ programming/(transaction cost issues) - 'technostructure' (principal/agent issues) -global governance -fixed currencies/ capital controls -managed 'free trade' -formal decolonization Internationalization of Productive Capital Circuits	-Keynesian developmental welfare state -projects of national development -credit, fiscal, monetary policy supporting mass consumption -class accords+ wage -vehement anti-communism

structures of consumerism promote a certain amount of development or underdevelopment is an empirical issue; though one which is contextualized by stage theory and where stage theory offers insights into the shape and realm of possibilities of development or underdevelopment. And, from the perspective of the Uno approach, analysis of particular situations of capitalist development also demands historical study of the pre-capitalist political economic milieu.

MARKET AND STATE IN THE DEVELOPMENT OF JAPAN AND SOUTH KOREA IN THE POSTWAR CAPITALIST STAGE OF CONSUMERISM

To be sure, apprehending Japan's historical process of capitalist development would require a combination of historical analysis and stage theoretic analysis of *imperialism*. Unique in Asia, Japan's pre-capitalist economy manifested similar transformatory impulses as those leading to the rise of capitalism in Western Europe (Preston (2000)). And, early twentieth century Japanese accumulation followed the 'late' catch-up development pattern of imperialist accumulators like Germany that struggled to meet the capital formation exigencies of a globally competitive steel industry. Japan's trajectory of colonization and militarism also recapitulates patterns of imperialism, where in Japan's case, bellicose territorial aggrandizement was viewed as key to it's balance of payments problems as it sought to import advanced technology from 'early' developers that had already colonized much of the world (Halevi (1999)). As well, Korea's history as a colony of Japan, something that also merits study through the prism of the stage theory of imperialism, is extremely pertinent to understanding aspects of Korea's later capitalist development.

What this article is concerned with however, is the way consumerism, the stage of capitalism following imperialism, shapes our understanding of Japanese and South Korean capitalism. This section combines stage theory and historical analysis as levels of analysis in Unoist Marxian political economy to contribute to an understanding of their development and the role of market and state in the development processes. Its procedure will be to trace out connections between the paradigmatic structures of capital in the stage of consumerism and those of Japanese and Korean capital and to offer commentary on the interfacing of these. The structures of capital to be treated are as follows: use value; form of capital; international dimension of capital; state and superstructure; capital/labor relation.

Use Value: The TPCS which constitutes a general, abstract theory of capitalism leaves use-value unspecified. Stage theory concretizes use-value by theorizing the interplay of capital's abstract logic and a stage specific form of use-value production. Consumerism, as a stage of capitalism, is characterized by the production of consumer durables with the automobile being the representative type. Automobile productions' expansive backward and forward linkages and its sheer material accouterment are unrivalled by any other capitalist production sector. The automobile industry constitutes the predominant industry in global trade, and one needs to look no further than the mainstream business press to appreciate the extent to which automobile production persists as the bell-weather industry of world capitalist accumulation.

As with steel in the late nineteenth century a national automobile industry is viewed as a hallmark of modern industrial development; just as the automobile is idiosyncratic of contemporary life (Law (1991)).

In use-value terms, as per the stage specific structure of consumerist accumulation, autos rapidly emerged as the core industry of Japanese capitalism. At the wars' end Japan was home to only 110,000 cars. By 1970 that number had rocketed to 17.8 million clearly stamping Japan as an automobile society (Westra (1998)). By the 1980's one in ten of all Japanese workers were involved in automobile production or industries directly related to it (Abegglen (1994, p. 32)). And Japanese automobile production would quickly soar to global prominence capturing 30% of world market share by 1981. As per the stage specific structure of consumerist accumulation autos rapidly emerged as the core industry of Korean capitalism. In fact, Korea 'compresses' the historical process of over a century of development experienced by the developed countries (including Japan) from light to heavy/chemical to consumer durable industry into a few decades (Watanabe (1992, pp. 103-8)). In the 1980's Korea's emergence as a prominent player in the world automobile industry embodies the dramatic shift that occurs in global automobile production during the last decades of the twentieth century (Bloomfield (1991)). While the export prowess of Korea is a well-documented subject it is not generally appreciated the extent to which Korea constitutes an automobile society ranking fifth in the world in 1998 in automobiles per 1000 population (163 in that year) and evidencing an exponential increase in automobile ownership of 2228.6% between 1980 and 1998–the largest of any country in the world during that period (Conybeare (2003, p. 66)).

Form of Capital: For capital to viably manage the production of a complex use-value such as the automobile it is necessary that it adopt an appropriate form. Corporate capital, the characteristic form of capital for the stage of consumerism differs qualitatively from both the entrepreneurial owner operated *industrial* capital of liberalism and *finance capital's* bank-dominated, bank/industry union of imperialism. Corporate capital shares the joint-stock form of finance capital but is marked by a series of novel stage specific features including: complex mixtures of vertically and horizontally integrated geographically dispersed production branches warranting the appellation multinational corporation (MNC), high degrees of management control, internalized intra-corporate transactions and transfer pricing, and an overall propensity toward economic planning and programming. Questions of the fit with Japanese and Korean capital may be dealt with through the lens of debate over so-called 'models' of post-war capitalism (Coates (2000)). The argument goes like this: Japanese *keiretsu* and Korean *chaebol* are marked by business networks and multi-subsidiary structures, draw increasingly upon personal relations and 'trust' among grouping affiliates to share investment responsibility and risk, spawn under the auspices of a single entrepreneur/family and flourish viz. political patronage. These features, it is claimed set East Asian capital apart from the impersonal modes of corporate governance of US capital with its more arms-length supply links and reliance upon a stock market dominated by individual investors for finance. However, in following Coates (2000, 149ff.), and striving to control for factors of historical catch-up, our response is this: first, US corporate capital at its inception also spawns around the entrepreneur/family (Ford. Carnegie, Rockefeller, etc.) and in its heyday certainly enjoyed political patronage comparable to that of East Asian capital. Second, the shift of *keiretsu* and *chaebol* into higher value-added production of consumer electronics and automobiles, characteristic of the stage of consumerism, has engendered a management technostructure and transformation in management style (Watanabe (1992)); a transformation currently being reinforced by government legislation to render businesses more accountable to individual shareholders. Third, on the question of ownership, as a noted business analyst explains (Abegglen (1994)), East Asian corporate capital is not alone in its structure of business groupings as European capital is marked by both the *keiretsu*-style bank-centered pattern and the *chaebol* form of entrepreneur/family control. Such configuring reflects the historical need of capital to tap into varying sources of investment. From the perspective of stage theory, both the so-called 'Nippo-Rhenish' model and Anglo-US model are simply variant responses to similar problems of managing transaction costs and that of principal and agent (Woo-Cumings (2001); Kester (1996)); problems stage specific to corporate capital given its development of the joint stock form and diversified horizontally and vertically integrated organizational structure. Fourth, on the issue of supplier links, indications are, particularly in the stage specific consumer durable/auto industry, that the tight coupling of tasks which optimally requires increased horizontal integration and fostering of long term relations with suppliers acts as a powerful force for industrial convergence across models of post war capitalism (Thelen and Kume (1999)). As Abegglen (1994, p. 205) puts it, 'this group versus individual characterization of East and West demands a good deal of qualification if it is to fit specific realities. But it does serve to identify what seems generally agreed to be a difference in fact, if in degree more than in kind'. And it is precisely the question of 'kind' that I argue is the crux of stage theory. Stage theory is required to theorize the form or kind of capital most representative of the stage and elaborate upon the stage specific modalities through which it is able to viably manage production of the characteristic use-value of a stage.

International Dimension of Capital: The Uno approach treats the unit of analysis problem of development theory through levels of analysis. At the level of stage theory, capital accumulation, including the international dimension of capital is theorized as an abstract type of capital idiosyncratic of capitalist development in the stage as a whole. Though stage theory is abstracted from the most advanced geo-spatial site of accumulation in a stage, it is *not* a theory of 'national' capital (US capital, for example, in the stage of consumerism) or of capital as a 'world system'. Rather it is a theory of the stage specific modalities of accumulation in all their dimensions. In commencing analysis with the view of capitalism as a world system, dependency theory occludes the paramount question of the extent to which capital is truly global across its history and that of the different forms international capital assumes.

If there is a signal distinguishing feature of international capital in the stage of consumerism it is the internationalization of production including:

foreign direct investment, international technology licensing, international subcontracting, leasing, management agreements and so on. Supporting the internationalization of production is the internationalization of finance and banking. It is the internationalization of production and spread of global commodity chains that creates a genuine international division of labor for the first time in the history of capitalism. In prior world-historic stages of accumulation international capital is characterized by the concentration of global industrial production in the hands of a limited group of core states. While Regulation-type mid-range theories explain the NIC phenomenon of industrialization largely in functionalist terms of core capitals' changing needs, an alternate framework is proposed here. The fact is, the exigencies of consumerist accumulation congealing around the mass production and mass consumption of a use-value complex of consumer durables (the automobile being the representative type)–whether approached in 'supply side' terms of the modalities of corporate capitals' integration of diverse economic sectors and production branches or in 'demand side' terms considering the requirement for capital to ensure ever-expanding effective demand–renders the geo-spatial dispersal of production a paradigmatic condition of accumulation in the stage of consumerism from the outset.

Again, the initial international thrust of Japanese capital at the dawn of the twentieth century requires stage theorizing of imperialism to contextualize. In the stage of consumerism however, immediately following the war, Japanese accumulation seemed to buck the trend of internationalization of production proceeding largely as a domestic project maintaining a low rate of export dependency (Itoh (2000, p. 4)). Behemoths of Japan's corporate capital had no foreign subsidiaries in 1962 while US MNC's had 1040. This however would soon change with 13 foreign subsidiaries of Japanese MNC's emplaced by 1971, 64 by 1983, 310 by 1991 and 2296, almost rivaling the US, in 1998 (Kentor (2005)).[5]

Korea connects with global commodity chains on the supply side initially as assembler and producer of low cost standardized products for mass consumption. In this process Korea benefits from the emergence in the 1960's of what has been proclaimed '[o]ne of the most significant developments' of the international economy–international subcontracting (Dicken (1998, p. 223)). In particular, Korean development is marked by two facets of this, Original Equipment Manufacturing (OEM) and Own-design and manufacture (ODM). Through OEM Korean firms first gain valuable technical and organizational expertise under the auspices of foreign companies that market their products. With ODM Korean firms 'reverse engineer' industrial processes, technology and components while producing under the design requirements of the foreign companies marketing the goods (Dasgupta (1998, pp. 268-72)). The growth in indigenous productive capacity which the foregoing engenders can be charted empirically in the upward spike of Korea's export-import ratio in trade of industrial goods with both Japan and the world, as well as in Korea's increasing rates of domestic investment as opposed to foreign investment (Watanabe (1992, p. 95-103)). With respect to the demand side of global commodity chains, as suggested by Halevi and Kriesler

(1998), the rise of Korea to the forefront of world market competition meets two vital challenges of the necessity of expanding effective demand in the stage of consumerism. On the one hand, it helps solve the problem of demand for Japanese industrial exports that plagued Japan in the pre-war period. On the other hand the rapid productivity growth of Korean *chaebol* in export industries results in a fall in prices of exports to the benefit of foreign consumers. Nevertheless, as Abegglen (1994) points out, a feature distinguishing Korea from other NIC's is the weight of domestic consumption. The international dimension of Korean corporate capital contributes to what Halevi and Kriesler (1998) dub 'full range industrialization' as opposed to the extroverted economy dependency theory claimed to be the fate of developing states.

State and Superstructure: The analytical separation of state and market in the study of capitalism resides in the tendency of capital toward reifying economic life. And that the meaning of 'development' as solely a product of the 'market' makes sense *only* in the context of the TPCS where it is assumed by *theory* that all use-value obstacles or oppositions to capital are neutralized and capital organizes a commodity economy solely according to abstract market principles with the goal of augmenting value. Though a pure capitalist society never emerges in history the TPCS is not invalidated: for it only extrapolates to conclusion tendencies of the deep inner logic of capital to optimally capture what it *is*. Stage theory works with knowledge of this constant of capitalism to explore ways the capitalist state *internalizes* or manages extra-economic, extra-capitalist externalities that beset capitalism in history. Stage theory thus concretizes the analysis of the TPCS to study capital as it accumulates with key types of use-value production and forms of capital supported by stage-specific policies.

The stage of consumerism characterized by the automobile industry of corporate capital represents the furthest move *away* from market principles by capitalism in its history. Obvious empirical indicators of this derive from the organizational modalities and scale/scope economies of corporate capital that compel it to rely less and less on external market transactions based upon market prices thus transforming the nature of economic competition (Korten (1995)). Further, the investment requirements of corporate capital increasingly saddle it with strategically managing the effective demand for its expensive consumer durables. Such a shift in the fundamental structure of capital expands both the range of externalities for the capitalist state to manage and the extent of extra-economic supports required by capital to successfully accumulate. To meet the policy challenges it faces the capitalist state of consumerism is equipped with an arsenal of interventions (see Figure 1). But, while state policy to manage the externalities of the dominant form of capital is the centerpiece of analyzing the superstructure in stage theory, as Albritton (1991) argues, particularly with regards to the stage of consumerism (though to complete stage analysis generally), it is vital to assess how other social practices such as ideology and politics coalesce with state policy in support of capital. Of significance here, and to be treated below, is the consumerist ideology of vehement anti-communism.

To be sure, the conceptualizing of a 'developmental state' in the context of NIC economic growth is not groundless. But the notion that its obverse in post-Second World War capitalism is a sort of 'night-watchman' state *is*. As Coates (2000, p. 223) puts it, no state can 'free either itself or its class base from the generalized logics of accumulation which characterized world capitalism as a whole'. And, if world capitalism in the stage of consumerism has a 'logic' shaping state action, it is one that operates within the international institutional parameters of the Bretton Woods monetary system facilitating state governed projects of national development. This 'economic nationalism' (Brown and Lauder (2001, p. 16)) in effect makes developmental policy of a sort a mainstay of state policy *per se* for consumerism. In fact, the US state consistently directs finance toward 'picking winners', specifically in defense and agriculture. Also, the US state maintains a de facto industrial policy in its proclivity to bail out corporate capital when required and regulate industry with an eye to international competitive outcomes (Coates (2000, pp. 202-3)). During the 1960's the US state resorted to varying forms of capital controls to support corporate capital's interests (Simmons (1999, p. 40)).

The role of the Japanese state in the post-war period falls clearly within the parameters of stage specific policy package of consumerism. For example, it maintained favorable rates of interest as an encouragement for investments in industry and subsidies for agriculture which facilitated not only a massive transfer of labor from that sector to industry but a substantial rise in rural incomes permitting the agricultural population to share in the middle class consumption of consumer durables. Further, on the heels of the oil shock, the Japanese government spurred an economic recovery with massive public expenditure in classic Keynesian fashion. Much, of course, has been made in the state/market debate over the thrust of neo-liberal reforms in Japan particularly as they were promoted under the auspices of Japan's so-called 'big bang' deregulations. However, neo-liberal reforms have not produced a diminution in state intervention in the economy but increased it as Japanese state public spending expanded to rescue financial institutions mired in neo-liberal policy induced debt (Itoh (2000)).

The view of the developmental state to which a so-called market economy is counter-posed in the Korean case is drawn from experience of the 1970's Yushin system of Park Chung Hee. In comparative perspective, it is precisely this period of the 'great spurt' where West European (and Japanese) development also manifest hypertrophied state participation in industry combined with authoritarian politics; a policy profile which then changes as these economies shift to consumer durable production (Kurth (1979)). With the receding of Korea's great spurt so state/business relations also begin to change. This process of transformation coincided with the US global pressure on developing states to adopt neo-liberal reforms. Nevertheless, actions like the merging of the Economic Planning Board in 1993 and International Monetary Fund pressure leading to Korea's equivalent of the big bang, the 'big deal' effort to reform the *chaebol* and privatize financial institutions, depends upon the state (Cherry (2005)). As such, neo-liberal deregulation in Japan and Korea does *not* reflect a transition to some a-historical 'market' development but the re-channeling of state power towards managing new externalities besetting capital as it struggles to successfully accumulate around consumer durable production with all the domestic and international ramifications of this.

In no stage of capitalism do extra-economic practices play such a prominent role in support of capital as in the capitalist stage of consumerism. With the spread of Soviet power internationally and the growth of giant collectivities such as the welfare/warfare state domestically, the ideology of anti-communism emerges as a cornerstone of accumulation for consumerism. Anti-communism paid handsome economic dividends to Japan. The 'reverse course' policy that led the US occupation to support Japan's re-industrialization and reassembling of its corporate conglomerates (*zaibatsu* to *keiretsu*) followed on the heels of Mao's victory in China. Direct military procurements from Japan by the US in 1952-56 equaled $3.4 billion and 25% of US commodity imports. Korean War demand would double output of Japan's major industries and spur development of an indigenous auto industry in Japan. Further, Japan was the recipient of generous technology transfers from the US and a politically articulated favorable yen/dollar exchange rate (Westra (1998)). The impact of the ideology of anti-communism upon Korean development is also momentous. In the years 1945-65 Korea obtained $12 billion from the US equal to 100 per cent of the Korean government budget during the 1950's. In fact, capitalist development in Korea emerges as the 'most significant...outside Japan because it was based on a deliberate linkage between the objective of creating a national capital in the country and the role of both Japan and the United States which accepted and sustained the above objective' (Halevi and Kriesler (1998, p. 88)). Korea's early export orientation was part of US strategy seeking to reduce the dependence on aid of its anti-communist partner. And the Vietnam War was also indispensable to Korea's industrial development. By 1967, it is pointed out (Halevi and Kriesler (1998, p. 86)), the share of Korea's total exports by sector going to South Vietnam was: steel (94.29%); transportation equipment (51.75%); non-electrical machinery (40.77%).

Capital/labor Relation: With a use value such as the automobile, an expensive consumer durable requiring a massive capital outlay for its production and secured market for its consumption, corporate capital is pressured to arrive at a *modus vivendi* with labor making consumerism the stage of the 'class accord'. Antagonistic class struggle is deflected by the inclusion of labor unions in projects of economic nationalism where sanctioned worker action revolves around bargaining over wage and benefit packages and unions are effectively de-politicized as a condition of inclusion. Maintaining consensual labor relations emerges as a major externality for capital which then draws in the state as its ultimate guarantor such that the class accord becomes 'tripartite' or 'corporatist'. The state also tops up the benefits for labor with a social wage.

As with the structure of corporate capital, labor relations in Japan represent small variation from the form of class accord characteristic consumerism. Japan's post-war labor relations were in fact imported from the US under the auspices of US brokered anti-communist reconstruction (Gordon (1998)). During 1955-70 real wages increased dramatically facilitating the mass consumption of consumer durables. That the rise lagged somewhat behind productivity increases was offset in the Japanese class accord by a system of life-time employment in dominant industries (Itoh (2000)). In 1973, the state would initiate a public social wage system with benefits comparable to other Western countries (Takahashi (1997)). In tracing out connections between the class accord of consumerism and Korean labor relations the important anomaly to recognize is the way these emerged under the auspices of an authoritarian state; though an authoritarian state that never sought to prevent union organization among workers, rather effectively co-opting and shaping it through 'state corporatism' (Choi (1989)). With the transition of Korean capitalism towards consumer durable production and subsequent democratization tripartite labor relations develop as in other consumerist states (Koo (2001)). Democracy also contributes to labor's ability to exact wage increases from capital (Jeong (1997)). And, in line with the consumerist capital/labor relation, democratization yields an expansion of state social welfare and insurance provisioning constituting what is dubbed a 'productivist welfare state' in Korea (Holliday and Wilding (2003)). Finally, neo-liberalism has paradoxically led to a fortification of Korea's social wage system (Kim (2005)); an outcome arguably flowing from the necessity of maintaining effective demand for consumer durables at the core of Korean capital accumulation as per the structure of accumulation of the stage of consumerism.

CONCLUSION

This article sought to make the case for mid-range theory and levels of analysis in Marxian political economy, as elaborated by the Uno approach, for rethinking questions of market and state in development theory. Signal article points are as follows: First, given the ontological structure of capital it is possible to theorize capitalist development as solely an outcome of unimpeded market operations under the assumption of total reification captured in the TPCS. Second, as capital is confronted by the exigencies of managing the real economic life of human society, though its reifying logic operates as a constant, the logic is refracted by a welter of oppositions to capital. Stage theory conceptualizes these in terms of world-historic architectures of accumulation that arise to manage stage specific forms of use-value production. Third, the article demonstrates how explanation of post-war development of Japan and South Korea flows through the prism of analysis of the stage theory of consumerism; a mainstay of the capital accumulation of which is extensive state management of burgeoning externalities. Finally, neo-liberalism constitutes a paradoxical amalgam of structures of consumerist accumulation yet with the state seeking to abdicate its responsibility for managing the externalities that capital required of it in its role as a *capitalist state* (Westra (2003b)). However, this does not represent a transition toward some a-historical 'market' capitalism; for the cases of Japan and Korea illustrate neo-liberalism has simply altered the duties of states. The question the Uno approach allows us to pose, however, is whether this heralds a wider process of the disintegration of capitalism rendering consumerism as the final stage?

NOTES

1. Uno (1980) is an English translation of an abridgement of Kozo Uno's two volume opus of the same name; the latter two available only in Japanese.
2. Sekine (1997) is an up-to-date two volume recasting of *Capital* which develops Uno's work further (see note 1), and engages with neo-classical adversaries.
3. On dialectics in Marxian political economy, see Kourkoulakos (2003).
4. Though debated among Unoists, Albritton (1991) is the most comprehensive English language effort to develop Uno's stage theory.
5. How Japan's consumerist internationalization dealt with supply side and demand side constraints will be touched upon in relation to the impact of consumerism's ideology of anti-communism.

REFERENCES

Abegglen, J. C. (1994), *Sea Change: Pacific Asia as the New World Industrial Center* New York, The Free Press.

Albritton, R. (1991), *A Japanese Approach to Stages of Capitalist Development*, London, Macmillan.

Amsden, A. (1989), *Asia's Next Giant: South Korea and Late Industrialization*, New York, Oxford University Press.

Amsden, A (1990), Third World Industrialization: 'Global Fordism' or a New Model?, *New Left Review*, 182, 5-31.

Bloomfield, G.T. (1991), The World automotive industry in transition, in C.M. Law (ed.), *Restructuring the Global Automobile Industry*, London, Routledge.

Brown, P. and Lauder, H. (2001), *Capitalism and Social Progress: The Future of Society in the Global Economy*, Basingstoke, Palgrave.

Cherry, J. (2005), 'Big Deal' or Big Disappointment? The continuing evolution of the South Korean developmental state, *The Pacific Review*, 18, 327-54.

Choi, J. J. (1989), *Labor and the Authoritarian State*, Seoul: Korea University Press.

Conybeare, J.A.C. (2003), *Merging Traffic: The Consolidation of the International Auto Industry*, Lanham, Rowman and Littlefield.

Dasgupta, B. (1998), *Structural Adjustment, Global Trade and the New Political Economy of Development*, London, Zed Books.

Dicken, P. (1998), *Global Shift: Transforming the World Economy*, London, The Guilford Press.

Evans, P. (1995), *Embedded Autonomy: States and Industrial Transformation*, Princeton: Princeton University Press.

Gordon, A. (1998), *The Wages of Affluence: Labor and Management in Postwar Japan* Cambridge, Mass., Harvard University Press.

Halevi, J. (1999), The accumulation process in Japan and East Asia as compared with the role of Germany in European post-war growth, in R. Bellofiore(ed.), *Global Money, Capital Restructuring and the Changing Patterns of Labour*, Cheltenham, Edward Elgar.

Halevi, J. and Kriesler, P. (1998), History, politics and effective demand in Asia, in J. Halevi and J.-M. Fontaine (eds), *Restoring Demand in the World Economy: Trade, Finance and Technology*, Cheltenham, Edward Elgar.

Holliday, I. and Wilding, P. (2003), *Welfare Capitalism in East Asia: Social Policy in the Tiger Economies*, Basingstoke, Palgrave.

Hoogvelt, A. (1997), *Globalization and the Postcolonial World: The New Political Economy of Development*, Baltimore, MD, Johns Hopkins University Press.

Hurtienne, T. (1989), Theories of Development, Differentiation of the Periphery and Development Strategies of the NIC's, in W. Vath (ed.), *Political Regulation in the 'Great Crisis'*, Berlin, Sigma.

Itoh, M. (2000), *The Japanese Economy Reconsidered*, Basingstoke, Palgrave.

Jeong, S. J. (1997), The Social Structure of Accumulation in South Korea: Upgrading or Crumbling?, *Review of Radical Political Economics*, 29, 92-112.

Johnson, C. (1996), *Japan: Who Governs? The Rise of the Developmental State*, New York, W. W. Norton.

Kentor, J. (2005), The Growth of Transnational Corporate Networks: 1962-1998, *Journal of World Systems Research*, 11, 263-86.

Kester, C.W. (1996), American and Japanese Corporate Governance: Convergence to Best Practice, in S. Berger and R. Dore, R. (eds), *National Diversity and Global Capitalism*, Ithaca, Cornell University Press.

Kiely, R. (1995), *Sociology and Development: The Impasse and Beyond*, London, UCL Press.

Kim, S. (2005), Economic Crisis, Domestic Politics and Welfare State Changes, *The Pacific Review*, 18, 375-91.

Koo, H. (2001), *Korean Workers: The Culture and Politics of Class Formation*, Ithaca, Cambridge University Press.

Korten, D. C. (1995), *When Corporations Rule the World*, West Hartford, Connecticut, Kumarian Press.

Kourkoulakos, S. (2003), The Specificity of Dialectical Reason, in R. Albritton and J. Simoulidis, *New Dialectics and Political Economy*, Basingstoke, Palgrave.

Kurth, J. R. (1979), The Political Consequences of the Product Cycle: Industrial History and Political Outcomes, *International Organization*, 33, 1-34

Law, C. M. (1991), Motor Vehicle Manufacturing: the Representative Industry, in C.M. Law (ed.), *Restructuring the Global Automobile Industry*, London, Routledge.

Lipietz, A. (1987), *Miracles and Mirages*, London, Verso.

Preston, P.W. (2000), Understanding Modern Japan: A Political Economy of Development, Culture and Global Power, London, Sage.

Sekine, T. (1997), *An Outline of the Dialectic of Capital*, 2 vols, London, Macmillan Press.

Simmons, B. A. (1999), The Internationalization of Capital, in H.P. Kitschelt, P. Lange, G. Marks and J.D. Stephens (eds), *Continuity and Change in Contemporary Capitalism*, Cambridge, Cambridge University Press.

Takahashi, M. (1997), *The Emergence of Welfare Society in Japan* Aldershot, Avebury.

Thelen, K. and Kume, I. (1999), The Effects of Globalization on Labor Revisited: Lessons from Germany and Japan, *Politics and Society*, 27, 476-504.

Uno, K. (1980), *Principles of Political Economy: Theory of a Purely Capitalist Society*, Brighton, The Harvester Press Ltd.

Wade, R. (1990), *Governing the Market: Economic Theory and the Role of Government in East Asian Industrialism*, Princeton, Princeton University Press.

Watanabe, T. (1992), *Asia: Its Growth and Agony*, Hawaii, University of Hawaii Press.

Westra, R. (1998), Periodizing Capitalism and the Political Economy of Post-war Japan, in E.R. Beauchamp (ed.), *The Japanese Economy and Economic Issues since 1945. Dimensions of Contemporary Japan: vol. 5*, New York, Garland.

Westra, R. (2003a), Social theory, economic crisis, and the Japanese political economy: a review article, *Review of International Political Economy*, 10, 363-73.

Westra, R. (2003b), Globalization: The Retreat of Capital to the 'Interstices' of the World?, in R. Westra and A. Zuege (eds.), *Value and the World Economy Today: Production, Finance, and Globalization*, Basingstoke, Palgrave.

Westra, R. (2006), The Capitalist Stage of Consumerism and South Korean Development, *Journal of Contemporary Asia*, 36, 1.

Woo-Cumings, M. (2001), Miracle as Prologue: The State and the Reform of the Corporate Sector in Korea, in J.E. Stiglitz and S. Yusuf (eds), *Rethinking the East Asian Miracle*, Oxford, Oxford University Press.

World Bank (1993), *The East Asian Miracle*, Oxford: Oxford University Press.

MACROECONOMIC POLICY IN THE 'LEADEN AGE' IN EUROPE: AN OVERVIEW

Constantinos Alexiou*

The golden age was a model of social market economy that focused on promoting co-operation both at international level between nation states and at national level between workers, employers, and governments. Within the EU region, the emergence of the new economic orthodoxy, as this is reflected by the prevalence of the neoliberal dogma, has spawned a new wave of criticism. The efficacy of the mechanism adopted to proceed to European Monetary Union provided the platform on which lingering doubters level their concern. In this paper a theoretical exploration of the new liberal thinking is being pursued in an attempt to unveil the rationale of the policies implied by the emerging consensus as well as provide alternative policy channels.

INTRODUCTION

Arguably, the demise of the economic regime established at Bretton Woods ushered in an era of volatile economic activity and poor economic performance, namely the 'leaden age'.[1] In spite of its infancy, the emerging economic system was quick to assert its authority by demolishing the then existing economic establishment, only to replace it with a system founded on 'free-market' economic structures.

In this paper an exploration of the new liberal thinking will be pursued in an attempt to provide a more lucid idea of the policies implied by the emerging consensus as well as the extent to which the EU economies have been affected by the new economic principles. More specifically, section 2 very briefly exposes the key mechanism that gave the Bretton Woods regime the means to tackle international problems. In section 3, an elaboration on the shift in economic policy across most of EU member states after the collapse of Bretton Woods will provide a further understanding of the repercussions that such a shift had on EU economic performance. This is further investigated in section 4, where the policy ramifications resulting from the prevalence of the neoliberal thinking in Europe, are assessed. More specifically, we focus on issues relating to industrial capacity and manufacturing, the role of the financial system and that of effective demand. These provide the reasons why, despite its apparent failure to address

* Department of Economics, City College, Affiliated Institution of University of Sheffield, Thessaloniki, Greece.

the soaring problem of European unemployment, the emerging doctrine insists on adopting a policy mix devoid of any effective employment measures. Section 5 concludes.

BRETTON WOODS AND ECONOMIC SUSTAINABILITY

The golden age was a model of social market economy that focused on promoting co-operation both at international level between nation states and at national level between workers, employers, and governments. The co-operative social and economic environment of the golden age, in a regulated national and international economy, provided the necessary long-term stability required for high rates of private investment, which in turn made possible high rates of productivity growth. Real wages rose in step with productivity and the share of profits in national income remained more or less stable during this period. In so far as the system was working it had a strong positive feedback mechanism, generating high rates of growth of production, consumption and employment.

During the golden age, the problem of the balance of payments surpluses and deficits between nation states was indeed resolved by high rates of growth of world demand, output, and employment. Eatwell (1997) argues that the Bretton Woods system worked not because of macroeconomic coordination but because of a framework of circumstances which permitted governments to pursue national macroeconomic policies without too much fear of international financial disruption.

The achievement of stable exchange rates was the main concern of the Bretton Woods regime. A modified gold standard formation was set up in an attempt to reduce the deflationary pressures that had become a feature both of attempts to restore pre-war gold standard and the successive international crisis as it broke up during and after the 1931 slump. To this end, the system provided that exchange rates could be changed where there was agreed to be a structural imbalance in a country's balance of payments.[2] It also accepted in principle that creditor as well as debtor countries had an obligation to ensure the necessary adjustments. Countries faced with difficulties in the balance of payments could turn to the International Monetary Fund (IMF) for some assistance. Subject to these provisos, however, a basic feature of this system was that demand management should be employed to remedy short-term imbalances. The most important achievement of the system was the promotion of co-operation as the means of dealing with the evolving problems of international payment. It was a regime in which fiscal policy tended to take precedence over monetary policy as the major instrument of macroeconomic policy.

The fixed exchange rate regime re-established at Bretton Woods eventually collapsed in the early 1970s when there was a general move towards sporadic floating rates. Since then, the approach entailing coordination between countries to tackle international economic problems has given way to free market ideology.

LIBERAL THINKING AND ECONOMIC PERFORMANCE IN EUROPE

A browse through history suggests that the process of liberalization of capital movements started with the collapse of the Bretton Woods regime and the introduction of flexible exchange rates in the early 1970s. Alongside it a novel term, 'globalization', came to dominate the economic environment around the world. Inevitably, a growing debate over the virtues of liberalization and globalization started to take up a substantial space on the agenda of governments in most industrial countries. The question whether liberalization and globalization[3] promote faster economic growth, both in rich and poor countries, has undoubtedly been in the forefront of the debate.

The notion that countries should reduce the role of the state and enhance that of the market has been one of the most distinctive features of the new economic establishment. Such a belief, for instance, can be detected in Mr. Lawson's[4] lecture in June 1984 where he expressed his belief in several of the basic tenets of monetarism. In particular, he emphatically stated that government measures to reduce unemployment should steer clear of demand management and concentrate instead on measures to promote price flexibility and the functioning of the markets. Moreover, it is often suggested that open trade leads to convergent rates of economic growth and that open economies successfully avoid balance of payments crisis.[5]

The authoritarian way by which the neoliberal school of thought commenced its campaign for a free market orientated economy was seen as a major threat to the welfare of the European economies *per se.* Among a number of scholars who did not subscribe to the neoliberal dogma, Ajit Singh (1997, p.13) maintains that 'it is not that liberalization and globalization promote economic growth, but rather faster growth of production and employment are essential for sustaining the new liberal economic order'. In addition, he observes that liberalization and globalization are to be held responsible for the slowing down of economic growth in developing countries. Deregulation of domestic financial markets might be another key factor that contributed to the establishing of this new state of affairs.

The flirtation with monetarism in the 1980s has given rise to a new orthodoxy supported by a number of finance ministers and bankers throughout Europe. The essential features of the new monetarism can be summarized as follows: the state should be deprived of the responsibility for formulating economic policy; inflation is a monetary phenomenon and can be controlled through monetary policy; interest rates should be used to control inflation, preferably by an independent bank; the focus of the government should be on how to balance the budget rather than to influence demand; the level of unemployment fluctuates around a supply determined equilibrium (NAIRU); it is the imperfections in the labour market that have to be dealt with, if unemployment is to be reduced. In achieving macroeconomic equilibrium, contemporary orthodoxy regards the fight against inflation as the key objective of economic policy. In this context, public deficit and national debt have been branded as inflationary which have to be reduced promptly.

Table 1 illustrates the path that the growth rate of government debt within the EU region has followed. More specifically, the upward trend that the growth rate of government debt exhibited over the first two periods reflects the

Table 1
Gross Government Debt (growth rates)

Countries	*1961-72*	*1973-78*	*1979-91*	*1992-98*	*1999-02*
Germany	9.1	16.4	10.0	10.5	1.5
France	N/A	17.8	11.6	10.4	3.8
Italy	15.4	25.6	19.5	6.9	1.6
Netherlands	6.7	9.9	9.9	3.1	-2.2
Belgium	8.7	12.7	12.2	3.3	0.7
Luxembourg	N/A	N/A	N/A	N/A	N/A
U.K	5.4	14.0	7.2	11.3	0.6
Ireland	N/A	27.7	15.2	2.8	-0.8
Denmark	N/A	N/A	12.6	4.1	-2.3
Spain	N/A	28.5	25.3	11.6	1.8
Greece	20.2	26.4	34.4	13.9	5.3
Portugal	9.6	37.2	30.6	6.1	6.8
Sweden	9.1	14.9	14.6	9.3	-4.6
Finland	9.2	18.4	15.9	19.1	0.6
Austria	7.3	23.0	11.2	7.6	1.9

Source: OECD, Economic Outlook.

expansionary nature of economic policies adopted by the majority of EU member states. Over the remaining periods the picture changes dramatically. The chief reason for such a shift could be attributed to the introduction of restrictive policies aimed predominantly at reducing budget deficits through public spending cuts. As we can observe, such cutbacks in spending are more pronounced in the relatively less developed economies (Greece, Italy, Portugal, Spain).

The new orthodoxy was embraced by those who wanted to restrict the role of the state, and its consolidation in the economic spectrum was only a matter of time. As a result, a new consensus was established throughout the European countries. Placing reliance on interest rates as means of conducting macroeconomic policy has become common practice in a number of countries in Europe. The stock of money is seen as exogenous to the private sector but subject to change by the authorities or the supply of money being manipulated by interest rates. International pressure to increase, rather than to lower, rates, comes from every direction (Homer and Sylla (1983)). Furthermore, the globalization of financial markets has given monetary policy a consistently deflationary bias.

The 1980s and 1990s have been marked not only by slower economic growth but also by a much more unstable growth. Advances in technology, rather than the current economic regime, are believed to be held responsible for the poor economic performance in recent years. The view that the pace of technological progress is a major threat to job creation has been paramount in a number of studies across the globe. However, emerging evidence for industrial countries refutes such contentions. As Boltho and Glyn (1995) stress, the reason for much higher unemployment in the post-1980s period is not 'jobless growth', but rather a much slower rate of economic growth. Furthermore, in so far as technological changes take place, productivity picks up as the new techniques reduce the labour input required per unit output.

Leading academics of the subject such as Professor Freeman (1989) suggests that the rapid advances in information and communication technology in fact constitute a new technological paradigm. This is not only because these innovations have led to the introduction of new products, but, more importantly, because they have the potential of reducing costs of production and raising productivity in most existing industries. Therefore these technological changes are regarded as constituting a far-reaching technical revolution. Thus, as far as 'the supply side' is concerned, the new information technology 'provides' an enormous potential for increasing production. However, the slow rate of growth of real demand and output over the last fifteen years has caused this potential not to be realized.

THE FAILURE OF MONETARISM AND ITS IMPACT ON EMPLOYMENT

The most conspicuous failure of the liberal economy in the recent decades has been with respect to employment. Monetarist and free-market thinking was established as the predominant economic consensus and in effect begun to dominate economic policy within the Euroland. The notion that inflation could be avoided by controlling the money supply was not a sufficient answer to the soaring problem of unemployment. In addition, deregulation of labour markets added to, rather than mitigated, the problem.

After enjoying more or less full employment during the 1950s and 1960s, leading European countries were faced with the spectre of mass unemployment in the 1980s and 1990s. Table 2 demonstrates the extent to which the unemployment rate in European countries has increased from a little over 3 per cent in the 1960s to nearly 10 per cent in the 1990s.

Table 2
Standardized Unemployment Rates, 1964-02 (Average Annual % Changes)

	1964-73	*1974-79*	*1980-89*	*1990-98*	*1999-02*
Germany	1.1	3.2	5.9	4.9	5.1
UK	3.0	5.0	10.0	9.1	7.2
Total G7	3.1	5.0	6.8	6.4	6.6
Total EU15	2.7	4.7	9.3	9.2	8.4

Source: OECD (1995), Historical Statistics (Paris), IFS.

It is interesting to note that even at times when inflation was brought under control the problem of unemployment was still there, gathering momentum. Grieve-Smith (1992) ascribes the latter firstly, to the fact that political attitudes had become more tolerant than to unemployment and secondly, to the irreversibility of rising unemployment when on the ascent. Moreover, high unemployment does not necessarily lead to government losing elections. In 1974, Kalecki warned that, 'The assumption that a government will maintain full employment in a capitalist economy, if it only knows how to do it, is fallacious.'

An upward trend in involuntary unemployment and lower effective demand was a prevalent feature of the 1980s. Structural changes in international financial relationships and their consequent impact on the structure of domestic macroeconomic policies share the blame for the slowdown in the growth of demand. The ensuing deep depression in the early 1980s rèduced investment in productive industries and impeded its recovery by dampening expectations. The ability of the economy to generate full-employment effective demand was further weakened by a redistribution of income from the poor, most of whose income is consumed, to the rich who save a high proportion of their income and who have a relatively high import propensity.[6]

Abundant undervalued labour has allowed firms to compensate for organizational and managerial inadequacies, delay the scrapping of obsolete capital equipment, and engage in destructive price competition. Tarling and Wilkinson (1997), and Grieve-Smith (1992) point out that the absence of wage discipline means that technologically and managerially backward firms can survive, and this helps prevent more progressive firms from expanding their share of the market. As a result, the average level of productivity drops and a slower rate of introduction and diffusion of new techniques and products occurs.

Inequality and poverty have detrimental effects on the balance of payments constraint, since resources are transferred to those with a higher propensity to import. It is well documented that a great deal of the share of the income of the working poor is met not by the employers but by the government. As a result, there is a considerable increase in the burden on public expenditure. Growing poverty and cutbacks in welfare provisions have aggravated social trends towards, for example, more single-parent families, and have increased the incidence of destitution in such households. Moreover, emerging evidence of a strong relationship between unemployment (poverty, social exclusion) and rising crime, (declining physical and psychological health), suggests that the more the problem of unemployment remains untreated the more detrimental to members of society it becomes.

FINANCIAL SYSTEM AND INDUSTRY: A LESSON STILL TO BE LEARNT

The collapse of Bretton Woods laid the foundations for a financial system that was left to its own devices; a system under which exchange as well as credit controls were abolished, and restrictions on cross market access for financial institutions were scrapped.[7] Short-term interest rates provided the platform on which monetary policy was conducted and monetarism was established as the predominant doctrine.

Governments nowadays tailor policies to suit the interests of the financial sector. A credible government is one that pursues 'market friendly' policies, policies in accordance with what markets perceive as 'sound'. Any divergence from monetary targets has to be met with harsh financial costs, which in turn will result in a major financial crisis. In other words, what actually determines the credibility of a government is the way that the speculative markets work.

In the 1960s, the way in which the international framework was managed encouraged the implementation of expansionary full employment policies as well as the adoption of measures to boost investment. Conversely, in the 1980s full employment policies gave way to policies favouring deregulation and financial stability, which has led to investment being choked off by sky-high interest rates.[8]

The notion that an economy's level of saving can have a profound impact on the pursuit of full employment, dominated economic analysis during the 1930s. The emergence of Keynes's 'General Theory' put an end to such claims, by setting in its place the argument, as Joan Robinson put it that 'firms are free, within wide limits, to accumulate as they please, and the rate of saving of the economy as a whole accommodates itself to the rate of investment that they decree' (1962, pp.82-3).

According to the Keynesian doctrine, stimulating investment, rather than seeking to increase the available pool of savings, is conducive to raising the level of output and employment. Even when policy focuses on financial markets and practices, the primary concern is not on saving behaviour, but rather on encouraging the channelling of funds towards productive activity and away from speculation (Pollin (1996)).

The role of the financial system in any national economy is to 'transform savings and investment and to allocate those funds among competitive users' (Zysman (1983, p. 57)). It is important that the relationship between the financial institutions and industry is such that both contribute to rebuilding industrial capacity and to creating full employment. The savings that the financial system generates should be allocated to companies on favourable terms to enable them to engage in investment activities. Capacity cannot expand nor output increase unless the latter argument holds. The European experience suggests that the conditions upon which the financial institutions have made capital available to industry over the years have been rather punitive. As a result, companies are faced with one of the highest costs of capital in the world.

Immediate profitability is the key word that provides the impetus for the financial system to pursue its objectives. 'The privatization of risk imposed substantial strains on the domestic and international system. The need to absorb and cover foreign exchange risk demanded the creation of new financial instruments, which in turn required the removal of many of the regulatory barriers which limited the possibilities of laying off risk, and a restructuring of financial institutions.'(Eatwell (1995, p. 278)).

The instability in interest rates observed in domestic money markets has a negative effect on policy. More specifically, it jeopardizes any future co-operation between countries to fight unemployment as, with exchange rates fluctuating, the distribution of the gains of such a concerted strategy is highly uncertain. Nowadays, there is much less economic co-operation between leading industrial countries. As a result, the financial markets have come to dominate. Moreover, the deflationary policies that these markets favour have caused the European economy to contract. Far more weight has been given to the perceived dangers of inflation than to the need to obtain full utilization of resources.

Even when the financial markets have sometimes been expansionary[9], their bandwagon and herd characteristics generate considerable instability for the real economy. According to Ajit Singh (1997) unrestricted capital movements provide enormous scope for destabilizing speculation, which in turn leads to high volatility of both monetary and real variables.

Investment is inclined to be affected by fluctuations of financial variables. In particular, investment is discouraged directly by the rising cost of capital, which is in part caused by volatility in financial variables. In addition, the overall uncertainty that increasingly characterizes the economic environment and the greater fluctuations in the components of final demand, have a negative effect on the corporate inducement to invest.

As Stiglitz (1994) has noted, unregulated financial markets are particularly prone to problems of co-ordination failure. Liberalized global financial markets have injured the economy in a number of interrelated ways. Moreover, the speed at which international financial transactions have grown is rather alarming. Zysman (1983) maintained that a 'capital-market' dominated market system, similar to that of Great Britain, in which 'financial institutions tend to manage portfolios of stocks, spreading their risks across companies that they nurture through hard times' (p.63). Substantial evidence points towards a short-term focus on dividends and capital returns rather than on investment plans that will bear fruit in the long run.

Despite the continual endeavour of the state to promote economic growth by using various policies, its attempt to reform and come up with an effective industrial policy has been subverted by the fact that the state 'has never controlled the channels of borrowing and lending that would facilitate the selective manipulation of credit allocation by the state' (Zysman (1983, p. 197)).

Minsky (1986) argues that, when an economy shows signs of recovery and full employment, 'euphoric expectations' take hold. It is then that the financial structure becomes increasingly fragile, as the growth rate of debt exceeds that of profits-for a given distribution of income between wages and profits, profit opportunities are constrained by the growth of productivity-whereas the extension of credit is not so constrained. An economy dominated by free capital markets, where government intervention is non-existent, is characterized by speculative[10] financial behaviour. Once the cycle has peaked, debt deflation and depression set in, which in turn create the condition for a return to financial robustness and recovery.[11]

Hutton (1995) contends that the fundamental weakness of the British system is the fact that high cost of capital and fears of inadequate return in the UK have acted as the most effective deterrent to long-term industrial investment. Ingham (1984) posits that the City's commercial interests revolve around the 'short term gains to be made in the trading of productive assets–in particular through take-overs and mergers–and not in the long term profitability of those units of industrial capital whose shares are bought and sold' (p. 62).

Effective Demand: A Key Factor to Redressing the Balance

Since 1960, European Union employment has increased by only 10 per cent, as opposed to an 80 per cent and 40 per cent increase in North America and Japan respectively. Evidently, the high rates of labour-force growth in North America and Japan have been matched by high rates of job creation. Of course, comparing rates of job creation does not mean much, as it would have been impossible for the European Union to create as many jobs as North America, simply because the European rate of population growth was so much lower. The fundamental question is not why European job creation has been low in absolute terms, but why job creation in Europe did not keep pace with its rate of population growth.

There are, of course, a wide variety of factors that may affect these trends, including the age structure of the population, government employment schemes, 'labour-hoarding', and employment in the 'black economy'. Eatwell (1995) argued, that whilst these effects may have some influence, the most important determinant of the common experience of growing unemployment has been the slow-down in the growth of aggregate demand in the 1980s throughout the G7. Moreover, he highlights the importance of labour-market policies by stating that 'it is the impact of labour-market policies which determine whether there is any employment in excess if that which might be expected from the growth of effective demand' (Eatwell (1997, p. 78)).

During the 'Great Depression' government intervention was a key element in the fight against unemployment. In the post-war era, the promotion of full employment was seen as an incessant endeavour to implement macroeconomic policies designed to manage aggregate demand. It is common knowledge in the circles of economists that Keynes and Kalecki independently came up with the principle of effective demand. Their discovery was based on the notion that the economy would not necessarily generate full employment of all resources.[12] According to their theory, the reason for this was not some market imperfection, such as rigidity of prices or wages, but rather, insufficient effective demand. In other words, in capitalist economies, there is not market mechanism that could guarantee full employment. Full employment is not feasible, unless some exogenous injection of demand is provided.

Unlike the labour-market flexibility approach, the demand growth strategy is a positive-sum game which benefits the rich as well as the poor countries. Thus, full employment in OECD countries and faster economic growth will help developing countries in several ways. Specifically, poor countries will gain from an acceleration in OECD growth through much the same channels by which they were disadvantaged by slower economic growth in industrial countries after the golden age. Faster OECD growth will have a positive effect on the demand for products of poor countries as well as on the terms of trade. It may also result in greater capital flows, both private and public from the rich to the poor countries. Other things being equal, all this should lead to faster growth of output and employment in developing economies.

The industrial world is faced with the problem of the creation of sufficient jobs with rising real wages. Solutions to the problem can be envisaged only if there is a sustained trend increase in the rate of growth of output and productivity in these economies.[13] The main concern is how to bring about a sustained rise in the rate of growth of real aggregate demand without risking unacceptable inflation.

Currently, policies to fight unemployment that favour labour-market flexibility seem to be the reason behind the dismal failure of the economy to deliver. The intellectual basis of this approach is rooted in the concept of NAIRU. The main cause of unemployment in terms of this theory lies in rigidities in the labour market and the provisions of the welfare state, which make it unattractive for people to seek work. (Layard and Nickell (1986); Layard (1991)). Hence increasing market flexibility can be achieved through means such as deregulation, reduction of trade-union power, and the pruning of the welfare state. In addition the whole concept of the NAIRU, which can be detected in the works of Milton Friedman (1968) and Edmund Phelps (1968), encouraged the idea that policy should be directed to establishing a minimum level of unemployment so that inflation remains unchanged - in other words, forget about the achievement of full employment.

Recent OECD analyses of changes in structural unemployment in the 1990s draw attention to the implausibility of the rigidities story explanation. As table 1 (see appendix) demonstrates, according to the OECD, the non-accelerating-inflation-rate of unemployment (NAIRU) rose in most European countries in the 1990s. In some instances, the increases were large. Between 1990 and 1999, the estimated NAIRU, for example, increased 5.4 percentage points in Finland, 3.0 percentage points in Sweden, and 2.7 percentage points in Germany (OECD (1999, p. 9)). Yet, by the OECD's own assessment (OECD (1999)), the 1990s were a period during which nearly all the European nations reduced labor market rigidities. As labor market rigidities have not increased during the 1990s, they cannot possibly explain the dramatic increases in unemployment over the last decade.

As Ajit Singh (1997) claims, the facts concerning inter-temporal variations in unemployment rates and real wages in industrial countries are much more easily explained by variations in the rate of growth of real demand rather than by the NAIRU approach. Drawing on the latter, Galbraith (1997) believes that 'the case for basing anti-inflationary policy primarily around the rate of unemployment was never persuasive... One need not object to the NAIRU as a purely mathematical construct. After all, a steady inflation-unemployment rate is merely an implication of models specified in a certain way' (p.106).

An alternative view, conceptualized by Keynes, is that a firm will expand its output only if it can be sure that it will be able to sell it. Keynes tried to conceptualise the involved uncertainty that money conveyed, by relating the demand for money as a store of value to uncertainty about future and showed how these features of the world in which we live affect investment, which is therefore subject to fluctuations: 'It is not surprising that the volume of investment, thus determined, should fluctuate widely from time to time. For it depends on two sets of judgements about the future, neither of which rests on an adequate or secure foundation - on the propensity to hoard and on opinions of the future yield of capital assets' (C.W. XIV, p. 118).

The fact that capitalists engage in production activity in order to make profits, constitutes a fundamental reason why entrepreneurs can decide to keep money idle and the economy can experience unemployment. The system's degree of liquidity preference is ostensibly, immediately, and directly related to entrepreneurs' expectation of profit, which is the driving force in a capitalist economy.

Employment will expand only if there is an increase in real demand and output, not just because there is a cut in wages. In the same line of argument, a reduction in wages in a closed economy could, in principle, reduce real aggregate demand through its adverse effects on business expectations and investment; hence the overall consequence may be a fall rather than a rise in employment.

As Alexiou (2001), points out, it is lack of demand rather than the need to cut the price of labour that inhibits the growth of output and employment. By lowering wages, purchasing power and costs are reduced at the same rate. Thus, it leaves unemployment intact. However, what is true about keeping real wages down is the fact that we can improve our competitive position and thus increase, for example, UK employment (at the expense of others). Grieve-Smith (1996), as well as Grahl (1997), argue that practices of the kind should focus on exchange rate policy rather than pay-bargaining one.

Manufacturing. Is there still hope?

In Europe, manufacturing employment has been dwindling alarmingly. More specifically, over the period 1976-86 the decline in manufacturing employment in EC accounts for a fall of almost 5.5 million jobs. The promotion of free-market orientation policies by European governments has taken its toll. Currently, attempts to restore competitiveness through product and labour deregulation have exacerbated the problem. Policies targeting the expansion of demand for manufacturers as well as industrial policies to improve competitiveness are conspicuous by their absence. Under-investment in manufacturing is a potential reason behind the rise in unemployment. Such a process of deindustrialization could have detrimental effects on the entire European economic life leading to additional hardships for its population.

In the UK, the fact that 1980s growth was skewed towards services, particularly financial services, raises the question of whether manufacturing matters after all. For Kitson and Michie (1996) the answer is 'yes, it does matter'. Their affirmative answer is based on the notion that the UK economy requires a large and competitive manufacturing sector in order to generate sufficient exports to pay for necessary imports. Moreover, both healthy manufacturing and reliable services are conducive to economic prosperity.

It is interesting to note that the decline in manufacturing, and particularly manufacturing employment, and the corresponding relative growth of services, is a predominant feature in both slow - and fast - growing countries (see Petit (1986)).

Trying to establish the causes of this rapid decline in manufacturing employment, a number of studies, including those by Fuchs (1968), Baumol (1967), Saxenhouse (1985) and Summers (1985), arrived at the conclusion that productivity differences are the main source of the decline in manufacturing employment, although others, such as Marquand (1979), maintain that services have lower productivity.[14] Furthermore, the relative decline in manufacturing and the relative growth of services stems from the changing structure of demand as income increases. Another explanation for the relative decline in manufacturing is the changing source of service provision, with activities that were previously undertaken by firms increasingly being contracted out.

Although Kaldor (1972) retracted a previously held view that employment in services may restrict the labour supply for manufacturing in favour of a demand constraint one, he retained the idea that services were not as dynamic as manufacturing. This was rooted in the views of Lewis (1954), Cornwall (1977), and others, that 'manufacturing is an engine of growth'.

The extension of the market for manufactured products would lead through the benefits of economies of scale to increased competitive advantage and hence to increased economic growth. This will have a positive effect on the expansion of the service sector, in terms of both output and employment. Nonetheless, should full employment be attained, there must be sufficient demand for manufactured products.

CONCLUDING REMARKS AND POLICY IMPLICATIONS

Economies throughout Europe have failed to deliver the prosperous economic future that the architects of the current economic systems had initially pledged to deliver. After the fixed exchange rate mechanism, established at Bretton Woods, had broken down, the world economy reverted to the pre-war state of chronic mass unemployment. The prevalence of monetarist and free-market thinking among the political leadership of the industrial nations effectively ruled out any major structural reforms in the management of the world economy. Indulging in neoliberal-type policies to expand productive capacity and stir the economy towards recovery has been once again an elusive objective.

Over the past two decades the commitment to full employment has been abandoned and mass unemployment has manifested itself as being an integral part of the capitalist world. The adoption of tighter fiscal and monetary policies to combat inflation caused unemployment to reach unprecedented levels, which in turn has caused a number of social problems such as the growth of poverty, homelessness to grow at a prodigious rate. As a result, Europe's economic and political stability has been under threat.

In the 1990s, the 'globalization of finance' started pushing its roots even deeper into the economic world. Maintaining sound finance was the main preoccupation of many governments around the globe. The only way to achieve such an objective was through the implementation of deflationary policies, of which the economic repercussions have been acute.

In Europe, industrial competitiveness has been sacrificed to inappropriate or inflexible exchange rate policies. In the 1980s, when demand was well below full employment levels, capacity throughout the EU was eroded by closures and inhibitions on investment in additional capacity. NAIRU, the idea of an inverse causal relationship between levels of unemployment and price inflation, is now so firmly entrenched that central bankers look with deep suspicion at any downward movement of unemployment, from any level, as signalling potential inflation and the need to increase interest rates.

In short, it has become rather apparent that the austere economic conditions experienced by the EU population over the last decades has been the result of tight economic policies implemented by the proponents of the free-market orthodoxy. Pursuing an alternative agenda, in which demand side policies topped the priorities, might be a policy option the fruits of which are waiting to be reaped.

NOTES

1. The term 'leaden age', which has been borrowed from Pollin (1997-1998), essentially, signifies the poor economic performance and financial instability that has permeated the capitalist economies for the past three decades.
2. However, the Bretton Woods regime did not eliminate foreign exchange crises. Speculation against currencies expected to devalue were still present; as well as deflationary policies prescribed, by the IMF, for countries in difficulties.
3. Braunstein and Epstein (1999) invoke Milberg's (1998) definition of 'globalization' –globalization is the deepening of international economic relations–to argue that it is erroneous to see 'globalization as synonymous with marketization and economic liberalization. Economic liberalization is one form globalization can take, and indeed, that is precisely its form in the current era–globalization is occurring in a neoliberal regime' (p.115).
4. The British Chancellor of the Exchequer at the time.
5. See World Bank (1991). For a critical analysis of the World Bank see for example Singh(1994, 1995a).
6. An extensive analysis of how aggregate demand is adversely affected by shifts in thedistribution of income can be found in Kalecki (1942, 1971) and Kaldor (1955/56).
7. Felix (1997-8) posits that international capital mobility is incompatible with full employment and economic growth.
8. 'Since modern capital markets came into existence, there have been such high long-term interest rates as we recently have had all over the world' (Homer and Sylla (1983, p.4)).
9. For a more detailed approach see Rodrik (1994) and Krugman (1995).
10. As Forrester (1999) points out, 'derivatives, which are now invading the economy, reduce it to casino games or bookmakers' practices... Now this new form of economy no longer invests: it bets' (p.80).

11. Minsky's position is perfectly consistent with that of Schumpeter and Marx; depressions are functional: they are a destructive but necessary mechanism–the 'slaughtering of capital values' as Marx put it–that returns financial structures to balance.
12. At the time, their discovery was contrary to all previous economic thought with the possible exception of Marx and the heretical under-consumptionists.
13. See further Boltho and Glyn (1995) and Singh (1995b).
14. There are substantial difficulties in measuring productivity in services, as in most cases no physical output is produced.

REFERENCES

Alexiou, C. (2001), Crafting a Post Keynesian Framework to Explain European Unemployment: Economic Evidence from European Union Countries, *Journal of Post Keynesian Economics*, 24, 59-80.

Baumol, W. (1967), Macroeconomics of Unbalanced Growth, *American Economic Review*, 57, 415-26.

Boltho, A. and Glyn, A. (1995), Can Macroeconomic Policies Raise Employment?, *International Labour Review*, 134, 451-70.

Braunstein, E. and Epstein, G. (1999), International Credit Rules and Investment, in J. Michie and J. Grieve-Smith (eds), *Global Instability: The Political Economy of World Economic Governance*, London, New York, Routledge.

Cornwall, J. (1977), *Modern Capitalism: Its Growth and Transformation*, Oxford, Martin Robertson.

Eatwell, J. (1995), The International Origins of Unemployment, in J. Michie and J. Grieve-Smith (eds), *Managing the Global Economy*, Oxford, Oxford University Press.

Eatwell, J. (1997), Effective Demand and Disguised Unemployment, in J. Michie and J. Grieve-Smith (eds), *Employment and Economic Performance: Jobs, Inflation and Growth*, Oxford, Oxford University Press.

Fuchs, V. (1968), *The Service Economy*, New York, Columbia University Press.

Forrester, V. (1999), *The Economic Horror*, Polity Press.

Freeman, R. (1989), New Technology and Catching Up, *European Journal of Development Research*, 1, 85-99.

Friedman, M. (1968), The Role of Monetary Policy, *American Economic Review*, 68, 1-17.

Galbraith, J. (1997), Time to Ditch the NAIRU, *Journal of Economic Persectives*, 11, 93-108.

Grahl, J. (1997), *After Maastricht*, London, Lawrence and Wishart Limited.

Grieve-Smith, J. (1992), Full Employment in the 1990s, *Institute for Public Policy Research.*

Grieve-Smith, J. (1996), Rebuilding Industrial Capacity in J. Michie and J. Grieve-Smith (eds), *Creating Industrial Capacity: Towards Full Employment*, Oxford, Oxford University Press.

Homer, S. and Sylla, R. (1983), *A History of Interest Rate*, New Brunswick, Rutgers University Press.

Hutton, W. (1995), *The State We're In*, London, Jonathan Cape.

Ingham, G. (1984), *Capitalism Divided? The City and Industry in British Social*

Development, London, Macmillan.

Kaldor, N. (1955/56) Alternative Theories of Distribution, *Review of Economic Studies*, 23, 83-100.

Kaldor, N. (1972), The Irrelevance of Equilibrium Economics, *Economic Journal*, 82, 1237-55.

Kalecki, M. (1942), The Essentials for Democratic Planning, in J. Toporowski (ed.) (1986), *Michael Kalecki: Selected Essays on Economic Planning*, Cambridge, Cambridge University Press.

Kalecki, M. (1971), *Selected Essays on the Dynamics of the Capitalist Economy, 1933-1970*, Cambridge, Cambridge University Press.

Keynes, J. M. (1964), *The General Theory of Employment, Interest, and Money*, New York, Harcourt, Brace and World.

Kitson, M. and Michie, J. (1996), Manufacturing Capacity, Investment and Employment in J. Michie and J. Grieve-Smith (eds), *Creating Industrial Capacity*, Oxford University Press.

Krugman, P. (1995), Dutch Tulips and Emerging Markets, *Foreign Affairs*, 74, 28-44.

Layard, R. and Nickell, S. (1990), Is Unemployment Lower if Unions Bargain Over Employment ?, *Quarterly Journal of Economics*, 105, 773-88.

Lewis, W.A. (1954), Economic Development with Unlimited Supplies of Labour, *Manchester School*, 22, 139-91.

Marquand, J. (1979), The Service Sector and Regional Policy in the United Kingdom, mimeo, *Centre for Environmental Studies*, London.

Milberg, W. (1998), Technological Change, Social Policy and International Competitiveness, *Working Paper on Globalization, Labour Markets and Social Policy*, New York, New School for Social Research.

Minsky, H. (1986), *Stabilizing an Unstable Economy,* New Haven, Yale University Press.

OECD (1999), The OECD Jobs Strategy: Progress Report on Implementation of Country-Specific Recommendations, *Economics Department Working Papers No. 196*.

Petit, P. (1986), *Slow Growth and the Service Economy*, London, Frances Pinter.

Phelps, E. (1968), Money-Wage Dynamics and Labour-Market Equilibrium, *Journal of Political Economy,* 76, 678-711.

Pollin, R. (1996), Saving and Finance: Real and Illusory Constraints on Full Employment Policy, in J. Michie and J. Grieve-Smith (eds), *Creating Industrial Capacity: Towards Full Employment*, Oxford, Oxford University Press.

Pollin, R. (1997-98), Theory and Policy in Response to 'Leaden Age' Financial instability: Comment on Felix, *Journal of Post Keynesian Economics*, 20, 223-33.

Robinson, J. (1962), *Essays in the Theory of Economic Growth*, London, Macmillan.

Rodrik, D. (1994), The Rush to Free Trade in the Developing World: Why so Late? Why Now? Will it Last?, in S. Haggard and S.B. Webb (eds), *Voting for Reform: The Policies of Adjustment in New Democracies*, New York, Oxford University Press.

Saxenhouse, G. (1985), Services in the Japanese Economy, in R.E. Inman (ed.), *Managing the Service Economy: Prospects and Problems*, Cambridge, Cambridge University Press.

Singh, A. (1994), Industrial Policy in Europe and Industrial Development in the Third World, in P. Bianchi, K. Cowling and R. Sugden (eds.), *Europe's Economic Challenge:*

Analyses of Industrial Strategy and Agenda for the 1990s, London, Routledge.

Singh, A (1995a), Competitive Markets and Economic Development: A Commentary on World Bank Analyses, *International Papers in Political Economy*, 2.

Singh, A (1995b), Institutional Requirements for Full Employment in Advanced Economies, *International Labour Review*, 134, 471-96.

Singh, A. (1997), Liberalization and Globalization in J. Michie and J. Grieve-Smith (eds), *Employment and Economic Performance: Jobs, Inflation and Growth*, Oxford, Oxford University Press.

Stiglitz, J. (1998), More Instruments and Broader Goals: Moving Toward the Post-Washington Consensus, The 1998 WIDER Annual Lecture, Helsinki, Finland.

Strange, S. (1986), *Casino Capitalism,* Oxford, Blackwell.

Tarling, R. and Wilkinson, F. (1997), Economic Functioning, Self - Sufficiency and Full Employment, in J. Michie and J. Grieve-Smith (eds), *Employment and Economic Performance: Jobs, Inflation and Growth*, Oxford, Oxford University Press.

World Bank. (1991), *World Development Report: The Challenge of Development*, New York, Oxford University Press for the World Bank.

Zysman, J. (1983), *Government, Markets and Growth: Financial Systems and the Politics of Industrial Change*, Ithaca, NY, Cornell University Press.

APPENDIX

Table 1
OECD Estimates of Structural Unemployment in the 1990s

Countries	*1990*	*1999*	*1990-99 (change)*
Finland	7.0	12.4	5.4
Sweden	3.2	6.2	3.0
Germany	6.9	9.2	2.4
Greece	8.2	9.8	1.6
Italy	9.7	10.6	0.9
France	9.3	10.2	0.9
Belgium	11.0	11.6	0.6
Austria	4.9	5.4	0.5
Spain	19.8	19.9	0.1
Portugal	5.9	5.8	-0.1
Denmark	9.2	8.6	-0.6
UK	8.5	7.2	-1.3
Netherlands	7.0	5.5	-1.5
Ireland	14.6	11.0	-3.6

Source: Author's analysis of OECD (1999).